# THE COMPLETE BOOK OF

# PARTIES

## CELEBRATIONS & SPECIAL OCCASIONS

# THE COMPLETE BOOK OF
# PARTIES
## CELEBRATIONS & SPECIAL OCCASIONS

A PRACTICAL STEP-BY-STEP GUIDE WITH OVER
650 PHOTOGRAPHS

## BRIDGET JONES

SMITHMARK

747.93
gon

Dedication:
To Neill, my favourite party partner

This edition published in 1994 by
SMITHMARK Publishers Inc.
16 East 32nd Street
New York
NY 10016

SMITHMARK books are available for bulk
purchase for sales promotion and premium
use. For details write or call the manager of
special sales, SMITHMARK Publishers
Inc., 16 East 32nd Street, New York,
NY 10016: (212) 532–6600.

ISBN 08317 1455 7

*Publisher:* Joanna Lorenz
*Project Editor:* Jennifer Jones
*Designer:* Adrian Morris
*Special Photography:* James Duncan
*Stylist:* Madeleine Brehaut
*Home Economist:* Sara Lewis
*Illustrator:* Kate Simunek

Previously published as
The Essential Guide to Entertaining

Typeset by MC Typeset Limited
Printed and bound in China

## PUBLISHER'S NOTE

All the projects in this book are easy and safe to make, but some general points should be
remembered for safety and care of the environment.

❖ Always choose non-toxic materials whenever possible; for example, PVA, strong clear
glue, and non-toxic varnishes.

❖ Craft knives, scissors and all cutting implements should be used with care. Children
love to help making things, but should only be allowed to use sharp tools under
supervision.

❖ Always use a cutting board or cutting mat to avoid damage to household surfaces (it is
also safer to cut onto a firm, hard surface.)

❖ Protect surfaces from paint, glue and varnish splashes by laying down old sheets of
paper or newspaper.

### MEASUREMENTS

Every cook or craftsperson prefers to work in the measurements of their choice – whether
metric, imperial or, where appropriate, cups. In this book the publishers have given all
these different measurement systems. Remember, the golden rule is to choose one set of
measurements throughout each project or recipe for accuracy and perfect results.

# Contents

# Entertaining with Ease

# PERFECT PLANNING

*$\mathcal{P}$ lanning is the cornerstone for success on every occasion, from the grandest of celebrations to the simplest of impromptu meals with friends. Thinking ahead about* *unplanned socializing may seem to be a contradiction, but the clever host or hostess always has some suitable refreshment to offer and a few good ideas for adding a sparkle to an unexpected opportunity for entertaining. This section concentrates on both preparing for specific dates and receiving guests at a moment's notice.*

### WHAT TYPE OF PARTY?

Deciding on the type of occasion is the obvious starting point for planning, yet it is not uncommon for what was originally intended to be a simple supper with friends to lumber ungracefully into becoming a more formal dinner or for a small buffet to evolve into a major party. Of course, both unplanned transitions may be extremely successful, but there is always the danger of unforeseen hitches or an oversight along the lines of communication which may spoil the guests' enjoyment or, more often, overtax the host and/or hostess. One of the classic sources of embarrassment to guests is turning up in the wrong style of dress, while the basic problem for a busy host or hostess is being overstretched at the last minute and neither spending sufficient time with the guests nor enjoying the party. Such occasions are always uncomfortable for everyone.

Many parties celebrate an event such as an annual feast, birthday, wedding, christening or anniversary; they can also take place for no special purpose at all other than to see friends. Whatever the occasion, it is most important to have a clear outline of the form of entertaining before beginning to work on any of the preparations.

Annual festivities, such as Thanksgiving, Christmas, New Year and Easter, often follow a traditional structure, but this does not free the host or hostess from planning ahead; it simply means that there are fewer decisions to make and that they all fall into an existing framework. For all other occasions, a decision on the type and size of celebration is the starting point and the usual pre-arranging has to follow. Begin by considering your likely budget, then clearly outline what sort of party you are planning within the financial restrictions. Work through the following points, and by the time you have made notes on these you will have a structure for planning all the details.

> **Party Planning Checklist**
>
> - **Time of day**
> - **Degree of formality**
> - **Dress**
> - **Numbers**
> - **Location**
> - **Food and drink**
> - **Invitations**

### Time of Day

Is the event going to be breakfast or brunch, lunch, afternoon tea, cocktails or drinks before dinner, early supper, dinner, late supper, or drinks after dinner? If the party is linked to some outside event, check the exact timing for that. Wedding ceremonies and christenings are the obvious occasions, but the same applies to other likely opportunities for social gatherings – graduation, opening night at the local theatre group, a visit to the theatre, concerts, a sporting event and so on.

### Degree of Formality

If you decide on a formal party, this will provide you with a set of clear-cut rules to follow. You may opt for complete informality, in which case you need to work out your own pattern of rules. However, many occasions fall somewhere between the two extremes. The important thing is to decide exactly how you want to entertain, let everyone know what to expect and stick to your decision by planning accordingly. Think in terms of dress, how you expect guests to participate and the type of refreshments, and pass all this information on to the guests.

The type of entertainment and refreshment must fit in with the level of party – delicate canapés or hors d'oeuvre are perfect for cocktails, but not when guests are dressed for a walk in the park followed by a hearty brunch; and coping with unsuitable food or boisterous indoor games is awkward when standing and chatting in evening dress.

The style of celebration will also dictate whether outside help is needed. Caterers, waiting staff and bar staff may be hired for formal occasions, such as weddings, and may also be employed for any large party or even for formal dinner parties. There are also several possibilities for commissioning outside entertainment on such occasions. These aspects of any party should always be planned at the outset, not as afterthoughts.

## Dress

Formal invitations will always state whether morning dress, white tie (full evening dress) or black tie (evening dress) are required. If none of these options is specified when a formal invitation is dispatched for a dinner party, then men should wear lounge (dress) suits and women should dress up without wearing evening dress. Generally speaking, if you plan a dinner party for a group of acquaintances and friends, then the mode of dress should be good suits for men and smart dress for women unless you specifically request some other style. When inviting close friends to a dinner party, the dress code is usually understood within the group; however, take special care when inviting a mixture of close friends, who are aware of your style, together with acquaintances who do not know you well. On such occasions, simply make a decision and let everyone know what to expect.

Informal dress, on the other hand, invariably demands some qualification

because it can mean different things to different people. When invited to an informal supper party some men will dress in a shirt, tie, sports jacket and trousers, while others will put on jeans and a sweater; to women informal

dress can mean anything from jeans and a sweater to a simple skirt and attractive shirt. The best way to deal with this is to let guests know what sort of clothes you intend wearing – and not to change your mind later!

## The Guests

Bringing people together for dinner parties is not always easy and deciding on the group of people to invite to larger gatherings can be difficult. Nevertheless, this is an essential and important first step in good planning. If you organize a dinner party for people who are strangers to one another, it is important to mix individuals who are likely to get on well together or at least express an interest in one another.

When inviting friends to larger gatherings, always ensure that there are groups who will know or can relate to one another. Sadly, family, friends and colleagues do not always have much in common and, worse, the differences can split a poorly planned party. In a large party it is a mistake to invite just one or two people who are unlikely to socialize easily with the majority.

Think back over your own social experiences and you will probably recall occasions when certain guests in the minority have obviously lingered on the fringe of a gathering awaiting the first polite opportunity to take their leave. Having made the point, it is equally important to stress that there are exceptions and we have all witnessed outstanding social successes in the most unlikely groups of people.

### Formal Dress

❖ Morning dress is worn for royal garden parties, Ascot and some similar events in Britain and other royal European countries, and at the request of the host and hostess at weddings all over the world. If you are planning a formal wedding, then make sure that all who are expected to wear morning dress are aware of the style which is being adopted. Black morning coat with striped trousers, grey tie and black top hat are traditional; however, there are variations on greys and blacks, as may be seen at any dress hire company. Women should wear hats to formal weddings, and *always* when morning dress is requested of the men.

❖ White tie is the traditional full evening dress, but it is now usually reserved only for grand balls and the most formal occasions. For the man, this means black tail coat, wing collar and white bow tie and black trousers, which usually have a double row of braid down the outside leg. Patent shoes are a traditional 'must', but not essential these days. Women should wear

long gowns on white tie occasions. Long white gloves may be worn with evening gowns, and these should come over the elbows.

❖ Black tie is the most common form of special dress for evening occasions and is simply referred to as evening dress. A black dinner suit (tuxedo) with white shirt and black bow tie is the conventional dress. A single-breasted suit may have a black waistcoat or a cummerbund; a double-breasted jacket is worn closed. There are many variations on this theme, with colourful waistcoats or cummerbunds and ties, even suits with various design details. However, many men do wear dark lounge (dress) suits with bow ties for evening wear. Women should wear evening dresses, which may be long or short.

*A marquee (closed-sided party tent) in the garden is perfect for entertaining larger numbers at home.*

### Location

Decide whether your party is to take place indoors or outdoors, and whether you have sufficient space on home ground or should consider holding it elsewhere. For indoor entertaining at home, the main considerations are the room arrangements. Similarly, for outdoor events such as barbecues and parties in the garden on a modest scale, take a practical overview of patio space. Consider likely seating for those who require it, areas for children, the alternatives should the weather let the party down and so on. Think about hiring a large grill or two smaller barbecues, if necessary.

However, for larger gatherings and events such as large-scale garden parties and picnics, you may need to consider a separate location or a marquee (closed-sided party tent) or open tent.

TENTS AND MARQUEES Unless the house is suitable for entertaining with ease in large numbers, an open-sided tent or marquee (closed-sided party tent) is the practical option for home celebrations. You do not have to have a vast garden (yard), as marquees can be comparatively small; however, you must have a flat area where the tent can be erected. Look through the telephone directory for hire (rental) companies which cover your area and ask for details from as many as possible to give you an idea of price range and the facilities on offer. Depending on the time of day and the season, you may need power for lighting and some form of heating. Remember when hiring marquees to establish exactly what is included in the way of flooring and internal lining or trimmings. Establish details about erection costs, timing for dismantling and so on.

PREMISES When considering hiring (renting) a room, club house or hall locally, thoroughly check the rules and regulations which apply to the use of the premises. For example, is the place suitable for music and dancing, will it have a bar, is the consumption of alcohol allowed, is there a time by which the premises have to be vacated, and what parking arrangements are available nearby? Check the availability of kitchen facilities for any catering requirements. Make sure that you have access to the area beforehand for all

### Numbers

It is vital to make sure that you can cope with the numbers for the type of party planned. This is largely a matter of space. For example, it is not practical to arrange a formal dinner party for eight guests if you can only sit seven around the table: the eighth person who is perched on a stool at the corner of the table will make everyone else feel thoroughly uncomfortable. The same applies to a barbecue for fifty when the only grill is a small hibachi; a cosy kitchen brunch for ten in an area which is cramped with six people; or a children's party for twenty-five in a house which is overfilled when half-a-dozen children are invited and where there is only a small garden.

Remember that the equation can work the other way and that for some types of gatherings, success depends on having the party area fairly tightly packed with people. This applies particularly to hired premises, where the capacity of the room must be tailored to the number of guests expected – too few people in too large a space is false economy as well as fatal to creating any kind of party atmosphere.

your preparations and find out whether there are any additional costs.

The vital point to remember is that the location must be suitable for the occasion. This does *not* mean you have to hire only the grandest of rooms for formal functions, rather that whatever the surroundings, they live up to the event. For example, a modest church hall with dull furnishings – or a plain marquee (closed-sided party tent) – can be transformed with a little flair by clothing drab tables in linen and adding flowers and foliage. You also need to agree when any decorations can be put up and removed – if a location is heavily booked you may not have much time for such transformations – which you'll also have to schedule in to your timetable. When you make your initial enquiries, always discuss such details of what you hope to do and make sure they are acceptable to the owners. Apart from the risk of causing serious offence within small communities, you may discover that there are objections to some of your ideas when it is too late to change locations.

*Pack a basket to picnic in style.*

**PICNICS** Picnics may be arranged around an event at a pre-determined location, such as an outdoor concert, theatrical entertainment or parade. However, they can also be occasions for meeting friends or other families, in which case a suitable site must be found and checked out in advance of making definite arrangements. Try to visit the place beforehand at about the same time of day as the intended picnic if at all possible. What seems an idyllic location on one occasion may be quite different when busy with weekend dog-walkers or early-evening jogging enthusiasts if it is a popular spot.

### Food and Drink

Whether the gathering is small or large, it is important to decide on the level of refreshments – nibbles (snacks), finger food, some form of buffet or a proper sit-down meal – and to make sure the food and drink are suited to the occasion. This must be considered alongside the time of day, numbers invited, budget and location, where appropriate. You can be quite individual in your choice of refreshments as long as they fulfil the requirements for the time of day and location and adapt well to the style of party.

The level of refreshment offered must also correspond to the expected length of the party. Light canapés or hors d'oeuvres may be served for a late morning or mid-day affair when guests are expected to depart fairly quickly, but if you anticipate entertaining for the whole of the afternoon, the range of canapés or hors d'oeuvres must be extensive and plentiful or more substantial refreshment should be offered.

Do not be afraid to make an unusual decision about the form of food, but do make sure it is adequate and that you can cope with the preparation or that caterers, if you are using them, do not need facilities which are not available.

### Invitations

Whether printed, handwritten or extended by word of mouth, an invitation should convey certain important information clearly to the recipient. It should state the names of those invited, the name(s) of the host and/or hostess, the occasion and the reason for it, the place, the time and an address to which replies should be sent. Written invitations often include the formula "RSVP" in one corner, which stands for the French "*Répondez, s'il vous plaît*" ("Please reply"), to remind guests that an answer is required.

Where appropriate, an invitation will specify the expected time for guests to depart. For example, if you expect guests to leave a drinks party at a certain time, then state on the invitation "6–8 p.m.". This is a good way of emphasizing that the occasion is simply for drinks, and dinner or a buffet will not be provided. Any special form of dress should be detailed on the bottom of the invitation. Many invitations to casual parties also include the instruction "Bring a bottle".

**TELEPHONE INVITATIONS** These are appropriate for dinner parties, informal luncheons and supper engagements or for drinks with friends and for arrangements made at short notice. Telephone invitations to a dinner party are often a case of "setting a date" rather than inviting friends for a pre-fixed date. The length of notice varies according to the group of people, but it is usually within a period of two to four weeks, sometimes longer when fixing a date with busy friends. It is a good idea to follow up with a card to confirm the date and time when planning a formal dinner party, and to phone a day or so ahead of an informal event.

**INVITATION CARDS** Ready-made cards where you write in the details yourself are available in styles ranging from formal to fun. You can also arrange to have cards printed specifically for an occasion. As with dress, there are systems of etiquette that govern printed invitations issued for weddings and similar formal occasions, and it is important to consult a detailed reference source on the subject.

**HANDWRITTEN INVITATIONS** For smaller gatherings and less formal occasions such as dinner parties, beautifully scripted invitations handwritten on a well-chosen card or interesting paper are quite sophisticated. If you choose paper rather than cards, then try any of the handmade papers which are available from art shops and fold them neatly before writing on the front. Some have matching envelopes available. Look out for coloured inks or pens, particularly in gold or silver. It is best to plan the content and presentation of the handwritten cards carefully on rough paper first.

## Christmas Star

This is the perfect invitation card to a Christmas party.

**YOU WILL NEED:** card (posterboard) for template, pencil, gold card, scissors, ribbon.

**1** Scale up the template to the size required and transfer the pattern onto the gold card (posterboard).

**2** Cut around the edges of the card using a pair of sharp scissors.

**3** Make a hole in one of the points of the star using the tip of a scissor. Cut a length of ribbon and thread it through the hole so that it can be used as a decoration by the recipient.

## A Masked Ball

An invitation in the form of a mask sets the theme for a fancy dress (costume) party. Make it life-size if you want to ensure that even the least creative of your guests will have no excuse for not coming in dress . Write the invitation on one side and decorate the edges of the invitation on the other side with beads, feathers and trimmings, if liked. Vary the decoration depending on the theme of the party.

**YOU WILL NEED:** card (posterboard) for template, pencil, thin coloured card, scissors, trimmings such as feathers and beads (optional), glue (if using trimmings), ribbon.

**1** Scale up the template to the size required and transfer the pattern onto the coloured card (posterboard). Cut around the edges with a pair of scissors and cut out two holes for the eyes.

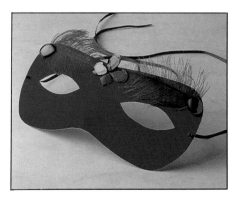

**2** Decorate the edges of the invitation with feathers, if liked. Attach with glue.

**3** Use a strong glue to stick decorative beads to the front of the mask, if liked. For a balanced effect, finish with a bead either side of a central cluster of beads.

**4** Pierce a hole on each side of the mask using the point of a scissor and thread a piece of ribbon through each hole. Knot the ribbon at the front to hold in place. Pinch the central part of the mask to follow the shape of the nose.

# Surprise Invite

Send this specially sealed invitation for a surprise party. The decorative seal in the centre can be adapted to suit the occasion, from a small rose made of silk fabric and attached with double-sided tape to a ready-made novelty self-adhesive paper shape depicting a fancy dress (costume) theme.

**YOU WILL NEED:** coloured paper, ready-made self-adhesive paper shape or sealing wax, ribbon (optional).

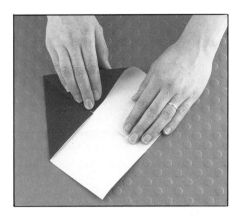

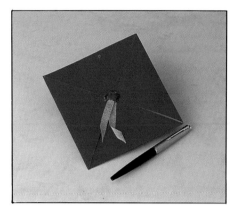

**1** Fold a piece of coloured paper, 20 cm/8 in square, in four (the size of the square can be adjusted to match the size of your envelopes, if using). Open out the paper and fold the corners into the centre to form a smaller square envelope shape. Press the paper with a cool iron to eliminate the previous fold marks.

**2** Write the invitation to the party inside the folds. Seal the four points where they meet in the centre with a self-adhesive paper shape or melted sealing wax.

**3** If using sealing wax, the seal can be made more decorative with the addition of some ribbon. Cut two short pieces of ribbon and place them on the seal. Carefully melt a little more wax where the ribbons meet in the centre to hold them in place.

# Stylish Hat

Novelty invitations are always popular. Make this stylish hat for an elegant summer party in the garden or for a romantic fancy dress (costume) party. Alternatively, design your own hat-with-a-theme invite to send out to guests. And there's no need to make the same hat for each guest — children in particular will love to receive their own special design.

**YOU WILL NEED:** card (posterboard) for the template, soft pencil, coloured card, scissors, range of coloured ribbons and ready-made bow in the shape of a rose, glue.

**1** Scale up the template to the size required — check that the finished size will fit into your chosen envelopes. Transfer the pattern onto the coloured card (posterboard).

**2** Cut around the edges with a pair of scissors. Cut a piece of ribbon to fit across the crown of the hat and stick in place. Cut lengths of coloured ribbons, fold in half and glue to one corner of the ribbon on the crown.

**3** Stick a rose bow over the join.

**4** Write the invitation details on the other side of the hat.

## GETTING READY

Once you have decided on the event, set about organizing the preparations. There is the location to get ready as well as the catering to be done, and any entertainment must be planned. Make a realistic assessment of how much of the work you are going to undertake yourself, and how much help you are going to bring in from outside – in the form of practical assistance, friendly or paid. Apart from the question of food and drink, you will also need to consider what equipment may need to be bought, borrowed or hired.

Lists and a timetable are essential. Make a separate list for each aspect of the party planning: guests, shopping, household tasks, outside help, equipment hire and so on. Keep them all together in a folder. Prepare a programme of work for the week running up to a large party, with an especially detailed list of tasks for the day before and for the day itself. As each aspect is completed, tick it off the relevant list.

### Catering Arrangements

Catering implies organizing the serving of food as well as its preparation. Catering companies will take the whole task off your hands, you can hand over some aspects to the professionals, or you can hire the services of

*Don't forget to leave enough time for the finishing touches such as arranging flowers.*

individuals to prepare the food and help in other ways. Alternatively, you may decide to undertake all the catering at home.

### Cooking at Home

It is very gratifying to be able to take the credit for having prepared a splendid meal yourself. Given good planning, it is possible for someone with the time and ability to organize quite a large spread from a domestic kitchen; other party-givers will find it more satisfying and relaxing to let someone else take the strain.

❖ If you intend dealing with the food yourself, be sure to plan a menu that you can prepare with confidence. Choose recipes that do not need too much last-minute attention. Take advantage of dishes that can be prepared ahead of time and frozen. Enlist practical help well in time, if necessary. Delegate friends and relations who are good cooks to make specific dishes. Alternatively, commission dishes from a freelance cook who may offer exactly the level of catering required to retain that 'best of home cooking' feel.

❖ Consider, too, the possibility of buying in a wide range of high-quality ready-prepared foods: smaller local delicatessens, for example, may be able to supply dishes if ordered in advance.

## Equipment
As you compile your ingredients shopping list based on your chosen menu, make a checklist of any special cooking equipment you will need. Cooking pots and pans, such as cake tins or pans, cutlery (flatware), china and linen, for example, can all be hired.

*A range of items can be hired for parties, including full sets of china.*

Make a list of requirements and approach local companies for a quote (in Britain glasses can usually be borrowed free from a wine merchant with charges made only for breakages). As ever, it is important to establish exactly what you need, to determine the rates and to book ahead.

## Preparing the Location
If you are hiring either a room or marquee, you are likely to have access to the place for only a limited amount of time before the event, and any de-

liveries or decorations should be scheduled into your timetable to take this into account. If you are holding a function at home, on the other hand, you may seem to have all the time in the world. It is all too easy to postpone paying any attention to the home itself, a mistake which can lead to extensive last-minute work just when you would like to devote time to the final details for the gathering. Think well ahead for large gatherings and make lists of things that have to be done.

CLEANING If you are hosting a formal function at home, then you may want the house thoroughly spring cleaned beforehand. This may be something for outside specialists to handle if you do not have a home help.

Fix the day for cleaning about five to seven days before the event, and even if you have a regular help, it is a good idea to suggest commissioning an outside agency to assist with heavy work. Make sure you have someone to freshen up all areas on the day before the party or early on the day.

DECORATIONS Allow yourself time to do the flower arrangements, and any more complicated projects such as swags or wreaths of flowers and foliage for formal gatherings. Even for

a small informal get-together, lay the table in good time to create a welcoming ambience for your guests.

## Confirming Details
Finally, well ahead of time, make a checklist of vital last-minute points to confirm. This will probably mean telephoning to check details of orders placed, services commissioned, friends who have roles to play and guests that may need assistance in some way.

### The Perfect Party-Giver
Always allow time for yourself, especially on important occasions when you have to front the whole show. You will be more efficient if you feel at your best, and more likely to enjoy yourself.

❖ Fix an appointment at the hairdresser's to have your hair cut or trimmed a week or so in advance. For a special party style, fix an appointment on the day.

❖ Decide what you are going to wear in plenty of time and make sure it is dry-cleaned or pressed if necessary and ready to put on.

❖ If you plan a facial, book it for a few days ahead (it can leave your skin looking blotchy on the day).

❖ Consider having a relaxing massage the day before, when plans are almost complete.

❖ Always allow plenty of time for

your personal preparations, including that essential soak in the bath or long, refreshing shower.

❖ Plan to be dressed, relaxed and sipping a cool, non-alcoholic drink 30 minutes before you expect the first guests to arrive.

# MEMORABLE MENUS

*The time and effort devoted to menu planning depends entirely on the type of party that you are organizing. At a dinner party, or similar meal-time gathering, the menu* and quality of the food is an important focal point, whereas some parties concentrate more on the entertainment and refreshments are kept simple.

*Memorable menus fit in perfectly with the occasion and style of entertaining, from a breakfast spread to cocktail snacks or the grandest dinner party. This section sets out guidelines for planning refreshments to suit all occasions.*

## CREATING THE PERFECT MENU

The food must complement the event, whether it is the whole point of the occasion, one of several key features or a pleasing aside. Bear in mind the following general rules:

❖ The style of the menu must reflect the impression given on the invitation. For example, if you plan a celebration buffet, the food must live up to the occasion: bowls of nuts, crisps (chips), pretzels, some olives and a few salads will not do.

❖ Make sure the menu fulfils its intended role. If hungry guests are invited for a meal, don't palm them off with a snack. On the other hand, if you invite friends to a light lunch, it is equally inappropriate to serve them a hearty feast.

❖ Plan dishes that will be convenient to serve and eat in the circumstances of the party. For instance, avoid presenting guests at a stand-up buffet with food which really requires a knife and fork, a firm table and comfortable seat to be eaten neatly.

### Special Diets

Dietary restrictions may be applied for health, religious or cultural reasons, or purely on the basis of personal preferences. If you invite acquaintances to a dinner party, the obligation falls on them to let you know of any significant dietary restrictions. It is always a good idea, however, when discussing an invitation over the telephone, to check with guests whether any foods are best avoided.

Religious dietary laws include the kosher rules which Jews follow; these are extremely complex, covering the whole process of food production and cooking, and many Jews no longer adhere to them strictly. However, pork and shellfish are not eaten, and dairy products – this includes milk, cream and yogurt – are not prepared or consumed with meat.

Muslims do not eat pork and they do not consume alcohol. Hindus do not eat beef or drink alcohol, and many Hindu sects follow a vegetarian or vegan diet. Buddhists are vegetarian.

These notes merely indicate certain restrictions that may apply. You will need to check with your guests (or with a well-informed third party) to find out exactly what is and is not acceptable.

A vegetarian diet excludes meat but usually allows dairy products such as eggs, milk and cheese. A vegan diet permits no animal products at all.

Providing vegetarian alternatives at a large buffet is easy. Egg and cheese dishes and salads of peas and beans such as chick peas (garbanzo beans) or green lentils are suitable for cold buffets, and vegetable gratins are ideal for hot buffets.

Menu planning takes a little extra effort when you invite one or two vegetarian guests to a very traditional dinner party. It is easy to prepare a vegetarian soup (remember to avoid animal stock) or other first course that everyone can enjoy. As a vegetarian main dish serve something like a ratatouille gratin, braised fennel with a gratin topping, stuffed courgettes or mushrooms, a terrine of celeriac (celery root) or vegetable couscous. Select the non-vegetarian dish next and choose other vegetable accompaniments that will go well with both main dishes.

❖ The taste, texture, colour and presentation of all dishes should be palatable and visually pleasing. These characteristics must be well balanced for each course and throughout the meal as a whole.

❖ If you are cooking the food yourself, consider your kitchen facilities and equipment, and plan a menu that will not overstretch either of these. Select dishes and quantities which you can prepare with reasonable confidence. Think about preparing some dishes ahead of time to freeze when cooking for larger gatherings.

❖ When catering for a large party or for people whom you don't know well, be prepared to accommodate some special dietary needs.

## Formal Buffets

A buffet is practical for large gatherings, such as weddings and formal parties. The buffet may consist of hot or cold dishes, or a combination of the two. Canapés or hors d'oeuvres may be served beforehand. Ideally, the buffet should consist of a choice of fish, poultry and meat dishes accompanied by a range of salads and vegetables.

It is usual to serve one course, just the main course – no starter (appetizer) – at a buffet, followed by dessert and perhaps cheese; however, an excellent alternative is to present a selection of light dishes, like those suitable for the opening course of a dinner party, together with one or two main dishes.

Guests may sit at formal dining tables, in which case the buffet can include pies, roasts and other foods which are eaten with a knife and fork. If there is limited seating and the majority of guests are expected to stand during the meal, then the food must be easy to eat with a fork.

Staff may include waiters and waitresses to help guests to dishes on the buffet and a chef or competent server to carve. Make sure there are staff ready to clear dishes between courses.

## Buffet Dances

A buffet for a dance may take the form of a light supper, served early on in the evening before the music starts so as not to detract from the main event, the dancing. In this case, it is wise to offer snack food very much later. On the other hand, the buffet may be more formal, as above, and this will precede

*A platter of crudités is a simple, light dish for a buffet table.*

the dancing but there will be equal emphasis on dining as well as dancing later. Alternatively, light snacks may be offered on trays by serving staff around the room or put out on tables for the early part of the evening and a breakfast buffet may be served in the

early hours of the next day, from midnight or 12.30 a.m. onwards.

There are many variations on these ideas, with snacks being followed by a midnight feast or light refreshments of a savoury nature being made available throughout the evening.

### Formal Dinner Parties

Serve good-quality bought or home-made appetizers with drinks before dinner. The meal itself may consist of four or five courses, or more. Supper dishes and one-pot dishes are usually avoided in favour of carefully sauced dishes with separate vegetables or salads. Serving a meal of many courses can be an excellent way of entertaining, particularly when guests appreciate the nuances of different foods and subtle flavours. As lighter eating has become the norm, the most acceptable way of serving such a feast is to present very small portions throughout the meal.

Caterers, butler and waiting staff may be hired for a very formal dinner party. Show the staff the facilities available beforehand, discuss the menu requirements with them in detail and provide a guest list with any notes relating to serving requirements.

The simplest of formal dinner party menus should include soup or a first course, a main course and dessert. In Europe it is also usual to serve a cheese course towards the end of the meal. A fish course or light appetizer may be served after the soup or a refreshing sorbet may be served between the first and main courses, and a savoury dish may be served instead of cheese.

### Informal Dinner Parties

Three or four courses are usually served at informal dinner parties. The opening course may be a starter (appetizer), salad or soup and the main course is followed by either dessert or cheese, or both may be offered.

Informal dinner parties can feature a more extensive menu even though the general approach to the evening is very casual. For example, the confident cook may invite guests to join him or her in the kitchen before dinner as the final touches are added to the food.

If the informal nature of the evening refers more to dress than to food, then the host or hostess may still offer four or more courses but the nature of the food is likely to be less classic, with supper-style dishes (such as pasta or risotto), perhaps with a national theme, included on the menu.

### Supper Parties

One or two courses may be adequate and the food can be kept very simple. The term supper indicates a casual approach to the evening in general, providing an excuse to indulge in favourite childhood dishes and an opportunity for friends to enjoy a cosy meal in the kitchen. Serving supper is an excellent way of catching up with old friends or colleagues, when everyone can feel thoroughly relaxed and allow time for conversation to drift without fear of ruining any culinary masterpieces.

### Party Events

Generally, these are larger events where the food offered is less central to the proceedings, although a formal buffet served for a wedding breakfast, for instance, involves the full panoply of a well-balanced meal. For most party events, offer a good range of nibbles (snacks) and finger foods.

---

**After-Theatre Supper**

Inviting guests back for supper after a theatre performance is a good way of entertaining simply but stylishly at weekends when everyone is happy to eat late and stay into the early hours. Select a menu that can be prepared ahead: any hot food should be quick to cook with the minimum of fuss. Alternatively, simply serve a splendid array of open sandwiches, prepared in advance ready for receiving their garnish, with salad; followed by a simple dessert.

*Colourful canapés for the cocktail hour.*

### Cocktail Parties

The food at cocktail parties is intended to whet the appetite rather than satisfy it – guests are intended to go on to a main meal elsewhere – although another school of thought decrees that cocktail snacks should be substantial to counteract the inebriating effects of the cocktails themselves. Canapés or hors d'oeuvres, nibbles (snacks) and dips are the usual refreshments. They should be served in bite-sized portions and all be easy to eat with the fingers while balancing a glass at the same time. Any messy foods should be served on cocktail sticks (toothpicks).

### Mealtime Events

These are occasions when an event provides the pretext for the meal, such as a Thanksgiving or Christmas get-together, and is the focus of attention. Its style can be as formal or informal as you please, but its content needs to reflect tradition and be appropriate for the time of day.

---

**Perfect Petits Fours**

Individual servings of petits fours artfully arranged will round off any meal. Arrange the petits fours in small fluted paper or foil cases.
❖ Use a standard meringue mixture to pipe button-sized meringues and dry them out in the coolest possible oven. Sandwich them in pairs by dipping their bases in melted dark bitter chocolate.
❖ Stuff fresh dates with marzipan (almond paste) and roll in caster (superfine) sugar.
❖ Sandwich pecan nut or walnut halves in pairs with marzipan (almond paste).

*Cream teas are a special treat.*

## Tea

Depending on numbers, afternoon tea may be simple or elaborate. When casually inviting one or two friends to tea, then sandwiches and cakes are ideal. Guests can sit in easy chairs indoors or out with plates on their knees and cups on occasional tables.

❖ For a special cream tea, offer guests scones with jam and Devonshire or clotted cream as well as sandwiches and cakes. This is an occasion for sitting around the table.

❖ A summer tea party in the garden provides an occasion to invite larger numbers – space permitting. In this case, a good selection of sandwiches and savoury foods may be offered. Cakes and biscuits, strawberries and cream or a more elaborate trifle or selection of fancy pastries may be served buffet-style.

❖ A traditional British high tea provides a great opportunity for family entertaining. This is a cross between tea and supper, and usually consists of a light egg, fish or meat course followed by teabread, buns and cakes, with tea to drink. Suitable dishes include quiche, cold meats with pickles and filled pastries.

## Lunch or Luncheon

This can be an occasion for meeting friends over a light snack, for sharing activities before or after a more substantial but less elegant snack, or for bringing together a larger gathering at a buffet meal.

❖ A cold buffet is ideal for luncheon parties. Alternatively, a hot dish can be served along with a selection of salads and cold platters.

❖ Serve a vast tureen of hearty soup,

*Serve light, easy-to-prepare dishes for an informal lunch gathering.*

some crusty bread and cheese for an informal lunch. Minestrone is the ideal winter soup; chilled Spanish gazpacho is refreshing for summer.

❖ A traditional British Sunday lunch – a roasted joint of beef, lamb or pork, followed by a hearty dessert – may be shared with family or friends. Offer three courses, and coffee to finish. A classic roast requires fairly careful timing, so this type of meal is best kept informal.

## Breakfast and Brunch

Breakfast parties are ideal for weekends and national holidays. The menu should reflect the time of day, with fruit, cereals, cold meats, breads and buns or muffins. Fruit juice, mineral water and perhaps a champagne drink to which orange juice has been added are suitable cold refreshments; coffee or tea should also be served.

Brunch is served somewhere between breakfast and lunch, usually mid-morning. It may consist of a two-

or three-course meal, or a buffet. Since guests are not expected to have eaten breakfast and the meal is not followed by lunch, brunch may well be more substantial than for a lunch menu. Alternatively, the menu may revolve around one food, such as waffles or pancakes served with a variety of sweet or savoury fillings and toppings.

## Children's Parties

Apart from a special cake, the food is not usually of great gastronomic concern when planning a children's party. A mixture of savoury and sweet foods may be served as a sit-down lunch or tea, or you could opt for a buffet-style spread, depending on the age of the children and the surroundings. It is best to prepare simple, traditional foods – most children prefer them – and to limit the amount of sweet or very rich items available. Excited children will be more concerned with activities and entertainments once they have satisfied their hunger pangs.

# HELPING HANDS

*ven if you are super-organized and extremely confident, you will probably appreciate help at some level when planning a party. For a small event at home you may simply seek the encouragement and moral support of a friend or partner at the planning stage and some practical assistance on the day. For a somewhat larger gathering you will almost certainly need help to make sure that the occasion runs smoothly and that you have a chance to enjoy it yourself. This is particularly true for large formal events, especially for* the ultimate in party organizing – a traditional wedding at home. Many people have nightmares at the thought of being responsible for guest lists, a menu, caterers, wine, the welfare of all the family and keeping everyone in the local community happy. The answer is to stay calm, research all the options and allow sufficient time to plan all aspects of the party. Then you can make sure you have enough of the help you need and can afford in the days leading up to the party and on the day itself.

*Whether your helping hands belong to family and friends or to hired professionals, good planning is vital. Compile a list of tasks and a timetable of what to do when so that you can brief your assistants quite precisely about their duties. Once you know these aspects of the event are in capable hands, you will be able to turn your full attention to your own responsibilities as host or hostess.*

---

### FRIENDS AND RELATIVES

When planning informal parties or small, formal gatherings, it is probably enough to draw on those about you for any help you need rather than hiring professional assistance. If you do ask friends or relatives for special help, or accept assistance when it is volunteered, it is vital to establish a clear and tactful understanding to avoid any time-wasting, confusion and offence later. Before allowing anyone to help, consult your lists of work to be completed, decide exactly what you want to do, and can realistically tackle, yourself, then look at the areas with which you need help. Never fall into the trap of gratefully accepting every offer of help without organizing the distribution of work, otherwise you may find that the party has started early while you run around trying to get all the vital finishing touches completed.

❖ Always enlist the support of the family or other household members. Even if they are not involved in the organization of the party they must at least be supportive and not cause any hindrance. This point applies particularly to children, younger teenagers and partners who are unused to helping with household tasks, as they can get in the way dreadfully!

❖ All adults in the household should play their part, if not with direct preparation for the party, then at least with making sure that the home is neat and tidy.

❖ Delegate responsibility for specific tasks only to those who are competent and enthusiastic. Do not force someone into something he or she obviously does not want to do, as you will end up having to pick up the pieces right at the last minute.

❖ Never feel obliged or forced to accept help from someone whom you do not want involved. Some people will eagerly, and often unthinkingly, try to take over the whole show, or take over a major part which you would prefer to play. It is best to divert their attention tactically to an area which you are prepared to delegate. Alternatively, firmly but pleasantly thank them for their offer and point out that the work is already in hand.

❖ When you do enlist the help of others, clearly plan their roles with them, making sure they understand what needs doing and how you want it done. This may seem to be a very pedantic way of handling volunteers, but it is practical.

❖ Remember to encourage and thank everyone who helps, no matter how small the contribution. Never dismiss or overlook good intentions.

❖ For occasions such as formal engagement parties and weddings, it is diplomatic to involve members of the partner's family or close friends. Never exclude them from plans. Welcome their input into the proceedings and offer assistance, and deal tactfully with any suggestions which may not fit in with the general flow of plans.

## PROFESSIONAL HELP

You may decide to employ a company to organize the party completely, leaving you free to concentrate on the guest list and the social side of the occasion. You will probably find several local companies offering comprehensive party services, from organizing a children's birthday party to formal dinner dances and weddings with live music or a disc jockey.

When paying for any help, it is a good idea to ask around among friends for recommendations. If you were impressed by outside staff at a gathering you attended and know the organizers well enough, then don't hesitate to ask for their comments.

### Cleaning Services

If you have a regular home help, then warn him or her of your party plans and book time for special preparations, and for clearing up afterwards. Some helpers will also assist immediately at the end of the party with washing up and clearing away.

If you do not have a regular cleaner, then you may consider using an agency or a company which moves in and spring cleans the house on an appointed day. Book a window cleaner shortly before the date of the event. For daytime parties and in summer particularly it is a good idea to have all the windows sparkling clean.

### Comprehensive Party Planning

Draw up a list of your requirements, then approach suitable companies in your area for their comments and a quotation. Look through their suggestions carefully and go back to those companies offering the most attractive and competitive packages with more specific queries. Ask about previous events which they have organized,

how long they have been operating and how far in advance you have to supply a firm booking. When planning a large wedding or similar function, many hosts or hostesses think in terms of contacting suitable companies up to a year ahead, especially for spring and summer weddings, when popular organizers quickly fill their diaries.

### Caterers

You can commission caterers to provide all or some of the food, to provide food and waiting staff, or to organize all aspects of the meal, including tables, seating, linen, crockery (china), cutlery (flatware), the menu, wine, chef or cook and waiting staff. Whether you opt for a large company or an individual cook depends mainly on the number of guests. There are many small caterering outfits which work from home, and which offer excellent quality buffets and service at gatherings for anything up to a hundred

people. Individual cooks can also perform well for dinner parties, and will sometimes wait at table.

It's best to approach a number of caterers initially, give them some idea of the function and numbers involved, and ask them what type of food and service they provide and what menus they would recommend, before getting quotes from a shortlist.

Discuss numbers, facilities for catering and serving food, the exact style of food and meal required and some indication of budget before receiving a menu suggestion. By making sure the caterer has all the necessary information you will avoid wasting time on discussing unsuitable menus. If you have queries or are unhappy about any aspect of the menu, then follow up promptly and come to a decision. Larger companies will provide a written order; if you verbally make any changes, then follow by writing a letter outlining them.

*If necessary, enlist a skillful hand with flower arrangements.*

You may want to hand over responsibility for the wine to the caterers; some may work on the premiss that they always expect to handle wine orders when organizing functions. However, the more economical option is to deal with this yourself, particularly as many good wine merchants will advise on fine wines; there is even more choice in the middle-market area.

If the cook or caterers provide waiting staff, china and so on, then you can expect them to organize staff and return the goods.

**Waiting Staff**
You may decide to employ a waiter or waitress for formal dinners which you prepare yourself, in which case it is important to find someone who is confident and capable enough to interact correctly with yourself while you cook and look after your guests. With careful planning, this arrangement can work very well and ease the burden on you. Pay attention to serving arrangements when planning the menu, selecting dishes which can easily be brought to table and served. The waiter or waitress should clear the table after the first course. Make sure the waiter or waitress is organized as far as the side dishes are concerned, then ask him or her to bring them in promptly once you have presented the main course. You or your partner may serve or carve the main course, leaving your helper to place vegetable dishes on the table. The waiter or waitress should clear the table and, depending on the dish, bring in dessert, then coffee.

If you wish food to be served to guests, make sure that the waiter or waitress is experienced in doing so correctly, presenting dishes to the diner's left.

At drinks or cocktail parties, trays of canapés and snacks can be handed around by a server, who will also remove used glasses and top up drinks. At a buffet, he or she may assist in serving certain dishes, top up drinks and remove used items.

Ask waiting staff to arrive 30–60 minutes before guests are due, to fit in with your own schedule and requirements. Explain the menu and facilities, and make a note to pass on any relevant information about guests that they may need to know. Offer a cup of tea or a soft drink if time allows.

### Hiring a Butler

Most special occasions that call for hired help will not, of course, include the services of a butler. However, some caterers do offer a butler service, and it's useful to know exactly what this entails. On the other hand, you may want to instruct one of the waiting staff to take on some of the functions of a traditional butler.

❖ The duties of the butler are to prepare the table for a dinner, to set out glasses and ensure that all drinks and wines are ready. If there are waiters, waitresses or bar staff, then the butler should oversee their work to ensure that all runs smoothly. The butler opens the door, takes coats and announces guests. During a sit-down meal the butler may carve or do all the serving if there are no waiting staff. He will also serve coffee and liqueurs.

❖ At buffets and any other large parties, the butler will top up drinks and generally ensure that all guests are well cared for; however, although he may hand out some canapés or hors d'oeuvre and remove used dishes, the butler is not expected to serve food at buffets.

❖ Make sure the butler is shown around before the party, that he arrives in time to lay a dinner table (and is aware of this duty in advance) and that he knows where to put guests' coats. Go through details of the area to which guests should be shown and how you would like guests introduced.

*Magicians and jugglers can liven up a party where children are present.*

**Bartender** Employing someone to look after the bar is only necessary if the function demands that cocktails are mixed. Waiters, waitresses and butler all serve drinks.

### ENTERTAINMENT
The form of entertainment depends on the guests and the occasion. The majority of dinner or drinks parties run perfectly smoothly without any formal entertainment; sometimes music and dancing are an essential feature of a gathering; and children's parties often rely on well-organized entertainment.

If you plan games, make sure all the equipment you need is ready to hand and assign someone who knows the rules to take charge of the proceedings. If you want music, whether it is for background interest or for dancing, it is a good idea to delegate the task of organizing it to someone enthusiastic and knowledgeable. They might prepare tapes beforehand, or act as a disc jockey, adapting the music to the mood of the party.

If you want guests to dance, then it is vital to make sure that there is a sufficiently large area cleared for the purpose. The host and/or hostess starts the dancing by inviting other guests to participate in the fun.

## Musicians
Live bands, pianists, string quartets and various musical groups may all be hired. Discuss the repertoire when booking and confirm details a week or so before the party. Live music is well suited to events such as weddings or large parties when a hall is hired or a marquee or tent erected. Unless you have a very large area in your home, then anything more than a pianist may be very overpowering as a form of general entertainment.

## Entertainers
Magicians and clowns can be booked for children's parties, and for adult parties where children are included. Their performance will revive any flagging spirits, particularly those of children who are bored among too many adults. If you intend to entertain all age groups, discuss this with prospective entertainers and make sure they have a suitable repertoire.

Entertainers of this sort are often used to working at functions where guests are seated, not necessarily in rows but at least at dining tables. They may not adapt easily to moving among guests who are standing. For parties where children and adults are invited or at weddings where there are lots of children, it can be an excellent idea to organize all the youngsters into sitting in the living room or a suitable place for the entertainment. Since they all sit quite happily on the floor this does not usually involve a great deal of work and a 20-minute show can provide a quiet gap which will be appreciated by adults as well as giving younger children a rest from running around.

## Outdoor Amusements for Children
Puppet shows provide the outdoor equivalent of the conjuring show, with a performance at a pre-set time that makes a rewarding focus for everyone's attention. Even though puppet shows are intended for children, many adults will happily break away from socializing to participate. An alternative form of entertainment to offer out of doors is "activity equipment" such as play centres. These are designed for children's parties, but most adults love to try them out, too.

When hiring any equipment of this kind, make sure you have a clear understanding about what the fee covers. Some companies sound extremely economical but leave the collection and process of erecting equipment to you.

## OUTSIDE ENTERTAINMENT
Local telephone directories list a variety of different entertainment possibilities, as do local newspapers and some up-market glossy magazines. Personal recommendations from friends are always helpful, particularly if you are thinking of employing musicians or other live entertainment such as a disco for an adults' party.

## Discos
Even though discos are sometimes thought of as noisy teenage entertainment, there are outfits that specialize in providing suitable music for weddings and family gatherings. Again, it is important to discuss the repertoire to suit all guests. Consider noise levels and ensure you do not cause offence to neighbours.

# STUNNING SETTINGS

*they pass through the hallway before dinner, the merest glimpse of arrangements should excite the dining instincts by hinting at the quality of the meal to come.*

*Whether crisp and sophisticated, softly flowing with lace and flowers, warm and homely, or refreshingly bright, the setting should confirm the guests' anticipation of the party and raise it to new levels. This section is designed to arouse your enthusiasm for scene-setting and to encourage artistic instincts. With flair and a sense of occasion you can be as individualistic as you wish, and carry off any event with outstanding success.*

*T*he first sight of the table plays a keynote for any meal, so it is essential that the setting is just right for the occasion. In contemporary living-dining rooms and at buffet parties the table is on display from the moment the guests arrive; if guests happen to pass an open dining room door as

**TABLE LINEN**

There is an enormous variety of table linen available, most of it far removed from traditional white linen. There are no rules about what is acceptable or otherwise, the only qualification being that the choice should suit the occasion. A chequered patio cloth and bright paper napkins are not worthy of a gourmet meal of classic dishes. Conversely white damask and fine glass would seem inappropriate for a casual invitation for a snack lunch . . . .

**White linen**

White linen is both versatile and practical, and there is nothing quite like crisply starched, large white napkins for a dinner party table.

Heavy, white damask tablecloths and napkins are expensive but they will last for years. It is always worth looking out for good-quality second-hand linen at auctions, flea markets and in antique or junk shops – as long as the fabric is not scorched, badly marked, worn or torn, then it is a good buy.

Although spray starch is adequate for a tablecloth, the only way to get a really good finish on napkins is by starching them with traditional starch which you mix with boiling water. A good compromise, instead of soaking

the fabric in the starch solution, is to mix a small quantity according to the packet directions, then keep it in a clean plant spray bottle. Spray dry napkins and cloths before ironing, leaving the moisture to soak into the fabric for about 30 seconds. The result

is just like proper starched linen.

Although plain white linen is unsuitable for casual table settings, do not feel that it always has to form the base for extremely formal table arrangements. Introduce a contemporary air with your choice of flowers or table

*White, damask table linen adds elegance to a formal dinner.*

*Choose brightly coloured table linen for an ethnic meal or theme party.*

centrepieces; instead of traditional white candles go for coloured ones or even scented candles; or neatly roll the napkins and use colourful napkin ties or ribbons with a small flower or suitable trimming to pick up on the rest of the table decorations.

## Plain and Printed Linen

Good linen in delicate pastel shades can be equally as formal as traditional white table settings. Deep colours can be more dramatic and stylish but just as formal, depending on the overall presentation. Strong colours can also make an eye-catching base for flamboyant themes, particularly when preparing an ethnic meal or for fancy dress

### Table Protection

Buy a waterproof protective covering to lay on the table under the cloth. This protects the table surface from plates and glassware, and from any spills. Do not buy a cheap brand if you have a good table; it is better to spend more and know that the table is safe.

(costume) parties and buffets.

Printed and woven linen varies enormously in quality. Smart checks and stripes are useful for informal picnics, barbecues, patio meals, breakfasts and brunches.

## Embroidered Linen and Lace

Colourful hand embroidery is ideal for breakfast cloths, and for table coverings for brunches, family teas and high tea. Fine work trimmed with lace and lace cloths are ideal for afternoon teas, parties in the garden, grand picnic parties and for weddings.

## Appliqué Napkin

Appliqué in the form of flowers or fruit makes decorative corner trimmings for plain tablecloths and napkins.

**YOU WILL NEED:** plain coloured napkins, thin card (posterboard) for template, pencil, colourfast red fabric, green felt, scissors, iron-on interfacing, dressmaker's marking pen, red and yellow thread, needle.

**1** Transfer the strawberry shape to the red fabric and the stem shape to the green felt. You will also need to transfer the strawberry shape onto a piece of iron-on interfacing.

**2** Cut around the lines using a pair of sharp scissors. Iron on the interfacing to the back of the strawberry cut-out. Mark where the seed details will go with a dressmaker's marking pen (this should be washable).

**3** Tack (baste) the strawberry cut-out in place on the napkin, then stitch all around the edge using buttonhole stitch or zig-zag machine stitch. This will prevent the fabric from fraying. Tack the stem in position, then hand or machine stitch in place using a straight stitch and yellow thread. Hand stitch the seed details using the yellow thread.

## Stencilled Table Linen

Wall stencils used as part of the dining room or kitchen decor can be picked up on cloths and napkins using fabric paints. Do not try to match colours, as it is unlikely you will be able to achieve the same shade with fabric paints. Select toning or contrasting colours instead. Follow the manufacturer's instructions for using fabric paint for a result which is lasting and washable.

**YOU WILL NEED:** plain coloured place mats and napkins; (for making stencil) paper, pencil, sticky (transparent) tape; clear acetate for stencil, waterproof black felt-tip pen, craft knife, fabric paints, paintbrush, rag.

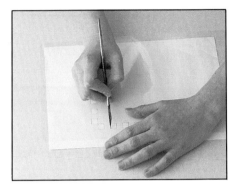

**1** If you are making your own stencil, draw your design onto a sheet of paper. Place the sheet of acetate on top and tape in position to hold the sheet firmly in place. Transfer the design to the acetate using a waterproof black felt-tip pen. Cut around the outline of the stencil design with a craft knife.

**2** Load the brush with paint. Keep a rag handy for wiping excess paint from the brush. For stencilling, you should not have too much paint on the brush as this can seep beneath the stencil. Holding the stencil firmly in place, press the brush over the pattern in the stencil keeping the brush vertical. Wait for the paint to dry before applying the second colour.

**3** To create a stippled effect, you will need some white or pale coloured paint and a clean brush. Lightly load the brush with paint and dab on the paint using a stabbing motion. Allow the paint to dry, then fix according to the manufacturer's instructions.

*A range of fine cutlery (flatware).*

*Collect a range of colourful china for informal entertaining.*

## EATING UTENSILS

It is usual to have a set of everyday cutlery (flatware) for kitchen use and to have a smart collection for dining room use. Silver or silver plate is the traditional material for eating utensils, but stainless steel is more popular and practical, and there are many elegant designs – both traditional and modern – in high-quality finishes.

For entertaining purposes, most cutlery (flatware) sets include meat knives and small knives for bread and butter; large forks and two sets of small forks, for first courses and desserts; soup spoons, dessertspoons and teaspoons; and possibly fish knives and forks, which are a useful addition. Serving spoons are essential; sauce and soup ladles can be useful.

Remember that cutlery (flatware) with wood or bone handles must not be immersed in water for any length of time, so they are not suitable for dishwashers. Make sure the handles are clear of the water if soaked.

*Simple designs are often the most elegant.*

## CHINAWARE

Traditionally, there is usually a set or mixture of crockery (china) in everyday use and a set reserved for smarter meals. China for special occasions consists of dinner and salad plates, soup bowls, dessert plates and bowls, and tea or coffee cups and saucers, usually of the best quality affordable.

❖ White china is practical and versatile as it may be dressed up or down by the table settings. It also allows plenty of scope for buying ovenproof dishes and serving dishes which do not clash with the dinner service.

❖ Build up a collection of bright everyday china, including soup bowls which double as pasta dishes, so that it can be used for informal entertaining.

❖ Good-quality old china can be attractive. Given that you collect china of a similar or complementary style, the patterns do not have to match. For example, large floral patterns on serving bowls, cake stands and dishes make a pleasing display on a buffet table.

❖ If you have a dishwasher, check when buying new fine china that any decorative finish will not be affected by the machine.

### Unusual Serving Containers

The most unlikely of serving dishes can often look wonderful, especially at large parties when your usual supply is stretched to the limit. Search in junk shops and antique shops for old, decorative china (check before you buy for cracks and chips) and use casseroles and vegetable dishes for pâtés.

❖ Large wash jugs and basins which are in good condition make attractive, exciting serving vessels: use the jug for outrageously fruity punches and fill the bowl with a dessert such as fruit salad.

❖ Dress up inferior glass cake stands with luxurious bows of ribbon and use the very readily available glass sugar bowls for serving salad dressing.

❖ If all else fails and you really cannot find suitable serving dishes, then buy some large white plastic trays and decorate them according to the food on offer or the party: cover them with paper doilies; tie ribbon bows and stick them on the corners; wire frosted flowers or fruit and tape them to the corners; or use festive decorations such as sprigs of holly or spring flowers.

## GLASSWARE

Choice of glassware is entirely personal and subject to budget. When buying inexpensive glasses, remember that it is always pleasing to be offered a glass that is suitable for the contents and comfortable to hold. Plain styles are generally preferable to ornate ones. Always hold each type (even if they are a special offer at the local hardware store) as you would if you were about to drink. Look at the way in which the stems join to the bowls – are they smoothly incorporated or is there an ugly link? – and always run your fingers around the rim to check there are no rough edges.

If you regularly have barbecues and parties which demand inexpensive, functional glasses, then it is worth buying a boxful of white wine goblets and storing them for such occasions.

Good-quality glass is always pleasing when drinking wine, but this does not mean having very expensive or decorative crystal; the simplest, fine-rim glasses, which are often the most inexpensive, are often the nicest from which to drink, especially when serving light white wine, which tends to be lost in heavily cut lead crystal.

The number of glasses provided at a dinner party depends on the wines served. Always provide water glasses and separate glasses for white and red wine. You also need glasses for serving pre-dinner drinks and for brandy, port or liqueurs after dinner.

Sturdy plastic tumblers are essential for children's parties and for any occasions when lots of children are invited. Although decorative plastic patio wear looks the part, it is not pleasing material from which to drink wine. A better option for outdoor parties and picnics would be inexpensive plain glasses – wrap them up well in tea-towels (dishtowels) when transporting them or keep them in the boxes in which they were purchased.

### Shapes and Sizes of Glass

Liqueur glasses are the smallest, followed by port, then sherry glasses. White wine glasses are smaller than those for red wine. Hock glasses originally designed for German white wine have tall stems and rounded bowls. Champagne and sparkling wines are served in flutes, tall slim glasses which conserve the gas in the wine. The once popular wide-topped champagne glasses did nothing for the wine, and they could also be very poorly balanced when filled! Water goblets are larger than red wine glasses.

There is a wide range of glassware for pre-dinner and after-dinner drinks, parties and cocktails. It is just as important to choose well in this area as it is when buying wine glasses. There are a few traditional shapes and associations.

❖ A jigger is a small glass which holds 45 ml/1½ fl oz and this is the standard measure used when mixing cocktails. It is ideal for serving very strong drinks, such as Polish vodka.

❖ Cocktail glasses are traditionally about 75 ml/3 fl oz (about ⅓ cup) capacity with steeply sloping sides. Sizes vary and there are some large cocktail glasses which can be lethal when filled with strong drinks!

❖ An 'old-fashioned' glass is a short, wide, heavy-bottomed tumbler, about 250 ml/8 fl oz (1 cup) capacity; this is ideal for the cocktail of the same name, consisting of whiskey (rye or bourbon) a little sugar syrup, Angostura bitters, ice, a cherry and lemon.

❖ A highball glass is a tall, slim, heavy-bottomed glass tumbler, about 250 ml/8 fl oz (1 cup) capacity.

❖ Beer and cider (hard cider) may be served in tall tumblers or stemmed glasses. The classic glass for light beers has a short wide stem and tall slim bowl (a lager glass). Goblets with short stems and large, often well-rounded, bowls are also used for beers. Very large, well-rounded glasses on tall stems (often intended for those who imbibe red wine with pleasure) are excellent for serving beers and ciders. Metal tankards and mugs are less elegant but there are many attractive glasses of this type.

❖ Punch may be served in a punch bowl with matching cups. Round-bowled glasses are also suitable or use short, fairly small water glasses.

❖ Brandy glasses have large bowls, narrowing at the rim, and short stems. They are designed for swirling and sniffing, to appreciate the aroma of the drink as well as its flavour.

❖ Irish coffee glasses are slim and tall, with short, wide stems and a handle. They are also useful for serving mulled wine as they are easy to hold even when the contents are very warm.

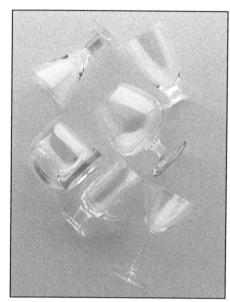
*Drinks glasses vary in shape and size.*

*Choose glassware that is suitable for the contents and pleasing to hold.*

*Brightly coloured china is extremely versatile. Dress it up or down according to the occasion.*

## TABLE SETTINGS

The way in which the table is set depends on the occasion and the type of food being served. The convention is to place forks to the left of the plate and knives and spoons to the right.

The forks are laid with tines pointing up and the spoons have bowls up. The base of each is about 2.5 cm/1 in from the table edge. Spoons and forks for dessert are sometimes laid across the top of the plate, along with the knife for cheese. A bread plate is placed on the left side and the napkin is usually laid across it. The napkin may also be folded decoratively and placed in the middle of the setting. Napkins are not placed in glasses for formal settings.

### Formal Settings

When you want to pull out all the stops and serve a number of courses laying a traditional table is simple.

❖ The rule is that the diner starts at the outside of the row of cutlery (flatware) and works inwards. Working inwards from the right: bread knife, soup spoon, fish knife or knife for first course, meat knife, dessertspoon. Working inwards from the left: fish fork or fork for first course, fork for main course, fork for dessert. This is the most formal method of laying place settings, the cutlery being suited to each course in turn. Knives and forks for fruit or a savoury offering at the end of the meal may be brought in when the course is served. If the dessert is eaten with a spoon only, it is usual to lay this on the table for formal settings.

❖ The spoon and fork for dessert may be laid across the top of the plate, spoon with handle to the right, fork handle to the left. This is still acceptable as a formal setting, but not quite up to traditional state dinner standards!

❖ The glasses are set out above the cutlery to the right of the place setting. They should be arranged in the order in which they are used, but the conventions relating to placing glass are not as rigid as for cutlery – make sure, however, that all glass settings are identical.

**FINGER BOWLS** These are provided, one to each guest, when the food has to be eaten with the fingers. For example, when peeling prawns (shrimp), cracking and cleaning lobster, eating globe artichokes and serving whole fruit at the end of the meal. The bowls should be fairly small and wide-topped; glass is ideal. The bowls are placed on small plates, saucers or delicate cotton mats. The water should be warm and a slice of lemon, rose petals or other suitable decorative ingredient may be added.

**SERVING SPOONS** Serving spoons and forks may be laid at intervals on the table and there may be heatproof mats ready for hot dishes. At formal meals where food is served to the diners by waiting staff this is unnecessary. When serving utensils are laid, these should follow the convention of having spoon handles to the right and fork handles to the left. Any special serving implements for the host or hostess should be laid near his or her place or brought in with the food.

## CRUETS AND CONDIMENTS

Traditionally, salt and pepper sets are placed on the table and several are laid for large gatherings. If the cook has carefully prepared and tasted the food for seasoning, however, then he or she may not provide salt.

Pepper can be another matter as there are times when freshly ground pepper enhances an ingredient, for example fresh figs, some melons, Parma ham (prosciutto), pasta dishes and goats' cheese are typical. A pepper mill for table use should be presentable and it is best to buy one especially for the purpose. Avoid buying an attractive case with a poor-quality grinding mechanism: look for a smart but workmanlike utensil instead. Mills are usually filled with black pepper.

Condiments such as mustard are laid to one side, and several containers should be placed on a large table.

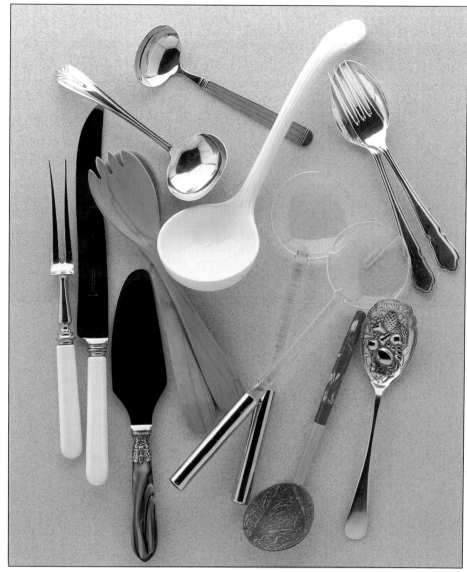

*Above: a range of serving utensils.*　　　*Below: a finger bowl with rose petals.*

*A garland of fresh flowers and foliage enhances an outdoor buffet table.*

## BUFFET SETTINGS

Buffet tables provide the perfect excuse for impressive settings, perhaps with swags of flowers or ribbons and posies as well as a large main decoration. All the food should be decorative too, and it must be arranged for ease of access when guests serve themselves.

The buffet may be placed against a wall so that guests move along in front of the table and serve themselves, or it may be situated in the middle of a room (or with space all around) so that guests move around the table. Whichever system is used, there should be an obvious starting point for serving and this is indicated by a pile of plates. On a large table, plates may be piled at both ends so that guests can work from both directions.

If the buffet is set against a wall, then the main decoration should be at the

*Small garlands look pretty above entrances.*

rear and positioned in the centre. If guests walk all around the table, then a centrepiece should be placed on the table.

Make sure all the dishes are easy to reach and that there are serving spoons nearby. If there is a ham or other food

which needs carving, set it in a position to one side of the table so that guests do not obstruct access to other dishes while they carve. It should be some-one's task to check the availability of foods, topping dishes up and tidying the buffet occasionally.

Set napkins and cutlery separately on a side table. Large paper napkins are usually used for informal buffets. If disposable plates are used, they should be sturdy and of good quality, as thin plates sag miserably and make eating difficult. Buffet-style plates are now available which include a holder for a wine glass. Alternatively, keep a large number of good-quality, large plastic plates, which are ideal for entertaining in large numbers. They are easier to rinse, stack and wash than china plates, and ideal for outdoor parties as well as for informal buffets.

**Themed Settings**

There are times when it is fun to abandon convention and go for something strikingly different in the way of setting arrangements. This is fine if you know the guests reasonably well, but it is not a good idea to confront business acquaintances or people you rarely meet with something out of the ordinary. Think of these setting styles as informal alternatives!

White and pastels tend to be favoured colours for table settings, but strong colours make a dramatic impact. A blue and gold setting, for example, could have a deep blue cloth and napkins, matching candles and a blue flower arrangement, such as hydrangeas, hyacinths, delphiniums, lavender or cornflowers. Wire dried autumn leaves and spray them gold, then use these with the fresh flowers.

Alternatively, try creating a lush green table using a white linen cloth as the base and limiting the other colour to green, including candles. Make a central arrangement of leaves: as well as cuttings from shrubs, take leaves from indoor plants, such as Japanese aralia and grape ivy. Create movement and interest by using leaves of different sizes and shapes.

A contrast setting could start with a black tablecloth and white dinner plates. Use black-and-white napkins, perhaps ones that have a strong, geometric pattern. To make an elongated napkin shape with points at the top and bottom, fold and press each

*Combine clean lines and black and white chinaware and table linen for a strikingly modern look.*

napkin into quarters, then give it a quarter turn and fold the opposite side corners over the middle so that they overlap. Press neatly and place one on each plate.

Use small white candle holders and short black candles, or small white saucers and black nightlights (votive-style candles) or small, rounded candles. Place several of these along the length of a rectangular table or around

the middle of a circular table. If using white saucers, press and fold two small squares of crêpe paper to sit under the candles: one black square to go on the saucer, then a white square offset on top to go under the candle.

Any central decoration should be simple and based on white flowers with dried leaves that are wired and sprayed black.

In complete contrast, a pretty lace

setting is ideal for a celebratory lunch party, for a small wedding lunch party or for a large buffet table. Lay a plain-coloured cloth or fabric over the table – pink is ideal for this theme. The colour should be reasonably strong but not garish. Lay a lace cloth over the plain cloth so that the colour shows through.

*Opposite: fine lace and small posies of flowers set the scene for a celebration lunch.*

*Candles and candle holders come in a wide range of sizes and colours suitable for every occasion.*

### Lighting for Effect

Fixing on the right lighting is crucial to the success of any scene-setting plan and the results can have marked effects on your guests. Just as people will feel uncomfortable in glaringly

bright surroundings more conducive to a dentist's office than to a dinner party, so they will also feel unnerved and depressed by lighting which is dim to the point of being gloomy.

For the majority of entertaining

the lighting should be soft enough to make your guests look their best and to suggest that everyone ought to be relaxed. It should, however, be bright enough for people to see what is being eaten and to read the expressions across the dining table.

### Candles

Candles really do give a room a pleasing glow. They should be used in conjunction with sufficient electric light to ensure that the surroundings are bright enough.

❖ Slim, tall candles are perfect for elegant dining.

❖ Chubby, bright candles are well suited to kitchen suppers and informal meals.

❖ Create different heights of light by arranging candles around the room. Place some on a fireplace hearth (set them to one side if the fire is lit, otherwise they melt and run), others on side tables and some at windowsill level.

❖ Arrange marbles or glass pebbles in a large copper or other metal bowl with nightlights. Place the bowl on a low table or footstool in a corner of the room.

❖ Wherever you place candles, make absolutely sure that they present no risk of fire and never leave lit candles unattended.

❖ Floating candles are designed for floating when alight. Select a wide-topped glass bowl and place some colourful stones, shells and artificial aquarium plants in the bowl. Float and light the candles.

❖ Combine floating candles and Japanese water flowers.

*Floating candles and rosebuds in a bowl.*

Set conventional place settings. Roll the napkins and tie them with satin ribbon and large bows.

Draw up the lace cloth at the corners of the table and at intervals around the edge (between place settings), then pin it in place so that it hangs in swags.

Prepare small posies of roses and tie them with flamboyant bows of satin ribbon to match the place settings. Pin the flowers on the cloth.

Arrange a large bowl of roses for the centre of the table. Make sure you have enough roses to lay one at each place

setting. Trim each stem and wrap with a leaf in a little moistened absorbent kitchen paper (paper towels). A final wrapping of foil will hold everything together and keep in the moisture. Place the roses under the bows around the napkins shortly before guests arrive.

### Candles

White candles are traditional at formal dinners but this convention depends entirely on the hostess and the setting. Tall candlesticks usually have short candles and short holders take long candles. The candles may be placed in the centre of the table or at intervals along its length. If there is the space, very effective settings can be created by flouting this convention and arranging low candles or nightlights (votive-style candles) towards the table corners.

### Ideas for Electric Lights

❖ Arrange fans or sunshades in front of floor spotlights to create a warm light.

❖ Make large paper lanterns and place very low-wattage bulbs in them (15 watt).

❖ Use coloured bulbs. These are especially good for lively parties,

where areas may be lit with bright red, blue or green by fitting the appropriate bulbs.

❖ Use a floor spotlight or standard spotlight to cast light from behind a large, exotic-looking indoor plant – the effect can be quite eerie.

❖ Place a low-wattage light on a windowsill to illuminate a hand-painted blind or unusual fabric.

**Patio and Garden Settings**

If you are entertaining outdoors, the patio must be swept clean and adorned with flowers. Tubs of growing plants and hanging baskets should be distributed. Table settings may be bright or pastel, as you prefer and according to the occasion: pastels are ideal for special celebrations; primary colours for fun events.

Entertaining outdoors can be just another day in the garden or the whole scene can be transformed by bringing out a few props and distributing them in a casual fashion. The key to success with this sort of scene-setting is to really go for it . . . do not feel shy about being flamboyant: anything less will not command the same stunning impact. Take a careful look at the arrangement of garden chairs and patio furniture. Bring out rugs and large

comfortable cushions. As well as a sunshade for the table, put up smaller sunshades and leave them lying around

*Transform a simple straw hat with a garland of fresh or dried flowers.*

for guests to use – Oriental sunshades are inexpensive and decorative. Buy simple straw hats, decorate them with ribbons and flowers and scatter them

around both as decoration and for guests' use. Decorate shrubs and trees with enormous bows of ribbon and balloons. Hang round flower or foliage posies around the outside of the house and from large standard sunshades.

If the party is planned for late afternoon or evening, then light garden flares (torches) and set lights among shrubs or trees – do not create a fire hazard, however. Outdoor candles can be purchased in special glass holders which withstand the heat and prevent the flame from blowing out in a breeze. Coloured glass holders create attractive shadows and colours.

*Candles in glass holders cast a warm glow on the patio once the sun has gone down. Be careful to place them in a safe position.*

# Gold Leaf Napkin Ring

Collect autumn leaves to make this elegant napkin ring. Dried beech leaves have been used here, but any medium-sized dried leaves are suitable. As an alternative, use silver spray to paint.

**YOU WILL NEED:** dried leaves, wire, gold spray paint, florists' dry foam (styro foam), heavy satin ribbon, needle and matching thread.

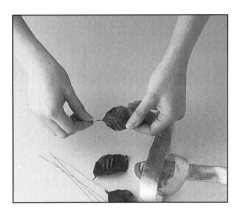

**1** For each napkin ring, wire 3 dried leaves onto 20 cm/8 in wires.

**2** Spray the wired leaves with gold spray paint on a well-protected work surface. Always work in a well-ventilated area. Stand each finished leaf in florists' dry foam (styro foam) to dry.

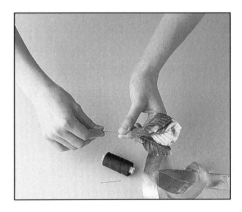

**3** When the paint is dry, twist the leaves together. Arrange the leaves so that the central leaf is higher than the other two leaves. Allow about 2.5 cm/1 in of wire to remain untwisted immediately below the leaves when they have been arranged.

**4** Wrap the end of the ribbon around the wire below the middle leaf, taking about 7.5 cm/3 in of the end and binding it around the twisted wire. Bind another layer of ribbon over this, then bind along the length of the wire.

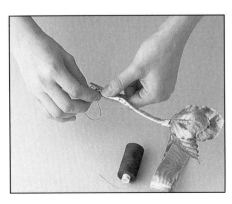

**5** Stitch the ribbon in place at the end of the wire with matching thread. Trim off any protuding ends of wire. Form the ribboned wire into a ring and secure the end under the leaves with a few stitches. Gently twist the leaves in place and flatten the ring to neaten.

# Greenery Chain

Make a simple chain of greenery to swag the table edge.

**YOU WILL NEED:** suitable foliage, plastic-covered tying wire or florists' wire, selection of herbs such as bay leaves, rosemary and thyme, needle and green thread, pins, green ribbon.

**1** Join lengths of foliage together with suitable wire cut into manageable strips.

**2** Wire sprigs of herbs and stitch them to the chain at intervals. Pin the chain to one corner of the table and then pin at each sprig of herbs to form swags. Trim with bows of green ribbon.

## Pomander Decorations

Orange and lemon pomanders are pretty hung around the kitchen suspended from ribbon, or arranged in a bowl as a table centrepiece. Stud them all over with cloves to keep longer.

**YOU WILL NEED:** oranges and lemons, soft pencil, cloves, ribbon, pins.

**1** Using a soft pencil, lightly mark segments lengthways on the fruit. Press the cloves along the pencilled lines, spacing them evenly.

**2** Take a length of ribbon and wrap it lengthways on the fruit, positioning it between two rows of cloves. Tie it off at one end. Repeat, tying off the second ribbon in the same position as the first.

**3** Take a separate piece of ribbon and thread it under the knot of the ribbon on the fruit. Tie it into a bow and insert a pin through the ribbon and into the fruit to hold it in place. The pin may be disguised by folding one loose end of the ribbon over the join and tucking it under.

# Garden Posy

Spherical posies of fresh, dried or bright tissue flowers on a length of garden cane (bamboo stake) and placed in flower pots can be arranged around the patio and garden to provide instant colour.

**YOU WILL NEED:** sturdy florists' dry foam (styro foam) spheres, garden cane, ribbon, flower pot, sand, gravel, moss, flowers and foliage.

**1** Place the foam sphere on the end of a cut piece of garden cane (bamboo stake) which has first been wound around with ribbon. Insert the cane into a flower pot filled with sand or gravel, then cover the top of the pot with moss. Begin to insert the flowers into the foam.

**2** Add foliage to fill any gaps.

**3** Finish by attaching a ribbon bow into the foam at the base of the arrangement.

# DRINKS FOR ALL TASTES

*The days of high-jinks and free-flowing cocktails have been replaced by comparatively sober gatherings; however, despite this practical approach, the whole business of liquid refreshment still adds a zing to many occasions. This is now balanced by a welcome safe attitude to alcohol, which means that there must always be appropriate soft drinks such as fruit juices and mineral water for those who are driving or, indeed, travelling by any means.*

*The following pages set out to boost the confidence of those who are unsure about what type of drink to serve and to encourage a cosmopolitan, adventurous attitude to wine. It is quite in order, these days, to nurture an individual approach to apertifs and drinks served with a meal but there are ways of doing this well, with a few reasons for observing some conventions on wine and food. Treat conventions as a framework for your own ideas, without allowing them to quell your likes and dislikes, and you will surely carry off the most formal occasions, with the most experienced of imbibers, with admirable style.*

## APERITIFS

An aperitif is a drink served before a meal, either luncheon or dinner, for the purpose of exciting the taste buds and arousing the appetite. For this reason, drinks served before food should, in theory, be dry and simple, almost with a zesty tang. Individual taste obviously tames this opinion and there are those who will always select a sweet drink regardless of the occasion. Drinks such as sherry, vermouth and some spirits are typical traditional aperitifs; wines are served more frequently these days and light beers should be available for anyone who wants to quench a thirst. White port and dry Madeira (Sercial) both make good aperitifs.

### Sherry

This fortified wine ranges from very dry to sweet. Fino sherries are dry, aromatic and pale; manzanilla is a very dry, fino sherry with a delicate taste and pale colour. Amontillado is medium dry, with a fuller flavour than the finos from which it is made. Oloroso is a very sweet sherry with a full flavour and rich, dark colour.

Cream sherry is also very sweet and traditionally dark and rich. Pale cream sherries are also sweet but they are not as rich as the dark cream wine. It is important to buy good-quality sherry for drinking.

Sherry is traditionally served at room temperature in a small glass or double-sized sherry schooner. The alternative method is to serve the wine, usually a dry or very dry type of sherry, on ice. Guests should always be given the option. A white wine glass or attractive stemmed aperitif glass should be used when sherry is served on ice.

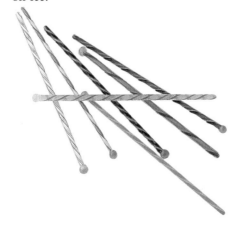

### Vermouth

Vermouth is a wine-based aperitif, usually flavoured with herbs. There are red and white types, the red being very rich and sweet, and the white available as very dry, dry or sweet. The quality of the drink varies according to the brand, although with less pronounced differences than for sherry.

Vermouth may be served on ice, usually with a slice of lemon. It is also often topped up with tonic or fizzy lemonade to make a longer drink. Mixed with gin, vermouth is used to make martinis.

### Campari

An Italian drink flavoured with bitters, this is a popular aperitif and usually served with ice and soda.

### Pimm's

A mixture of spirits, this drink is topped up with lemonade and served with ice and lemon, orange and cucumber slices. Mint sprigs are also added to make a long aperitif. There is more than one type of Pimm's and the mixture of spirits varies accordingly.

## Whisky

This spelling denotes Scotch whisky, which is distilled from barley or other grain. Malt whisky is made from the malted grain. There is a wide variety of whisky, varying in flavour and quality, and forming something of a serious hobby with connoisseurs.

Whisky may be served straight, with ice, soda water or still water; it is best to offer the water separately so that it can be added to taste. Although even a moderate connoisseur will choke at the very thought, whisky is also drunk with lemonade; however, it would be a waste to treat a fine-flavoured malt whisky in this way.

## Whiskey

This is the Irish drink, and the American spirit too, bourbon being one of the most famous varieties of the American whiskeys.

## Gin

A spirit flavoured with juniper, gin is usually drunk with tonic on ice and with a slice of lemon. Balancing the gin with the tonic so that it is neither drowned nor too dominant is a skill which is acquired with practice. Slightly less than half gin to tonic seems to do the trick, but taste varies and many people prefer a weak drink in which the flavour of the gin is largely lost.

## Vodka

Vodka which is used with a mixer is flavourless and it simply lends a kick to the mixer. It may be served with fruit juice, such as orange, or with fruit cordials, such as lime. For those who like a very dry drink, vodka may be served with a little fresh lime juice, ice and a slice of lime.

Russian vodka is served neat, very cold and in small glasses which are traditionally downed in one. Caviar, dark rye bread and soured cream are almost an accompaniment for vodka in

such circumstances, rather than the other way around. Polish vodkas come in many subtle flavours and these are not served with mixers. They are served very cold, in small glasses.

## Rum

White rum is the type offered as an aperitif; however, it is not as popular as other spirits. It is an ingredient in a variety of cocktails and can be used to make a refreshing long drink when combined with fruit juice.

## Wine as an Aperitif

Red wine is not usually served as an aperitif but white wine is popular. Dry white wines fulfil the traditional requirements, but some of the medium dry wines and very fruity wines make pleasing drinking on their own, and they are not too sweet to kill the palate before a meal. Even if you normally serve dry wines, this is a good opportunity to sample medium-dry and fruity wines, such as those from the Alsace region of France and German wines, such as the Moselles.

Champagne makes a terrific aperitif for a special occasion and it has the advantage of being perfectly suitable for serving throughout the meal too,

given that you are prepared to research the subject sufficiently to procure a wine of the correct type to match your menu or, conversely, to marry the menu to the champagne. Served in limited quantity before a meal, champagne does not have to be too costly; serving it throughout a meal will stretch the purse strings.

There are many excellent sparkling wines which are far less expensive than champagne and equally acceptable as an aperitif. Look beyond the "*méthode champenoise*" labels from the French tradition to discover excellent, well-flavoured dry sparkling wines from Australia, Spain and California. Slightly sweeter sparkling wines from Germany and Italy are also an option, but it is as well to reserve the sweet sparklers for a dessert course.

Look out for the semi-sparkling frizzante wines, too. Chardonnay frizzante, for example, is flavoursome without being too sweet, and refreshingly fizzy.

## Beers as an Aperitif

It is a good idea to have beer in the refrigerator as many guests may be thirsty when they first arrive. Light, good-quality lager is the usual option.

**DRINKS FOR ALL TASTES**

### Soft and Low-alcohol Drinks

❖ Sparkling mineral water (seltzer) and flavoured mineral waters should be available before and during the meal. As well as fruit and herb mineral waters which are sweetened, look out for some of the drier flavoured waters of the same type. Serve with plenty of ice.

❖ Fruit juices and low-alcohol or alcohol-free beers and wines are also suitable for serving before the meal. A mixture of dry white wine and soda or mineral water makes the popular long drink known as a spritzer.

A choice of red and white wine is the norm at the majority of drinks parties, often offered with a fruit cup or some form of punch. Beers, mineral water and other non-alcoholic alternatives should be available.

If you are looking to buy a couple of cases of red and white wine for a party, try to sample some bottles yourself in advance so that you can make your choice according to personal taste as well as the name and price of the product. Taking advice from a wine merchant is a good idea. Do not be shy about pointing out that you want to keep the cost at a reasonable level; anyone can buy at the upper end of the price range with reasonable confidence, but the merchant's expertise can be particularly valuable in advising you about the moderately and lower-priced alternatives.

### WINES WITH FOOD

The popular rules of white with fish and chicken and red with red meat and cheese should not inhibit the knowledgeable or adventurous cook from making alternative pairings. The wine must neither dominate or destroy the flavour of the food nor be completely eclipsed by its taste. It is thus a great mistake to offer a delicate white wine to accompany a robust casserole of game, as the flavour of the wine will be lost after a small sample of the food. Similarly, it would be quite wrong to pour a full-bodied red wine with dark tannin overtones to accompany a delicate dish of poached scallops or a plate of the first asparagus of the season, as one good draught of the wine would totally overshadow the subtle taste of

the food. Whites and reds should not be dismissed as delicate and robust respectively, however, as there are examples of both types in each camp.

Wine is not usually served with a first course of soup, nor is it offered with extremely spicy meals – for which beer or cider is more suitable. Perhaps the sensible suggestion is not to present a fine-flavoured wine with a dish like curry but to offer something inexpensive, usually white and not too dry.

Crisp, dry white wines usually complement delicate fish and seafood dishes. Stronger fish, such as grilled mackerel or sardines, and salmon cooked with a sauce, take more distinctive white wines or light red wines. Seafood dishes are often best accompanied by a light red wine.

Chicken and turkey take either white or red, depending on the cooking method and flavourings used. Mild-flavoured cheeses, such as Brie and smooth, musty Gruyère, are well matched by fruity white wines.

Red wines are usually served with meat, with the more robust and full-flavoured wines reserved for well-marinated cuts and dishes dressed with rich sauces. Pork and veal, which can be less rich than lamb and beef, also take white wines, but again a lot depends on the sauces and stuffings served. Duck is definitely a bird for red wine and game birds are also accompanied by strong reds.

When serving risottos, pasta dishes, stews and braises, then consider the overall flavour of the dish before deciding on the wine. Garlic, strong herbs, tomatoes and strong cheeses may kill a white wine, whereas a medium-bodied red wine will really bring out the best in the food. Similarly, a good strong cheese such as mature Cheddar is well complemented by a rich red wine.

Sweet dishes make too great a contrast for dry wines and the result can be quite unpleasant. Many of the sweet dessert wines, such as Sauternes, are very heavy and not to everyone's liking at the end of a meal. However, less rich sweet wines complement desserts without being too rich to drink; some of the medium-sweet wines of German origin may be served. Marsala and Madeira (Sercial) may be served with dessert. If you do want to serve a dessert wine, and particularly a good one, then plan the meal around the final course to make sure that the diners feel neither too full nor that they have imbibed sufficiently by that stage in the meal.

Port may be served with cheese. It is a classic accompaniment for Stilton, particularly when a vintage or tawny port rather than a ruby wine is selected. Ruby port may be served with some desserts, if wished.

44

## SERVING WINE

### White Wine

Dry and medium-dry white wines should be served chilled. Up to 1 hour in the refrigerator is sufficient if the wine has been taken from a fairly cool place of storage. If the wine has been in a warm shop or left out on a hot summer day, then it may be chilled for slightly longer. Over-chilling white wine is a common mistake. When the wine is left in the refrigerator for several hours its flavour is completely dulled. Very sweet wines can be chilled for slightly longer than dry wines. Champagne taken from a cool place after storage can simply be placed straight in a bucket with plenty of ice and water and left for 30 minutes before drinking. To chill in the refrigerator, leave it there for up to an hour.

Unopened bottles may be placed in the freezer for 10–15 minutes only, but do not leave them for longer as the wine will be cold and flavourless.

### Red Wine

The majority of red wines should be served at room temperature. This means taking the bottle from storage and leaving it to stand in a warm, but not hot, room for up to a couple of hours before opening. If the wine is placed in a very warm room, for example a busy kitchen or near a radiator, then it will probably be fine after about 45 minutes.

If you have to warm red wine in a hurry, then the best method is to stand the bottle in a bowl of hand-hot water for 10 minutes. Despite all the experts' advice to the contrary, at least you can warm the wine by these means and it is preferable to serving a chilly red.

### Opening Wine

Ideally, the wine ought to be opened a while before it is served so that the air has time to get at it and to bring out the flavour to the full. Anything up to an hour is said to be suitable. In practice, this is obviously more important when dealing with better wines. Sparkling wines are opened when you are ready to pour them.

### Decanting

The vast majority of wines do not need decanting. The purpose of doing this is to draw off the wine from any sediment at the bottom of the bottle. This technique need only be applied to fine old red wines which have developed a sediment – there is nothing wrong with the wine and the sediment is often an inherent sign of the quality and age of the product. Vintage ports are the classic example of wines which have to be decanted.

Wine should be decanted into a thoroughly clean and dry glass decanter. The bottle must be carried gently on its side, just as it was stored, to avoid disturbing the sediment. Tilt it carefully and pour the wine steadily. The final 1–2.5 cm/½–1 in of wine in the bottle is not poured. A special funnel may be purchased for the decanter and the dregs may be passed through a fine sieve or muslin. (Strain the leftovers from ordinary wine into a sauce to set aside for some other cooking.)

---

### After-dinner Drinks

Brandy, port or liqueurs may be offered when coffee is served. Port may be served earlier with the cheese. There are numerous liqueurs but the following are some of the traditional ones:

**SOUTHERN COMFORT** Based on bourbon whiskey, this is flavoured with orange and peach.

**APRICOT BRANDY** Sweetened brandy flavoured with apricots.

**BENEDICTINE** A brandy-based liqueur which is flavoured with herbs. It takes its name from the French monastery where it originated.

**CHARTREUSE** A very sweet liqueur manufactured by Carthusian monks. Both green and yellow types are available.

**COINTREAU** Brand name for orange-flavoured liqueur.

**CRÈME DE MENTHE** Mint liqueur.

**DRAMBUIE** A Scotch whisky-based liqueur.

**GRAND MARNIER** Orange liqueur.

**PARFAIT D'AMOUR** A scented violet-flavoured liqueur of the same colour.

# AN INTRODUCTION TO ETIQUETTE

*Etiquette, the term for the rules which apply to social interaction, is an ever-evolving framework into which the majority of social activities fit and which may be called upon as a source of reference. The dramatic changes which* *have taken place during the last century have made deep impressions on many of the old forms of etiquette, particularly with regard to the changing role of women and their relationship with men.*

## ETIQUETTE

Generally, in all but the highest echelons of society, social form is infinitely more flexible than ever before and the emphasis is on good manners rather than strict observance of ancient etiquette – a subtle, yet vital, difference. Therefore, to a large extent the surviving rules are even more relevant and important. Most people check up on etiquette in relation to specific occasions, such as weddings, and there are many thorough books which deal with such subjects.

Think of this section as an opportunity to ponder the customs and courtesies which surround the whole business of entertaining and socializing in today's fast-moving world. If some of the ideas seem superficial or unnecessary, then others are equally obviously essential for the smooth running of a million and one minor occasions. All the little everyday customs we take for granted link eventually by the same framework to the more rigid rituals which apply to formal occasions. Modern manners, rarely acknowledged, yet readily accepted, are designed to ease the process of coping with our fellows in even the most difficult of situations.

## INVITATIONS

### Telephone Invitations

Telephone invitations are quite acceptable for informal dinner parties and other forms of entertaining. It is both practical and pleasant to confirm in writing. However, instead of sending a written note, the party-giver may ring guests a day or two before to remind them and confirm details of timing.

### Invitation cards

There is a wide range of pre-printed invitation cards available from card shops to suit most occasions. Written invitations are usually sent when the event is a more formal one, such as a formal dinner party, or when the guest list is long and telephoning would not be practical.

Alternatively, use specially printed cards that show the name, address and telephone number of the host and/or hostess, and specify "RSVP" (for the French "*Répondez, s'il vous plaît*" – "Please reply"). The names of guests, and the date, time and nature of the event can then be written in by hand. This form of printed invitation card is very useful and easily adaptable for most occasions.

### Invitations to Special Occasions

If invitations are issued for a special celebration, then the wording usually indicates the reason for the invitation. These may be issued by a couple or an individual.

**(name) and (name)**
**request the pleasure of your company at**
**a party to celebrate their wedding anniversary**
**on Saturday 30th October at 8.30 pm**

**RSVP**
**(address and telephone number)**

This is a standard form for wording invitations to parties and the necessary information may be substituted. For example, if there is a theme for the party then this should be written out. If a code of dress is expected, this should be written at the bottom of the invitation – "black tie" or "fancy dress (costume)". The name of the guest(s) invited is written at the top of the invitation.

## Wedding Invitations

Traditionally the bride's parents host the occasion and send out invitations six weeks before the wedding. The following form of wording is usually adopted:

**(names)**
**request the pleasure of your company**
**at the marriage of their daughter**
**(name)**
**to**
**(name)**
**at (location of ceremony)**
**on (date)**
**at (time)**
**and afterwards at (place of reception)**

**RSVP (to parents' address)**

There are often wedding circumstances which differ from this tradition; for example, the bride and groom may be taking sole responsibility for organizing their wedding, in which case the invitation will be issued from them. Detailed publications on the subject also advise about invitations issued by divorced parents or for the remarriage of divorced individuals. Some guests may be invited only to the reception or to an evening party following the reception, in which case a different form of wording should be used from that on the invitations to the ceremony.

## Addressing Invitations

Husbands and wives are traditionally addressed by the husband's forename and surname: Mr and Mrs John Smith. This is still common practice but some women find this dismissal of their individuality quite unsuitable. Although this is a safe means of addressing strangers and casual acquaintances, if you are aware of views on the subject, then it is polite to observe them and to write both first names, possibly dropping the "Mr and Mrs". If a married woman has not taken her husband's name and you are aware of this, then invitations should be addressed to both parties: Ms Joan Brown and Mr John Smith.

*Good-quality writing paper and envelopes always send out a stylish message.*

## GREETING GUESTS

Either the host or the hostess greets the guests on their arrival. At a small, informal occasion, the one who does not open the door joins the other and the guests promptly afterwards, allowing time for leaving guests who have already arrived. The guests are relieved of their coats and drinks are offered. While one party takes the guests in to meet the rest of the company, the other organizes drinks. Introductions may not be necessary, but the host or hostess should still make some opening remark of conversation to bring the new guests into the group.

At a larger party, the host and hostess may be too busy with the gathering to spend much time with guests when they first arrive. In this case, they should be shown or told where to take their coats and allowed to look after themselves, then they should be greeted properly when they come to join the group. Drinks should be offered and introductions made to at least a few of the other guests. Always remember to let guests know where the party is gathered if it is not immediately obvious, ". . . we're out on the patio, through the living room"; clearly indicating the location of the party will ensure that guests do not feel shy about wandering down and through the house unattended after leaving their belongings.

The conventions of making introductions dictate that the man is always introduced to the woman first and the junior to the senior, either in age or status. If a couple are introduced to a group, then they should always be named as individuals, never as "Mr Smith and his wife" or "Mr and Mrs John Smith".

Introductions should not be left as bald statements of name. It is useful to make some opening remark which will offer the guests an opportunity for beginning conversation. These remarks should be general, perhaps some reference to the link between the guest and host or hostess or a comment on the journey to the event. It is not a good idea to introduce guests by their occupation, as people often want to avoid talking about their work and the mention of some professions can immediately bring about a series of unwanted queries from other (less-than-thoughtful) guests.

### Party Conversations

It really is as much the duty of the guests to make an effort to participate in conversation as it is for their hosts. However, the host and/or hostess has a responsibility for keeping an eye on the progress of topics at small gatherings, particularly when the invited company do not know each other well.

If there are subjects which the host knows are likely to be controversial or cause offence to any of the guests, then it is important that they are skilfully diverted. The subject should be changed subtly and moved on in the required direction without dropping any drastic and irrelevant comments into the conversation. Sometimes, if the situation has reached a stage at which an immediate change of direction is required, the best course of action is to dismiss the previous topic completely and throw open a whole new idea more widely, picking a popular theme which is likely to be quickly expanded upon by several guests.

## SEATING ARRANGEMENTS

Traditionally, the host and hostess sit at the head of the table, with the most important female guest on the right of the host, the most important male guest on the right of the hostess. Traditionally, in households where women would always be 'taken in' to dinner and where staff looked after the business of serving food, the host takes the most important female guest into dinner first, followed by the other guests and the most important man takes the hostess in to dinner last. The remaining ladies would be escorted in strict order of rank by the men, also in order of rank, and the next most important lady would sit on the left of the host, the next most important man on the left of the hostess. The remaining guests

*Use small pieces of card with guests' initials on to work out a seating plan.*

would fill the table in order of rank away from the hosts, with men and women occupying alternate seats.

Modern dinner parties are often smaller and definitely less complicated. Since the majority of hostesses prepare the food and they are usually helped by their partners when serving, even the tradition of their taking the head places at table is waived since many dining rooms are too small for the host to leave his seat discreetly, pass all the guests and absent himself to assist with serving the meal without causing chaos. Therefore the host and hostess may sit together at one end of the table but the tradition of alternating male and female guests is usually observed and partners are often split to encourage conversation.

Men should wait until the women are seated before taking their places and it is still courteous, if space allows, for a man to hold the chair for his female neighbour.

## SERVING FOOD AT DINNER

Women are served first. Men assist the women by offering them vegetable dishes and so on. It is also courteous for women to do the same.

Guests are not expected to wait until the hostess has served all the company before they begin to serve themselves with vegetables, as this only causes delay and allows the food to become

*Serve freshly made coffee and after-dinner chocolates to round off the evening.*

cold. It is quite correct for guests to begin eating before all are served, though it is not necessarily considerate. It is more helpful if guests who have served themselves with accompaniments are ready to assist in passing plates or dishes. However, they should begin once it is clear that everyone is about to be served and their help is no longer useful.

The host usually pours the first glass of wine and it is his responsibility to keep an eye on glasses and to refill them as necessary. Often, particularly at larger dinner parties, the guests are invited to serve themselves from bottles distributed on the table. It is polite for guests to offer to top up their neighbours' glasses, particularly for men to look after women.

### After Dinner

Coffee may be served at the table or in the living room. The choice is entirely up to the host or hostess. Moving from the table can break up a dinner party which is going very well, in which case it is best to allow conversation to flow and to serve the coffee and liqueurs at the table.

Liqueurs should be set out at one side so that guests can see what is offered, or they may be offered by name. Port and brandy may be placed on the table. If smoking is welcomed, then guests may be invited to take cigars; however, this is far less common these days.

Traditionally, the women left the table at a nod from the hostess (to the chief female guest) and departed to the drawing room for coffee. The men then indulged in port or brandy and cigars for a period of 15 minutes before joining the ladies – although the rules of etiquette clearly advised the men should not linger longer, it is difficult to believe that they abandoned their port so quickly.

If coffee is taken elsewhere it should be set out before the guests leave the table, then they should be invited to move by the host or hostess.

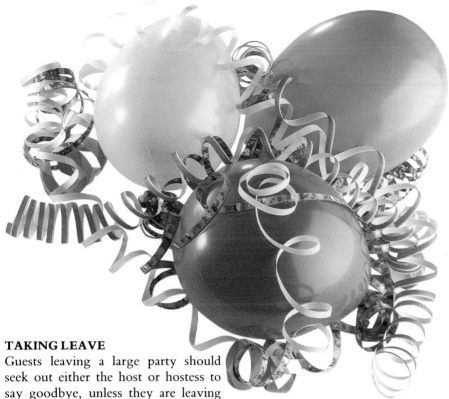

## TAKING LEAVE

Guests leaving a large party should seek out either the host or hostess to say goodbye, unless they are leaving early, when this can be disruptive. Usually a guest who has to leave early should let the host know on arrival, if not beforehand.

After a dinner party, the host and hostess should see the guests to the door, helping them with their coats, then speedily return to remaining guests and encourage conversation if the dinner party is to continue.

## CHILDREN

When you invite couples who have children you must decide whether the children are invited or not and make it clear on the invitation, either by including their names or by naming the couple and excluding the children.

You should be prepared for guests who may double-check that their children are not invited. Do not allow

yourself to be cornered into inviting one set of children, as this will cause offence to other couples whose families have not been invited. Try to make as little as possible of the fact by simply saying that on this occasion it is an adults-only party. However, it is worth remembering that unless there is a good reason for making it an adults-only event, then many couples may have difficulties in finding someone to care for their children.

If children are included, do make plans for them as well as for other guests. Do not include them on the invitations simply with the intention of ignoring them – think in terms of the food and drinks they are likely to consume, special plates and plastic tumblers, entertainments and so on.

### Helping Guests to Leave

There is no easy way of dismissing guests who are lingering longer than required. Allowing conversation to lapse at the end of a dinner party is a good way of indicating that you want guests to leave and this should be accompanied by gentle yawning, with comment on how busy you have been or how tired you are.

❖ Blow out candles which are

getting conveniently short to indicate that the party is over. Allow a fire to burn very low, saying, ". . . it's not worth putting another log on now".

❖ Comments about plans for the next morning, especially if an early start is involved, may work.

❖ It may be time to start doing the washing up – there's nothing like the crashing of crockery to break up a dinner party.

❖ At worst, try asking about last trains/taxis/the length of the drive home/whether the car starts well on cold evenings and other pointed topics on transport.

❖ As a last resort, clear away the cups and return with the coats: ". . . I thought I'd bring these in since you were just about to get them; it's draughty in our hallway so you may like to put them on here. It has been lovely to see you again."

## Standing Place Cards

Place cards are always laid at formal or large dinners. Simple, elegant cards are best for such occasions. Lay them in a suitable position on the setting, such as on a side plate or with the napkin.

**YOU WILL NEED:** card (posterboard); (for making stencil) paper, pencil, sticky (transparent) tape; craft knife, stencil or sheet of acetate, waterproof black felt-tip pen, gold paint, stencil brush, thin coloured ribbon.

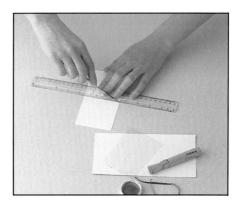

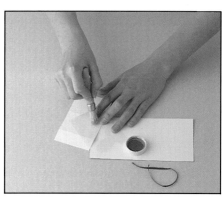

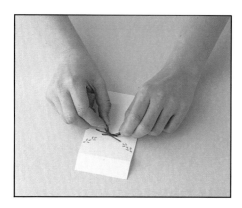

**1** Cut a strip of card (posterboard) measuring 15 × 7.5 cm/6 × 3 in. Mark a fold across the centre of the card and a 2.5 cm/1 in fold at each end of the strip. Lightly score the folds with a craft knife, but be careful not to cut through the card.

**2** If you are making your own stencil, draw your design onto a sheet of paper. Place the sheet of acetate on top and tape in position to hold the sheet firmly in place. Transfer the design to the acetate using a waterproof black felt-tip pen. Cut around the outline of the design using the craft knife. Lightly load the brush with gold paint. Holding the stencil firmly in position, press the brush over the pattern in the stencil keeping the brush vertical.

**3** To attach the ribbon, mark and then cut two small slits in the card. Thread the ribbon through and tie into a bow. Trim the ends of the ribbon if necessary.

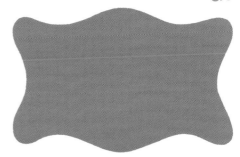

# Cut-out Place Cards

Use patterned card (posterboard) for these attractive place cards: special marbled, coloured, gold or silver card is suitable.

**YOU WILL NEED:** plain card, patterned card, tracing paper, pencil, craft knife, glue.

**1** For each place card, you will need a strip of patterned card (posterboard) measuring 20 × 10 cm/8 × 4 in. Trace the pattern for the cut-out area onto tracing paper. Using a soft pencil, shade the area underneath the tracing. Mark a fold across the centre of the card and a 2.5 cm/1 in fold at each end of the strip. Lightly score the folds with a craft knife, but do not cut through the card. Lay the tracing shaded side down on the reverse of one half of the patterned card, positioned centrally. Using a sharp pencil, follow the line of the design.

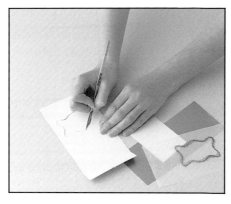

**2** On a hard surface, use the craft knife to cut out the shape.

**3** Push the cut-out area from the right side of the card, *not* from the back. Take care to push out any intricate designs carefully.

**4** Cut out a strip of plain card measuring 9.5 × 7 cm/3¾ × 2¾ in. Stick the plain card behind the cut-out area on the patterned card with glue.

# NAPKIN ART

*C*risp, *freshly laundered napkins are an essential feature of every well-set table. They may be pressed in large, plain squares and laid at each place with the minimum of fuss and for the maximum effect. Alternatively, they may be* *folded in a variety of ways to complement the food, table layout and occasion. Try some of the ideas in the following pages and use them as a source of inspiration for developing your own individual napkin art.*

## PERFECT NAPKINS

Regardless of the simplicity of the meal, fabric napkins must be spotlessly clean and well pressed.

❖ Plain white linen napkins may be embroidered by hand or by machine with a monogram of your initials. This may be surrounded by a wreath of leaves or some other decorative embroidery. Fold monogrammed napkins very simply to display the embroidery.

❖ Press embroidered napkins on the wrong side to make the pattern stand out attractively.

❖ Decorative napkins, trimmed with embroidery or lace or with a prominent self pattern, should be folded very simply; plain fabric napkins or those with a small decorative border are more suitable for elaborate folding.

## NAPKINS FOR BUFFETS

If you are preparing a buffet for a comparatively small number, that is, under fifteen guests, then it is a good idea to use linen napkins if possible. The fabrics do not have to be the same and a virtue can be made of their differences by combining contrasting colours or patterns in an attractive arrangement.

❖ For larger gatherings or when there are lots of children around, it is an advantage to have lots of spare paper napkins to deal with any spills. Bear in mind that guests rarely retain their napkins after the main course and many may take a second for dessert.

❖ Elaborate folding methods are not used for buffet presentation as the emphasis is mainly on the practicalities of carrying a plate, napkin and cutlery (flatware). There are a number of standard options for placing napkins.

❖ Roll a knife and fork in a napkin. If the number of guests is small and space on the buffet table limited, the cutlery and napkins may be fanned out attractively, near the plates. It is often more practical to pile them in a basket, or two, and place them near the plates or on a separate side table with condiments or bread. Do not roll cutlery for

---

### Paper Napkins

Paper napkins are more practical than fabric ones for parties. Choose those that are large, absorbent and fairly thick; the thin, small paper napkins that disintegrate easily are more hindrance than help. The exception to this rule is Japanese paper napkins.

**BRIGHT PAPER NAPKINS** For fun parties use a selection of different coloured paper napkins: pastels or primary colours both work well. Fold them in half, then overlap them in a large basket and fold one napkin into a water lily shape for the centre of the arrangement.

Paper napkins are a practical option for informal barbecues, especially when sticky spareribs and other finger foods are served. When laying a garden table, allow two or three different coloured napkins for each place setting. They may be fanned out simply or pairs of contrasting colours used double for folding shapes such as a water lily or roll-top design.

**JAPANESE PAPER NAPKINS** Look out for fine paper napkins which are very thin but quite strong. They are often delicately patterned and may be round or square, with fluted or gilded edges. As well as being used on their own, they may be used in conjunction with linen napkins for courses which are eaten with the fingers as part of a formal meal, especially when finger bowls are provided. Fold them attractively with the linen napkins, then clear the paper napkins away after they have been used.

*A tartan bow holds a neatly rolled napkin and spoon for a dessert course.*

dessert in the napkin; this should be offered separately.

❖ Stack a napkin on each plate.

❖ Fold the napkins in half diagonally to make triangles and overlap these on one side of the buffet table.

❖ Roll the napkins and stand them in a wide jug or arrange them in a basket.

## TIPS FOR SUCCESSFUL FOLDING

For folding purposes, heavy linen is best, as it becomes firm and crisp when starched. Plain dinner napkins measuring 45–50 cm/18–20 in square, or more, are best and are essential for many complicated folding techniques.

❖ The napkins must be cut square and the fabric must be cut straight on the weave so that the napkins will not pull out of shape easily.

❖ Linen should be washed, starched with traditional starch (spray starch will not give a sufficiently crisp finish) and ironed while damp. When ironing, gently pull the napkins back into shape if necessary to ensure they are perfectly square again.

❖ It is best to iron napkins on a large surface; an ironing board can be too narrow when pressing large napkins. Protect the surface with a folded thick

towel, which should be covered with a piece of plain white cotton.

❖ Dampen napkins which have dried before ironing. Traditional starch may be mixed and sprayed on linen using a clean plant spray. Allow it to soak into

the fabric for a minute or so before ironing for best results.

When folding napkins into complicated shapes, press each fold individually for best results. Soft folds should not be pressed.

## SIMPLE PRESENTATION

To form a neat square, press the napkin, making sure all the corners are perfectly square. Fold it into quarters, pressing each fold. A large quarter-folded napkin may be laid square between the cutlery (flatware) at each place or it may be turned by ninety degrees. This is fine on large tables.

❖ To make a simple triangle, fold the square in half diagonally and press the resulting triangle neatly. Lay the triangular-folded napkin on a side plate, with the long side nearest the place setting. The triangle may also be laid on top of a plate in the middle of the setting.

❖ For a simple oblong, fold a square napkin in half again. This is an ideal way of displaying a decorative corner on the napkin. Plain napkins may be folded and pressed into quarters, then the sides folded underneath and pressed to make an oblong shape. Lay the hemmed edge on the short side at the bottom of the place setting.

❖ Rolled napkins may be kept in place with napkin rings or tied with ribbon or cord. If the napkins are rolled carefully and laid with the end underneath, they will usually sit quite neatly.

## Place Mat

A large, square, cloth napkin can be used as a pretty place mat.

**1** Fold the four corners into the centre.

**2** Place a hand over the middle to hold the corners in position and turn the napkin over.

**3** Fold all four corners of the napkin into the centre again and carefully turn the napkin over for a second time.

**4** Fold each centre corner back to meet the outside corner, and press.

# Bishop's Hat

This is a very traditional method of folding large dinner napkins. The proportions are important, so it may be necessary to adjust some of the folds as you work it through.

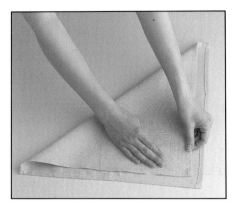

**1** Starting with the corners of the open napkin top and bottom in the form of a diamond, fold the corner nearest to you to just below the corner furthest away from you to form a triangle.

**2** Fold up the two corners nearest to you until the edges align.

**3** Bring the newly created bottom corner up and away from you so that its top edge sits just below the first corner when folded.

**4** Fold down the front edge.

**5** Bend the left and right corners backwards and interlock one half into the other to form a tube that will not spring open.

## Spreading Fan

An elegant yet simple design that is
suitable for all occasions.

**1** Fold up the edge nearest to you to meet the top edge.

**2** Rotate the napkin so that the folded edge is on your right. Make equal-sized accordian pleats all the way up to the top of the napkin, starting with the edge nearest to you.

**3** Insert the napkin into the ring, or tie with ribbon or cord and spread out the pleats.

# The Crown

The crown is one of the better-known traditional napkin folds and is often seen in restaurants. It can be used to cover a warmed bread roll at each place setting, or could hide a surprise for each guest.

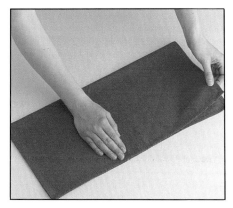

**1** Fold the edge nearest to you to meet the top edge.

**2** Fold the bottom right corner of the napkin up to the middle right.

**3** Fold the top left corner down.

**4** Turn the napkin over. Make sure that the long folded edges are directly facing you top and bottom. Fold over the top edge — the edge furthest away from you — to meet the edge nearest to you.

**5** Release the second point which is still tucked under so that there are two triangles at the top.

**6** Tuck the bottom left point under the edge of the right triangle. Carefully turn the napkin over and repeat the step.

**7** Gently open out at the bottom to form a circle and stand the crown up.

# Diagonal Pockets

A smart design suitable for any occasion. Use the pockets for decorative accessories, such as a small flower, a sprig of herbs or perhaps a small gift.

**1** Fold the napkin into quarters, making sure that all the open corners are at the top right-hand side. Roll the top layer back diagonally towards you as far as it will go.

**2** Press the roll flat to form a thin band.

**3** Bring the second layer back and tuck the corner behind the first band until the folded edge forms a parallel band the same width as the first.

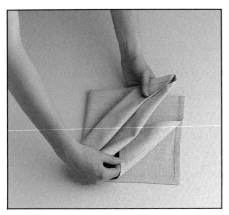

**4** Repeat the process with the third layer.

**5** Fold the sides under to the back to form a neat rectangle.

# Water Lily

This design requires a well-starched napkin to make the cup shape. It can be used to hold a bread roll, a small gift or seasonal decorations such as small fir cones and holly at Christmas, chocolate hearts for Valentine's Day, or a tiny posy of spring flowers.

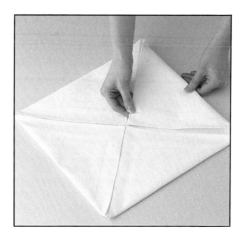

**1** Fold the corners of the napkin into the centre and press flat.

**2** Repeat the process a second time.

**3** Holding the centre points together, carefully turn the napkin over.

**4** Fold the four corners into the centre again, but do not press.

**5** Holding the centre firmly, partly pull out the previous fold from under each corner and gently pull them upward to make the petals.

**6** Pull out the corners from underneath between the petals, to form the base leaves of the lily.

## Table Basket

A cloth napkin can become an attractive basket for breadsticks, crackers or even a dried-flower arrangement.

**1** Fold down the edge furthest away from you by a third. Repeat with the edge nearest to you so that the napkin forms a narrow rectangle one-third its original width. Turn the napkin over so that the free edge is underneath and facing away from you. Fold the right edge to the centre, then fold the left edge to meet the newly formed right edge.

**2** Pull out the first fold made in step 1.

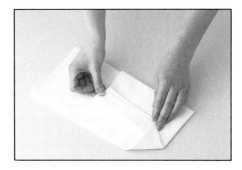

**3** Lift the top edge of the top fold and turn it down by one-third, forming a triangle at the top.

**4** Repeat with the bottom edge of the top fold to form a thin flap. Press.

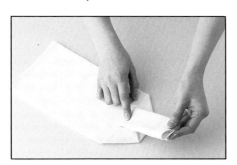

**5** Fold the narrow flap to your left.

**6** Now fold the wide right edge to meet the narrow left edge.

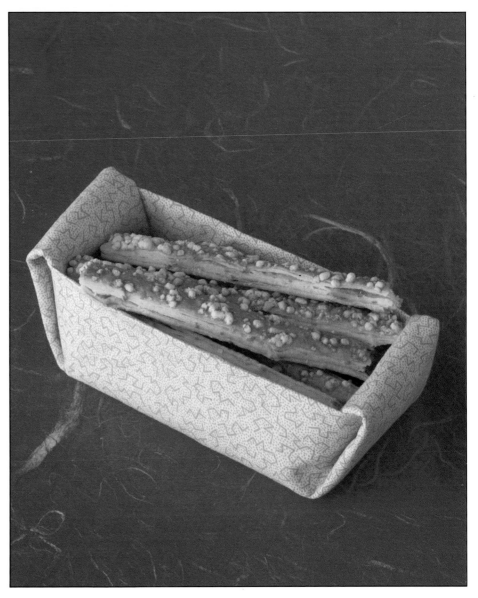

**7** Follow steps 3 and 4 on the second side.

**8** Fold the narrow flap on the second side to your right.

**9** Holding the flaps at the centre, turn the napkin inside out. (The flaps form the lining of the rectangular basket.)

## Roll-top

This is an easy napkin fold that will grace both an informal and formal table setting. The 'pockets' are ideal for presenting name cards, or perhaps a small gift on special occasions.

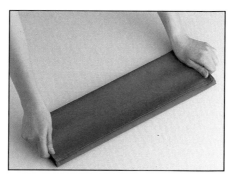

**1** Fold down the edge furthest away from you by a third. Then fold up the edge nearest to you in the same manner so that the napkin forms a narrow rectangle one-third its original width.

**2** Fold the left and right edges over by about 5cm/2in towards the centre — adjust the size of this band according to the size of the napkin.

**3** To form the first 'pocket', bring the right side of the napkin across to the left, leaving the left-hand band uncovered but its raw edge concealed.

**4** Fold from the right side again, making sure that each 'pocket' measures the same width.

## Iris in a Glass

This design can create a very striking display if folded with a large, colourful napkin.

*Opposite: Iris in a Glass.*

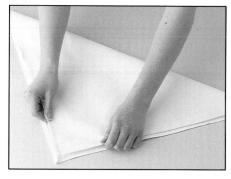

**1** Starting with the corners of the open napkin top and bottom in the form of a diamond, bring the point nearest to you up to the top point to form a triangle.

**2** With a finger at the centre of the fold line, fold up the two corners nearest to you so they are level with the centre top point and slightly to each side of it.

**3** Fold the newly formed bottom point part-way up towards the top point, as shown.

**4** Make accordian pleats across the napkin from left to right. Position the napkin in the glass and fan out the petals of the iris.

## Fan on a Plate

Use a carefully starched linen napkin for this elegant design.

**1** Fold the napkin in half to form a rectangle. Starting at the edge nearest to you, make eight fairly small, accordian pleats. Press each pleat as you work. Use two-thirds of the rectangle for pleating.

**2** Fold the napkin in half so that the two edges meet on the left and the pleats are on the outside bottom edge.

**3** Fold the top edge — the edge furthest away from you — down to make a small band. Then bring top left corner down to the bottom right and tuck it under the pleats. Turn the napkins so that it stands on the right edge. Then, holding the bottom with one hand, fan out the pleats.

*Above: Japanese Pleat.*

## Decorative Pocket

This clever design makes an attractive pocket in which to place anything from eating implements to flowers.

**1** Fold the napkin into quarters so that the free edges are facing away from you. Fold the first layer down so that the top corner is just above the bottom corner nearest to you.

*Above: Decorative Pocket.*

**2** Repeat this process with the second layer, again positioning its top corner just above the one before.

**3** Fold under the side corners until they just overlap at the back.

## Japanese Pleat

You will need a large starched napkin for this design.

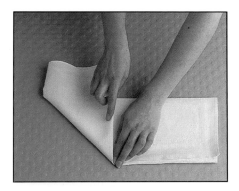

**1** Fold down the edge furthest away from you by a third. Fold up the edge nearest to you in the same manner so that the napkin forms a narrow rectangle one-third its original width. With a finger at the centre top, fold down both sides towards you so that the edges meet at the centre.

**2** Holding the diagonal edges, turn the napkin over so that the tip now points towards you and the top layer forms a triangle. Roll down the two extending rectangles towards you until they come just above the **base** of the triangle.

**3** Grip the rolls firmly with two hands and turn the napkin over again so that the tip of the triangle is facing towards you. Fold the two top corners down so that their edges meet in the centre.

*Below: Gathered Pleat.*

## Gathered Pleat

Using a simple technique and a napkin ring, create a stylish design for an informal table setting.

**1** Grasp the centre of the napkin and lift it off the table so that the material hangs in soft but clearly defined folds.

**2** Thread a napkin ring onto the end you are holding and slide it towards the centre. Spread out the folds to form an attractive shape.

## Fanned Bow

The fanned bow is perfect for festive occasions, especially if you use a highly decorative napkin ring or shiny ribbon tied into a bow.

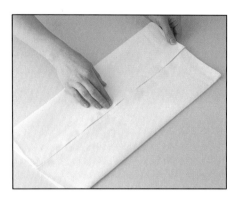

**1** Fold the top and bottom edges of the napkin to meet in the middle to form a rectangle.

**2** Rotate the napkin so that the shorter edges are facing you top and bottom. Starting at the edge nearest to you, accordian-pleat the napkin, pressing each pleat as you work.

**3** Thread a wide napkin ring along to the centre of the napkin, or tie with ribbon. Fan out the pleats to make a circular bow.

# Fanned Pleats

This is a quick and easy design for the beginner.

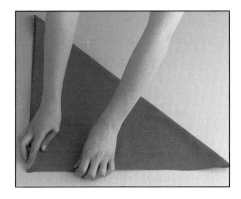

**1** Fold the bottom left corner of the napkin to the top right corner.

**2** Fold the resulting triangle in half, bringing the bottom right corner up to the highest point, with the top point of the napkin slightly to the left of the bottom point.

**3** Fold the triangle in half again to create three points, bringing the top point up and to the right of the other two points.

**4** Fold the top left corner under the napkin to give it a slender, elegant shape.

# FLOWERS FOR ALL OCCASIONS

*F*lowers are the most popular of centrepieces and decorations for any party occasion, from a simple bowl of daisies on a kitchen table to a breathtaking arrangement for a buffet table or a reception area. This section can only hint at the variety of designs that can be achieved for home entertaining, but it will provide a source of inspiration and ideas for inexperienced flower arrangers who want to experiment with traditional arrangements.

As well as fresh flowers, remember to make the most of the wide range of foliage and dried and preserved flowers available. The advantage of preserved material is that the arrangements can be prepared well ahead of a party without any need for time-consuming last-minute attention.

Finally, do not underestimate the time needed to create complex decorations. Swags, wreaths and garlands all look beautiful, but they cannot be put together in minutes. Always prepare as much as possible in advance, leaving only the finishing touches to be done on the day.

## BASIC EQUIPMENT
Take full advantage of the many items of equipment that are readily available at garden centres and florists, as they make life easier even when trying to prepare a simple bowl of flowers for an informal table centrepiece.

### Bases
**FOAM BASES** These are the most practical, as they can be cut to any shape and size required. They come in two basic forms: dry foam (styro foam), which is used for dried and preserved flowers, and wet foam, which has to be soaked and is used for fresh flowers.

**HEAVY SPIKED BASE** A heavy spiked base may be used to hold a foam base, lending it weight and stability. This is particularly useful for arrangements of dried flowers, which tend to be light.

## Containers

Almost anything can be used as a container for flowers, from formal cut-glass vases and ceramic vessels to pots, jugs and bowls. Waterproof containers must be used for fresh flowers. If you want to disguise a container, consider placing it inside a basket or swathing it in fabric.

## Florists' wire

This is available ready-cut and in various gauges. Fine wire is suitable for delicate flowers and for paper tissue or crêpe paper flowers. Thicker wire is required for wiring foliage and sturdy stems. Don't worry if, as is sometimes the case, the packet or bundle of wires does not specify the gauge. By comparing the different wires, it is fairly obvious which types are suitable for the flowers to be arranged. Plastic-covered wire used for the garden is also extremely useful for all sorts of craft tasks, such as making garlands. You will need wire cutters and fine pliers for cutting and twisting wire.

*Conceal wire stems with floral tape.*

### Bases for Wreaths

Circular bases for wreaths are available ready-made in rigid foam (styro foam) or cane (willow).

Cane rings are ideal for arrangements using heavy foliage and large blooms, and the canework is decorative enough to be treated as part of the overall finished look, and not completely disguised.

Rigid foam rings are better for flowery wreaths made from dried, silk or fresh flowers. Fresh flowers must be left up to their necks in water overnight and wired just before they are used, otherwise they will not look their best.

*Trim off excess foliage and shoots before arranging.*

### PREPARING PLANT MATERIAL

Trim excess leaves and side shoots which will get in the way of an arrangement. Snip the ends off the stems of flowers and foliage which have been cut for some time or have been bought. With a heavy object, crush or slit the ends of firm stems, such as the stems of roses and carnations. Place the materials up to their necks in a bucket of water in the shade for several hours before arranging them. Rinse and dust foliage and shake out flower heads, as they often contain insects which can creep out on the dining table only to make their social debut at one of your most important dinner parties!

### Wiring Flowers and Foliage

For posies and floral sprays, especially for decorating swags on tablecloths and for wiring into wreaths or garlands, it may be necessary to cut off the stem 5 cm/2 in from the flower. Bend the end of the wire into a small hook. Thread the straight end down through the flower head and into the stem so that the hook catches firmly in place. This is suitable for flowers such as chrysanthemums. Alternatively, push the wire through the stem as far as the flower head, then twist it gently around the stem to hold the wire in place. Cover the wires and flower stems with florists' tape. This method is also useful for any floppy foliage.

*Crush thick woody stems with a heavy object.*

### Balls and Bells

An arrangement does not have to be limited to flowers, foliage and ribbon. Give your imagintion a little freedom when you look around craft shops and stores, particularly at Christmas time, as there are lots of exciting materials which may be used in centrepieces.

**GLASS BALLS** These come in all sorts of colours that are far removed from the traditional Christmas colours. Peachy pinks, dusky mauves, pearly whites and lemon yellows are just a few examples of the opaque balls that can be found. They add an interesting and attractive dimension to corner decorations for tables as well as to flower ropes and garlands.

**BELLS** Similarly, some of the beautiful glass bells and slippers which are readily available at Christmas, and which can also be found in specialist craft or sugarcraft stores the rest of the year, have a place among floral decorations. Bells are ideal for silver and golden wedding anniversaries as well as weddings. Slippers are considered to be a charm for good fortune in some countries, and are frequently seen on wedding cakes and incorporated into floral decorations.

### SHAPING AN ARRANGEMENT

It is important to decide on the shape of the arrangement to suit the table and the materials used. The finished arrangement should look well balanced from all sides and this can only be achieved if you plan the outline first.

Place the first pieces of foliage or buds at the extremities of the arrangement so that the outline is clearly established. These should have firm lines to give definition to the shape.

Next, place a bloom or foliage at the required highest point of the arrangement – this does not necessarily have to be the centre, as the design may slope in a tear-drop shape. However, remember to consider the table when planning this shape – an off-centre high point may look good towards one corner of a buffet table, for example, but it could look strange from either end of a dining table.

Once you have established the key points, gradually build up the shape of the arrangement, working all around and from the base. Never allow the arrangement to extend beyond the length, width and height set by the first pieces of material or you will lose the overall structure and balance.

Do not fill up the arrangement completely from the base. Once you have sufficient material to see a clear shape, fill in from the top of the arrangement and from the sides.

Remember to balance the size of blooms to the shape of the arrangement. Place larger flowers in the middle – or two or three key blooms in a smaller decoration – then work down in size as you move out.

Gaps and hollows should be filled as appropriate. Always stand well back from an arrangement and walk all around it to check the shape. Sometimes it helps to go away for 15 minutes, then come back and look at the arrangement with a fresh eye.

### BOWLS OF FLOWERS

Not all arrangements have to be stiff and formal, even for important occasions. Looser arrangements often look charming, but they still need a little attention. Select a pretty bowl or small low flower holder and place a piece of wet foam in the base. If the flower holder already comes with a glass base with holes for stems, position a piece of foam on top or cover the base with a small piece of crumpled chicken wire. The holes are rarely designed for the flowers you use or the shape you want!

Gradually build up the arrangement, making sure it looks attractive on all sides. You may want to cover the container completely, in which case choose curved or dropping shapes that will naturally fall down over it. To avoid ending up with a stiff round shape, make sure you always bring some greenery or material down over the edge of the container in a few places, to soften the shape.

# Yellow and Peach Table Centrepiece

When working on a table arrangement to be seen from all sides, it's a good idea to keep viewing it from different angles to make sure that it looks equally good all round. This oval arrangement is asymmetrical but evenly balanced.

**YOU WILL NEED:** a container, a block of wet florists' foam, flowers and foliage (wired as necessary), ribbon loops.

**1** Establish the overall width and length of the arrangement using sprays of leaves as a foundation. Next place three or five flower sprays at key points to create the outline shape and height.

**2** Fill in the central shape using clustered heads of tiny flowers.

**3** Position larger shapely flower heads to add drama, maintaining the overall shape. Insert smaller flowers and ribbon bows to finish.

## Cushion Posy

Neat and charming, this little dome-shaped arrangement takes up very little space.

**YOU WILL NEED:** a container, a cylinder of wet florists' foam, flowers and foliage (wired as necessary), ribbon loops.

**1** Establish the basic outline with a radiating arrangement of foliage. Position key flowers symmetrically around the perimeter and in the centre to show the highest point. Add leaves between the flowers at the edges.

**2** Fill in the gaps with smaller blooms, clusters of tiny flowers and ribbon loops, maintaining the overall domed shape.

## Ribbon Loops

Ribbon loops in toning colours enhance any flower arrangement. Make sure the ribbon is stiff enough to hold a loop without flopping. Choose wide or narrow ribbon, and experiment with loops of different sizes to suit the proportions of the arrangement.

**YOU WILL NEED:** stiff florists' ribbon, scissors, fine florists' wire.

**1** Fold the ribbon into pairs of loops of the required length. Trim off excess ribbon.

**2** Holding the loops near the base between thumb and forefinger, make two small snips towards the centre through all layers of ribbon. Twist wire around the ribbon in the snips to secure the loops. Push the end of the wire into the arrangement.

## Wired Bows

Wired bows are quick to make and can be scaled up to any size by using wider ribbon, or even paper.

**YOU WILL NEED:** ribbon, scissors, fine florists' wire.

**1** Fold the ribbon into a bow shape and hold the crossover between thumb and forefinger. Twist a length of wire around the middle to hold in shape.

**2** Make a small loop in the ribbon to hide the join. Secure with wire, then cut off excess ribbon.

# Hanging Spherical Posy

The charm of this pretty posy is its perfect ball shape. It is sometimes easiest to hang it by its ribbon when adding the flowers to the underside.

**YOU WILL NEED:** a dry florists' foam (styro foam) sphere, florists' ribbon, florists' wire, scissors, flowers.

**1** Make a hanging loop from florists' ribbon and secure the ends with a length of wire. Push the end of the wire through the foam sphere.

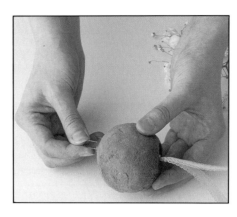

**2** Bend the end of the wire back towards the sphere to prevent it from slipping out.

**3** Wire individual blooms and trim the wires to about 2.5–3.5 cm/1–1½ in. Push the wired stems into the foam to cover it evenly.

**4** Make little bundles of smaller flower heads, wire them in the same way and insert them between the larger blooms.

## Flower Basket

A wide range of wicker baskets and trugs frame flower arrangements attractively, but freestanding wire baskets make subtle containers that allow the flowers to speak for themselves.

**YOU WILL NEED:** basket with wet florists' foam base to fit, sphagnum moss, flowers, trailing ivy, reindeer moss, florists' wire, scissors.

**1** Stand the soaked florists' foam base in the wire basket on a plate to catch any drips. Cover the top and sides with damp sphagnum moss.

**2** Select two or three flower heads of similar toning colours and arrange them attractively.

**3** Wire the flowers together into little bunches.

**4** Push the wired flower stems into the foam base, working around the outer edge.

**5** Insert single ivy leaves here and there between the flowers.

**6** Wind trails of ivy around the perimeter between the flower heads, pushing the ends firmly down into the foam base.

**7** Fill the centre with wired tufts of reindeer moss to create a high domed shape.

# Spiky Paper Flowers

Use paper of a single colour for each bloom, or make each layer from a different shade — for example, from pink through mauve and violet to blue — for a glowing, luminous effect. Crêpe paper makes suitably chunky leaves to contrast with the delicate flowers.

**YOU WILL NEED:** 20 cm/8 in squares of tissue paper in flower colours and crêpe paper in green, florists' wire, small paper scissors, needle.

**1** Bend a small loop in one end of a length of wire. Fold four sheets of tissue paper together into quarters. Beginning about 2.5 cm/1 in away from the central corner, cut a circle of spikes radiating out towards the outer edges of the paper.

**2** Open out the folds and use a needle to make a hole through the centre. Push the straight end of the wire through the hole. Separate the tissue paper layers and rotate them slightly to stagger them.

**3** Turn the flower over and gently gather the petals over the wire loop. Holding the bottom of the flower between thumb and forefinger, twist the wire two or three times around the centre of the paper to secure.

**4** Fold the sheets of crêpe paper in half and cut out leaf shapes. Wire these in the same way and arrange between and around the flowers.

# Flower Rope

A single flower rope adds decoration to an awkward panel of wall — beside a door for example. A pair looks elegant framing a fireplace. Alternatively, a series of ropes can be suspended at links in paper chains or swags of ribbon. Hung from table edges, they create a very festive atmosphere.

**YOU WILL NEED:** green raffia, florists' wire, florists' tape, pins, flower heads such as orchids, lilies etc, foliage such as ivy, ruscus etc, narrow and wide matching ribbon.

**1** Tie a knot at one end of the bundle of raffia, divide the strands into three and plait (braid) loosely. Trim the end to length and secure.

**2** Make a loop at one end of a length of florists' wire and wire individual ivy leaves.

**3** Hold an ivy leaf and an orchid together and twist the wire around both stems. Bind both stems together with florists' tape.

**4** Wire and tape together other flower heads and leaves. Insert an orchid and ivy leaf near the top of the raffia rope.

**5** Insert a second wired flower head into the raffia rope below the orchid, positioning it at an attractive angle to add width.

**6** Continue to add further flower heads and leaves, alternating the angles to achieve a balanced effect. Position one flower head to conceal the end of the raffia rope.

**7** Wind a trail of ruscus leaves around the raffia rope, tucking it in behind the flowers. Make little long-tailed bows with narrow ribbon, and curl the ends.

**8** Attach the little bows to the raffia with pins. Arrange a spray of ivy to add width at the top of the rope and wire in place. Attach a large ribbon bow at the top.

# Herb Cone

Many aromatic-leaved herbs will last well out of water to make an unusual focal point. Contrast their foliage textures with the warm tones of spices, and add ribbon bows in a harmonizing colour. For best results, crush the ends of the herb stems and stand them in water for 12 hours before beginning.

**YOU WILL NEED:** a cone-shaped dry florists' foam (styro foam) form, herbs such as rosemary, bay and thyme, pins, florists' wire, spices such as whole cloves and cinnamon sticks, ribbon bows, raffia, reindeer moss, a plate.

**1** Working downwards, pin bay leaves to the cone. Overlap the leaves and position in a spiralling shape, wider at the base than the top.

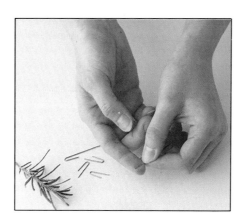

**2** Cut short lengths of florists' wire and bend them into hooks. Cut short sprigs of rosemary.

**3** Use the wire hooks to pin sprigs of rosemary to the cone, following the spiralling curve of the bay leaves.

**4** Attach a spiralling line of thyme sprigs to the cone in the same way. Pack cloves tightly together to infill the spaces between the herbs. Place the covered cone on a plate. Surround the base with tufts of reindeer moss, ribbon bows and bundles of cinnamon sticks tied with raffia.

# Miniature Vegetable Garland

Choose colourful, shapely whole vegetables such as baby carrots, small onions, artichokes and aubergines (eggplants) and chilli peppers, and mix them with florets (flowerets) of broccoli and sprigs of herbs for contrast. The plaited (braided) raffia is easy to hang as a garland but also looks good simply laid on the table.

**YOU WILL NEED:** raffia, florists' wire, darning needle (optional), small vegetables, sprigs of herbs, twisted paper ribbon.

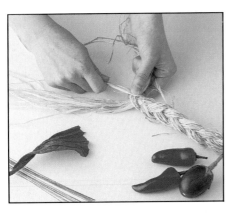

**1** Plait (braid) three bundles of raffia together loosely to make a rope of the required length. Secure the ends with a strand of raffia.

**2** Wire the vegetables individually. Use a darning needle to pierce holes for the wires if necessary, or wrap wires securely around the stalks.

**3** Wire little bundles of vegetables together. Insert the wire through to the back of the raffia and secure inconspicuously there.

**4** Wire little bunches of herbs together. Wire these into the raffia in between the vegetables.

**5** Untwist a length of ribbon for a bow. To make the loops, fold the ends to the centre and staple in place.

**6** Wrap a second length of ribbon around the centre of the bow, leaving the ends dangling as tails. Staple in place. Make a second bow in the same way. Fold the ends of the raffia rope under to neaten, tie with raffia and trim. Attach a ribbon bow to either end with wire.

*Miniature Vegetable Garland.*

## Garlands

Garlands can be long and made from flexible material, such as raffia or twisted paper, and hung across · walls, tables, down staircases and so on, or keep them short for placing above mirrors or doorways.

### LONG FLEXIBLE GARLANDS
Measure the length you require – if the garland is for a swagged tablecloth you may prefer to make a series of individual garlands to string between each swag. The raffia or twisted paper needs to be plaited (braided) first, so you will need three lengths, each one slightly longer than the required length. Tie a knot at one end of the raffia or twisted paper and plait (braid) loosely. Trim the end to length and secure. Fold the rope in half and mark the lowest, or mid-point in the sweep. Wire the decorative material, then thread it through the

garland, always ensuring that everything faces the mid-point. Secure the material at the back of the garland. Finish by securing a trio of flowers with leaves at the mid-point. Secure a wire loop at each end of the garland for fixing in position if necessary.

### SHORT GARLANDS
Prepare a base as before measuring 50–60 cm/20–24 in long. If you want to add large items to the garland, such as large cones and sprays of holly, the base must be at least 5 cm/2 in wide. Run a double thickness of sturdy tying wire through the base so that it can be easily curved into a neat shape that will hold its form before adding any decoration. Add a wire loop at each end as before for fixing. Begin by wiring in key material, such as large flowers or cones, then fill in the gaps with background material. Stop and check as you go along that the arrangement is well balanced.

Add bows at the ends to conceal the wire loops.

### CHAIN GARLANDS
Chain garlands are made by forming interlocking rings made from raffia or twisted paper, which comes in a variety of colours. A length of about 35 cm/14 in should be prepared for each link in the chain and secured in a circle. When one circle is formed, the next length is threaded through it before being secured. It is best to secure two or three links at a time, then wire the decorative material onto these before adding the next few links and so on. Lay out the chain on a long flat surface or on the floor as you work up the chain.

Remember to secure hanging wire loops at the ends and at points where the chain will be strung up. These may be concealed with bows and trailing ribbon ends in appropriate colours.

# Special Occasions

# THE ART OF FOOD PRESENTATION

*The first all-important impression of many a dish is a visual one, so it is essential to create a tempting appearance which stirs up a sense of anticipation for the delights to follow. Regardless of the simplicity or sophistication of a*

*recipe, there is no excuse for less-than-perfect presentation. This brief section runs through some practical points on preparing and serving dishes for the table, and ideas for garnishing and decorating a range of foods.*

### SIMPLE RULES FOR SERVING

There are a few basic rules of food presentation that are practical, as well as decorative. These are the first steps in ensuring that food arrives at the table looking appealing.

❖ Oven-to-table dishes must be in good condition. Always clean the outside of dishes and the rims before taking them to the table. Take care, however, not to crack a hot dish by wiping it with a wet cloth. Clean up the dish during the cooking process to avoid any baked-on residue.

❖ Plates should be warmed before serving hot food.

❖ If soup is served, try not to slop it about in the bowl on the way to the table as this creates an unattractive tide mark on the side of the bowl.

❖ If a cold first course is plated in advance, do not leave it to dry out before serving; keep each plate covered with cling film (plastic wrap).

❖ If the main course is plated and sauced before being taken to the table, always wipe away any small drips or spills before presenting the dish.

❖ When serving the main course at the table, plan one that is easy to carve or serve, or be prepared to cope with the problem in advance. For example, it may be prudent to slice or cut up the food in the kitchen before taking it to the table to serve.

❖ Food which is meant to be served hot should be just that; chilled food should be left in the refrigerator until just before it is served.

### A GUIDE TO GARNISHING

The garnish should fulfil two functions: to complement the ingredients in a dish and to make it look pretty. Recipes often specify a particular garnish for these reasons, one that is integral to the dish, not merely an afterthought. Garnishes don't have to be fancy or complicated to achieve the desired effect – adding a sprig of dill to a fish dish, for example, often completes the picture and will add to the flavour. However, do avoid the ubiquitous lettuce leaf and tomato quarter if at all possible.

### Useful Cutting Techniques

**CANELLE STRIPS** Use a special canelle knife to pare long, fine strips of skin or rind (peel) along the whole length of cucumbers, oranges or lemons. This produces a decorative cog-wheel effect when the vegetable or fruit is then sliced.

The pared strips of lemon or orange rind can also be used as a garnish if they are simmered first in water until tender, then drained well on absorbent kitchen paper (paper towels).

**JULIENNE STRIPS** Also known as julienne, these are matchstick-thin strips, usually cut from vegetables such as carrots, celeriac (celery root), celery, turnips, white radish and courgettes (zucchini). First cut the vegetables into thin slices and neaten the ends, then cut the slices into short, very thin strips.

**VEGETABLE SHAPES** Thinly slice carrots, potatoes, celeriac (celery root) or swede (rutabaga). Cook the slices in boiling water until just tender, then drain well. Use aspic cutters to stamp out shapes. Use this attractive garnish for chaudfroid dishes, terrines, aspic-coated foods and mousses.

## Salad Garnish

Prepare these spring onion (green onion) curls in advance and set them aside in a covered bowl in the refrigerator to keep them crisp and fresh. Add to the plates at the last minute. This is a particularly effective garnish on Chinese-style dishes.

**1** Shred the green part of an onion, leaving all the strips attached at the bulb end.

**2** Place in a bowl of iced water for at least 30 minutes in the refrigerator and the shredded part will curl. Drain well on absorbent kitchen paper (paper towels).

## Fleurons

These are small crescent shapes of puff pastry. They are delicious served with soups, sauced dishes and other savoury foods that are enhanced by a contrasting crisp texture.

Roll out the pastry (dough) thinly and use a crescent-shaped cutter to cut out the shapes. Brush each shape carefully with a little beaten egg and place them on a damp baking sheet. Bake at 220°C/425°F/Gas 7 for about 10 minutes, until well puffed and golden. Cool on a wire rack.

## Melba Toast

Serve melba toast with pâtés and savoury mousses. The toast will keep for several weeks stored in an airtight container.

Lightly toast medium-sliced bread on both sides under a hot grill (broiler). Remove from the grill and cut off the crusts. Using a sharp knife, cut through the centre of the toast to form two thin slices. Place the untoasted side face upwards on the grill pan and toast until golden brown.

**CARROT FLOWERS** Peel a carrot, then cut thin strips out of the side, working lengthways. When the carrot is sliced, the slices will have decorative edges. Blanch in boiling water until tender before use.

**VANDYKE CUTTING** Use this technique to give tomatoes, lemons, oranges, limes and radishes a fancy edge. Cut around the middle of the fruit with a small, fine-bladed knife, cutting a zig-zag pattern and in as far as the middle of the fruit. When cuts are made all around, pull the two halves apart to reveal the decorative zig-zag surfaces.

### Bread and Pastry Garnishes

**CROÛTONS** Cut thinly sliced bread into small shapes, such as dice, triangles and small circles. Heat a mixture of butter, olive oil and garlic (optional) until sizzling hot, then fry the croûtons until golden brown all over. Drain well on absorbent kitchen paper (paper towels). You can make these in advance and store in an airtight container. Sprinkle on soups and salads.

**CROÛTES** These are pieces of fried bread larger than croûtons, which are served around a casserole or under

portions of fried food, such as steaks, to absorb the juices. Prepare as for croûtons. Store in an airtight container

**PHYLLO FLAKES** A good way of using up broken or slightly dry sheets of phyllo pastry. Snip the pastry into small irregular shaped pieces, then place on a thoroughly greased baking sheet. Trickle a little oil evenly over the pastry. Bake at 180°C/350°F/Gas 4 for 20–30 minutes, turning the pieces occasionally. The cooking time depends on how much pastry is on the baking sheet and the thickness of the layer. Use hot or cold as a crunchy topping.

## Marbling

This is a technique for decorating sauces and soups, combining soft mixtures which will be left to set.

Flood a plate with a dark, coloured sauce, such as a chocolate or fruit sauce. Trickle a little cream at random over the sauce. Use the point of a fine metal skewer to drag the cream through the sauce, swirling it to achieve an attractive marble effect. Alternatively, use a pale custard sauce with a contrasting dark sauce to make the marbling.

## Feathering

An alternative to marbling.

**1** Flood a plate with dark, coloured sauce. Fill a piping (pastry) bag fitted with a small nozzle (tube) with cream. Pipe dots of cream evenly spaced around the edge of the bowl.

**2** Use the point of a fine metal skewer to drag the cream through the sauce to form a 'tail'.

# An Ice Bowl

Use the ice bowl when serving ice cream and sorbets. To make, you will need two freezerproof mixing bowls, one much smaller than the other. The smaller bowl should be plastic.

**1** Boil sufficient water to fill the larger bowl and leave it to cool. Place the larger bowl in the kitchen sink and pour in the cool boiled water. Float the plastic bowl inside the larger bowl and weigh it down so that it is partly submerged. Use freezer tape to keep it in place. Place both bowls in the freezer.

**2** When the water between the bowls begins to freeze, push rose petals and other edible flowers and herb leaves down between the two bowls. Use a metal skewer to do this. Do not try to push too many flowers or leaves down at once or the decoration will be all bunched together and the result will be less attractive.

**3** When the water has frozen, remove the bowls. Dip the bottom bowl in hot water and twist off. Quickly fill the top bowl with hot water, pour it out again and twist off.

# Frosting Fruit and Flowers

Use these to decorate cakes and desserts. Remember to use only edible flowers. Gum arabic is available from specialist cake decorating supply shops.

Brush the outside of soft fruit, such as grapes, strawberries, raspberries and blackberries with a little lightly beaten egg white, then sift with caster (superfine) sugar or roll them in the sugar. Use the same technique for frosting flowers. If preferred, for a crisper finish, the flowers can be brushed with gum arabic mixed with water instead of egg white.

*Frosted Fruit and Flowers.*

## Chocolate Caraque

Use to decorate desserts or cakes. Chill if not using straightaway.

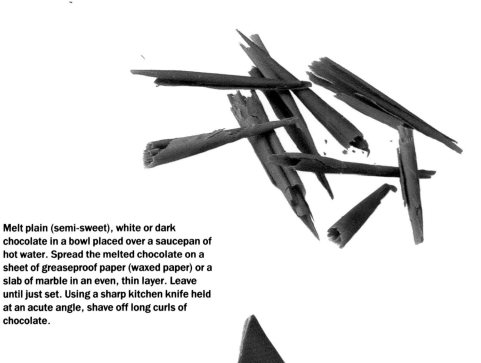

Melt plain (semi-sweet), white or dark chocolate in a bowl placed over a saucepan of hot water. Spread the melted chocolate on a sheet of greaseproof paper (waxed paper) or a slab of marble in an even, thin layer. Leave until just set. Using a sharp kitchen knife held at an acute angle, shave off long curls of chocolate.

## Chocolate Shapes

Use to decorate cakes. Again, they can be placed on the cake at once, or stored in the refrigerator until required.

Melt plain (semi-sweet), white or dark chocolate in a bowl placed over a saucepan of hot water. Spread the melted chocolate on a sheet of greaseproof paper (waxed paper) in an even, thin layer. Leave until just set. Use aspic cutters to stamp out shapes. Alternatively, use a sharp kitchen knife or scalpel (razor knife) and ruler to cut out strips, then cut the strips across into squares. These squares can then be cut in half diagonally to make triangles.

## Chocolate Rose Leaves

Choose any non-poisonous leaves, such as rose leaves, to make this attractive decoration for cakes and desserts.

Melt plain (semi-sweet), white or dark chocolate in a bowl placed over a saucepan of hot water. Using a small brush, brush a thin layer of melted chocolate on the underside of each leaf. When the chocolate has dried, it will easily separate from the leaf.

*Marzipan Fruits.*

## Marzipan Fruits
Use bought white marzipan (almond paste) and colour it using paste food colours (food colouring). Mould small balls of paste of the appropriate colour into miniature fruits. Finish oranges by rolling them on a nutmeg grater to achieve the correct texture and add the end of a clove for a stalk (stem); paint bananas with brown food colouring; use pale green paste for pears and dust them with red powder food colouring; use cloves for stalks on apples or on a bunch of grapes. Arrange the fruit in paper cases (cups) and serve them as petits fours or small gifts.

## Stuffed Dates
Stuff fresh dates with marzipan (almond paste) and roll in caster (superfine) sugar. Candied dates may also be stuffed and included among a box of chocolates.

## Toasted Nuts
Toasted flaked almonds, chopped hazelnuts and desiccated (shredded) coconut are ideal to sprinkle over desserts and for pressing on the side of cakes. Lay the nuts on a foil-lined grill (broiler) pan and toast well away from the heat, turning the nuts often so they brown evenly and do not burn.

## Crushed Crumbs
Place plain biscuits (cookies) in a clean plastic bag and crush them with a rolling pin. Crushed crumbs are delicious sprinkled over soft desserts to add a little crunch or use them as coating for cakes covered in a buttercream or soft icing.

## Strawberry Fans
Part-slice strawberries, cutting thin slices and leaving them attached at the stalk (stem) end. Gently ease the slices apart sideways. This fanning technique may be used for savoury ingredients such as baby carrots, small cucumbers and gherkins (pickles).

# BREAKFASTS AND BRUNCHES

*E*ntertaining first thing in the day is not everyone's style and many people prefer not to be sociable before lunch, so breakfasts should not be formal, early morning affairs. Decide whether you want your party to be extremely lazy and relaxed – a good idea for breakfast gatherings – or bright and cheery, a better option for brunch. Guests can be invited any time from 10 a.m. to 11.30 a.m. at the latest for a brunch party.

A breakfast party can be a good way of getting a special day off to a social start. You may invite friends for a casual breakfast before setting off for a day trip into the country, or before the local carnival, town parade or other similar festive event. Linking breakfast in this way means that you can allow guests to lounge around without having to indulge in deep conversation because everyone will have plenty of opportunity to chat later. Allow a couple of hours before everyone has to leave the house.

## LAZY BREAKFAST

Make this party easy on yourself as well as the guests. Keep the cooking to a minimum by preparing a large continental-style breakfast platter. Make croissants in advance and have them warming in the oven. Warm bagels and serve them with bowls of cream cheese and smoked salmon (lox). Include doughnuts or Danish pastries for those who enjoy sweet treats and have an enormous basket of fruit as a centrepiece so that everyone can help themselves. Keep the coffee and tea brewing all the time.

❖ Arrange a large flat basket full of unusual teas as alternative drinks – fruit tea sachets, bundles of herb teas and sprigs of rosemary, lemon balm and different types of mint. Place small glass dishes of thinly sliced lemon, orange and lime around the basket, with tongs for guests to serve themselves. Remember to set out a bowl of sugar lumps, too.

❖ Make sure you are well stocked with different fruit juices and prepare a jug of an early morning awakener: orange, lemon and lime slices, thin cucumber slices, mint sprigs, rosemary sprigs and several good dashes of bitters. Top up with sparkling mineral water (seltzer). Serve this on its own or use it as a mixer for topping up glasses of chilled sparkling wine.

### Breakfast and Brunch Checklist

- Cereal
- Fruit
- Savoury dishes
- Milk
- Sugar
- Coffee
- Tea
- Sparkling wines
- Fruit juices
- Any special dietary needs?
- Table linen
- Cutlery (flatware), china and glassware
- Flowers
- House cleaning and tidying

*A cooling glass of mint tea.*

### Table Style for Brunch

Select sunny colours – yellows, oranges and greens.

❖ Arrange bowls of fresh, fragrant herbs around the room.

❖ Make lots of pomanders using oranges and lemons. Stud the fruit all over with cloves, then pile them high in colourful pottery bowls and distribute them around the house.

❖ Decorate a plain cloth with ribbon flowers, arranging them in groups of three on the corners or around the edge of the cloth. Sew on silk leaves, tucking them under the flowers. Make ribbon rosebuds and stitch small groups of them at intervals around the cloth, between the larger flowers.

### BRIGHT BRUNCH IDEAS

As a complete contrast to the laid-back breakfast, opt for a livelier feeling when entertaining mid-morning. Move the party out into the garden on summer mornings or have all the windows open and tie back curtains with bows of spring-coloured ribbons.

❖ Serve two or more courses or lay out a buffet for larger gatherings. Greet guests with Buck's Fizz (Mimosa, a mixture of sparkling wine and orange juice), wine spritzers or kir (sparkling wine flavoured with cassis) .

❖ Make simple fruit salads and cock-tails and have bowls of yogurt to serve with them.

❖ Serve pitted, ready-to-eat prunes wrapped in bacon and grilled as a hot starter (appetizer).

❖ Have a kitchen brunch and cook waffles, blinis or pancakes as they are needed. If you have the batter all mixed and ready to cook, then encourage guests to fix their own. Make sure you have at least a couple of pans or electric waffle irons ready to heat. Alternatively, make stacks in advance and let your guests heat their own.

❖ Organize a seafood brunch: serve smoked salmon, prawns (shrimp) marinated with herbs and lemon, grilled oysters, smoked mackerel and scallop kebabs (scallop kebabs are delicious wrapped in a piece of bacon, for example). Serve dressed crab, grilled lobster and poached salmon for an extra special brunch occasion.

*Take a Scottish theme, and use tartan cloth for the table and serve a bowl of hot porridge (oatmeal).*

# BREAKFAST FRUIT COCKTAIL

———— SERVES 4 ————

This zesty fruit cocktail is the perfect first course for a sit-down brunch party or it is ideal for a breakfast buffet table.

*1 mango*
*2 pink or yellow grapefruit*
*3 oranges*
*1 charentais or cantaloupe melon*
*mint sprigs to decorate*

TO SERVE
*Greek yogurt or fromage frais*
*runny honey*

**1** Peel the mango, then slice the fruit off the stone (pit) and cut it into bite-sized pieces. Prepare the grapefruit and oranges: slice off the peel and pith from the top and bottom of each fruit, then use a sharp serrated knife to cut the rind and pith off the sides in wide strips, working all around the fruit.

**2** Once all the peel and pith is removed, slice the grapefruit and oranges, and cut the slices in half. Halve the melon, discard the seeds, then cut the halves into quarters. Cut the flesh into strips with a knife, then across into pieces (still attached to the skin). Cut between the skin and the melon flesh to form neat pieces.

**3** Mix all the fruit and add the mint sprigs. Cover and chill for at least 30 minutes, preferably a couple of hours. Pick out the mint sprigs and arrange them on top of the fruit before serving. Offer the yogurt or fromage frais and honey separately.

*Breakfast Fruit Cocktail.*

# SEEDED CROISSANTS

———— MAKES 8 ————

Home-made croissants really are worth the effort, especially as they can be made in a large batch and frozen before or after baking. This recipe is slightly different from traditional croissant recipes, having a small proportion of wholemeal (whole-wheat) flour and a crunchy topping of poppy seeds or sesame seeds.

*350 g/12 oz (3 cups) strong plain (bread) flour*
*100 g/4 oz (1 cup) wholemeal (whole-wheat) flour*
*1 teaspoon salt*
*1 teaspoon caster (superfine) sugar*
*400 g/14 oz (1¾ cups) butter*
*1 sachet (envelope) easy-blend (quick-rising) dried yeast*
*250 ml/8 fl oz (1 cup) lukewarm water*
*1 egg, beaten*
*poppy seeds or sesame seeds for topping*

**1** Mix together both types of flour, the salt and sugar in a bowl. Rub in (cut in) 50 g/2 oz (¼ cup) of the butter. Divide the remaining butter into 3 equal portions and shape each into a 10 cm/4 in square. Chill. Stir the yeast into the flour mixture .

**2** Bind the flour mixture with the water to make a firm dough.

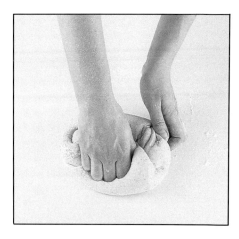

**3** Turn out the dough onto a floured surface and knead well for about 10 minutes, or until it feels very smooth and elastic. The dough is kneaded sufficiently when it springs back quickly if pressed with a fingertip.

**4** Roll out the dough into an oblong shape measuring about 30 × 12.5 cm/12 × 5 in. Place a square of chilled butter in the middle of the dough, then fold the bottom third portion of the dough up over the butter.

**5** Fold the top third of the dough down, then seal the edges by pressing them with a rolling pin. Chill the dough for 5 minutes.

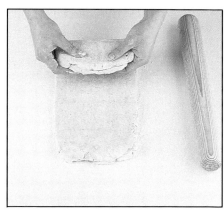

**6** Roll out and fold the dough a further 2 times the same way to incorporate the remaining butter, chilling between each rolling. Then repeat the process again without any butter so the dough has been rolled and folded 6 times in all. Chill the dough well at the end of rolling.

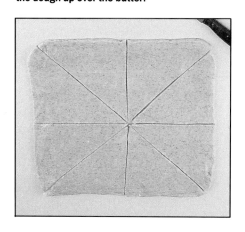

**7** Grease 2 baking sheets. Cut the dough in half. Roll out one portion into a 30 cm/12 in square and cut it diagonally into quarters, then cut into 8 triangles.

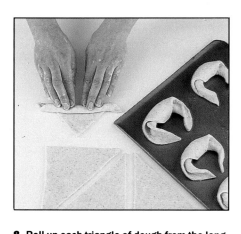

**8** Roll up each triangle of dough from the long side towards the point. Place on a baking sheet and curve the rolled portions of dough to shape the croissants. Repeat with the remaining dough. Cover the dough loosely with oiled plastic or place in a large plastic bag and leave to rise in a cool room for several hours. Alternatively, leave the croissants in the refrigerator to rise overnight. If the croissants are placed in a warm room, the butter will melt and they will become greasy and poorly risen.

**9** Set the oven at 220°C/425°F/Gas 7. Brush the tops of the croissants very gently with beaten egg and sprinkle generously with poppy seeds or sesame seeds. Bake for 15–20 minutes, until the croissants are risen and golden. Cool on a wire rack.

*Seeded Croissant.*

**FREEZE AHEAD**
To freeze the croissants before baking, allow them to rise completely, then open freeze them on their baking sheets and pack them in freezerproof bags when they are firm.

To freeze the baked croissants, leave them to cool completely before sealing in a plastic bag. Either way, the croissants benefit from being stored in a rigid container to prevent damage. Bake raw croissants from frozen, allowing about 5 minutes extra baking time.

## Wheat Basket

Bring new life to an old or drab wire basket by trimming it with wheat and toning buff-coloured paper ribbon. Wire containers intended for kitchen use look good decorated this way.

**YOU WILL NEED:** wire basket, twisted buff-coloured paper, dried wheat and other grass heads, dried poppy seed heads, raffia, scissors.

**1** Thread a length of twisted, buff-coloured paper at intervals through the loops around the basket edge. Open out some of the paper once it is in position.

**2** Tie the ends of the paper in an attractive knot or bow. Tie small bundles of wheat and grass heads together with raffia, including a poppy seed head in some of the bundles.

**3** Position the bundles of grasses around the edges of the basket, between the opened-out sections of paper. Bind in place with raffia, tying neat knots and trimming the ends.

# EUROPEAN BREAKFAST PLATTER

──────── SERVES 4 (see Cook's Tip) ────────

A platter of cold food looks great on a brunch buffet. It is also excellent for a sit-down breakfast with overnight guests, as it is simple to prepare and especially easy to serve, allowing you to relax and late-risers to share the meal without any last-minute cooking and embarrassing fuss. Of course, you do not have to follow rigidly the combination of ingredients used here — vary the selection of cold meats and fruit according to taste, but ensure that the display is colourful, neat and attractive. Ideally, poach the apricots the night before to allow them plenty of time to cool down and absorb flavour.

225 g/8 oz (1⅓ cups) ready-to-eat dried apricots
100 ml/4 fl oz (½ cup) unsweetened apple juice
2 tablespoons cider vinegar
2 cloves
1 cinnamon stick, 7.5 cm/3 in
4 eggs, hard-boiled, shelled and quartered
1 tablespoon chopped fresh dill
2 tablespoons soured cream
about 1 tablespoon milk
salt and freshly ground black pepper
4 ripe tomatoes, sliced
8 slices mortadella
4 slices cooked ham
12 slices salami
225 g/8 oz Gruyère or Emmenthal (Swiss) cheese, thinly sliced
100 g/4 oz feta cheese, cubed
100 g/4 oz Edam or Gouda cheese, cubed
50 g/2 oz (⅓ cup) black (ripe) olives, stoned (pitted)
8 cocktail gherkins (pickles)
sprigs of dill, to garnish (optional)

*European Breakfast Platter.*

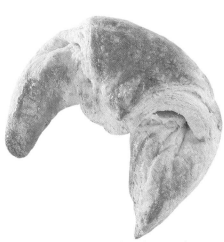

*Serve a European Breakfast Platter with a range of breakfast breads, such as croissants, seeded rolls and French-style baguettes.*

Place the apricots in a small saucepan. Add the apple juice, cider vinegar, cloves and cinnamon stick. Heat gently until the liquid boils, cover the pan and simmer for 7–10 minutes, until most of the liquid is absorbed. Leave to stand until completely cold.

Arrange the eggs at one end of a large serving platter. Mix together the dill and soured cream. Stir in just enough milk to give a thick pouring consistency. Add a little seasoning, then trickle this dressing over the eggs. Arrange the tomatoes, cold meats and cheeses on the platter, then add the olives and gherkins (pickles) as appropriate. Garnish with sprigs of dill, if liked.

Keep or discard the spices from the apricots, as liked. They can be served in a separate bowl or add them to the platter to separate the meats from the cheeses.

---

**COOK'S TIP**
The quantities given apply when the platter is served as the main dish for a sit-down breakfast; the amounts do not have to be multiplied in proportion when preparing a buffet for a larger gathering as guests will eat less from the platter.

# LUNCHEON OPTIONS

*T**he majority of lunchtime entertaining is concentrated into weekends and holidays, and what better opportunity for meeting friends and families, forgetting about formalities and relaxing with simple food in good company. Keep the menu unfussy and plan to meet friends for some* form of activity in the morning, perhaps a shopping session, or to participate in a favourite sport, or organize a swim at the local pool with adults and children.

*Larger gatherings can be successful too – make sure you provide for young guests as well as adults and take advantage of fine weather to keep children happy outdoors. If you invite several families with children of roughly the same ages, then you will not have to bother about organizing games. As soon as introductions are over, shyness fades fast and children quickly establish common interests using their imagination to create their own entertainment. As long as it's not disruptive, let it happen and concentrate on the adults.*

**INVITATIONS**

Formal lunches are fixed for 1 p.m. and you may want to invite guests half an hour earlier so that you can offer them an aperitif. Cards do not have to be sent to a small group, simply ring around one or two weeks in advance to reserve the day.

**LUNCH MENUS**

Two courses are adequate for any lunch, perhaps together with a cheese board. Unless you are serving a roast Sunday lunch, the menu should be light and fairly delicate. A light soup and some grilled fish or poultry with seasonal vegetables or salad are suitable. A vegetable terrine with salad and new potatoes or quiche lorraine with salad are all typical dishes.

**HEARTY WEEKEND LUNCHES** Quite different from delicate social affairs, these are for action-packed weekends when everyone is planning to get out in the fresh air and expend some energy before lunch or later in the afternoon. Chunky soups, warm breads, hearty pasta and rice dishes and full-flavoured pâtés all fit the bill.

**SUNDAY LUNCH** This is not a snatched meal – especially if serving up a roast – and plenty of time should be set aside to linger over the dessert, cheese (if serving) and coffee. Three courses may be served, or offer a light dip and crudités with drinks beforehand instead of a first course.

A rib of beef or standing rib roast has to be the ultimate joint for such occasions. Cooked to perfection, served with rich gravy, mashed or golden roast potatoes, creamy mashed parsnips, glazed carrots or crunchy steamed Brussels sprouts, this is what traditional Sunday lunch is all about!

For dessert consider apple pie and custard (custard sauce) or ice cream; creamy baked rice pudding served with a compote of plums or smooth orange syllabub.

To cook a roast to perfection, it is important to have everything well planned in advance: peel potatoes and prepare vegetables and keep them covered with water (not a good idea for everyday cooking as you lose precious vitamins but practical on occasion), cook and mash parsnips ready to reheat and have the dessert prepared.

## Lunch Checklist

- Nibbles (snacks)
- First course
- Main course
- Dessert
- Wine and/or beer
- Alcohol-free drinks
- Ice
- Coffee
- Any special dietary needs?
- Table linen
- Cutlery (flatware), china and glassware
- Flowers
- House cleaning and tidying

# LITTLE EMPANADAS

------ MAKES 24 ------

These tiny empanadas, or turnovers, are ideal for handing around with drinks. They also look attractive arranged on individual plates, with a small garnish of salad; however, for a less elegant result simply shape the dough into 12 small turnovers.

450 g/1 lb (4 cups) strong white (bread) flour
1 sachet (envelope) easy-blend (quick-rising) dried yeast
1 teaspoon salt
1 teaspoon caster (superfine) sugar
275 ml/9 fl oz (1 cup plus 2 tablespoons) lukewarm water

FILLING
2 tablespoons olive oil
1 onion, finely chopped
1 garlic clove, crushed
1 small green pepper (sweet bell pepper), seeded and finely diced
1 small red pepper (sweet bell pepper), seeded and finely diced
450 g/1 lb boneless chicken breast, skinned and finely diced
2 tablespoons black (ripe) olives, stoned (pitted) and chopped
salt and freshly ground black pepper
1 teaspoon dried oregano
2 teaspoons ground coriander
1/4 teaspoon chilli powder
3 tablespoons raisins (optional)
1 egg, beaten, to glaze

*Gazpacho.*

Prepare the filling first: heat the oil in a saucepan. Add the onion, garlic, green and red peppers, and cook, stirring occasionally, for 5 minutes. Stir in the chicken and continue to cook until the chicken pieces are firm and lightly cooked. Stir in the olives, seasoning, oregano, coriander, chilli powder and raisins (if used), then cook for 2 minutes. Remove the pan from the heat and set aside.

Grease 2 baking sheets. Mix together the flour, yeast, salt, sugar and water to make a firm dough. Turn out the dough on to a lightly floured surface and knead it thoroughly for about 10 minutes, until it is smooth and elastic. Divide the dough in half. Keep one half covered with plastic while you work with the other, first cutting it into 12 equal pieces.

Flatten a small piece of dough into a circle measuring about 8.5 cm/3½ in across. Place a little of the chicken mixture in the middle of the dough and dampen the edge, then fold the dough in half to enclose the filling completely in a semi-circular pasty. Pinch the edges to seal in the filling. Continue shaping the pasties, placing them on the baking sheets as they are filled. Cover with oiled cling film (plastic wrap) and leave in a warm place until the dough is risen. Meanwhile, set the oven at 220°C/425°F/Gas 7.

Brush the empanadas with beaten egg and bake them for 15–20 minutes, until golden brown. Transfer to a wire rack to cool.

# GAZPACHO

------ SERVES 6 ------

This Spanish soup, flavoured with garlic and vegetables and thickened with breadcrumbs, is usually served chilled. It is perfect for a summer lunch on the patio, and the quantities can easily be multiplied for a large party.

75 g/3 oz (1½ cups) fresh breadcrumbs
100 ml/4 fl oz (½ cup) water
2 tablespoons cider vinegar
250 ml/8 fl oz (1 cup) tomato juice
1 onion, chopped
1 cucumber, peeled and roughly chopped
2 garlic cloves, crushed
1 kg/2 lb ripe tomatoes, peeled and seeded
1 red pepper (sweet bell pepper), seeded and roughly chopped
2 teaspoons caster (superfine) sugar
6 tablespoons olive oil
salt and freshly ground black pepper
cayenne pepper

GARNISH
croûtons
black (ripe) olives, stoned (pitted) and sliced
1 green pepper (sweet bell pepper), seeded and diced
1 onion, chopped

Place the breadcrumbs in a bowl. Sprinkle the water, cider vinegar and tomato juice over and leave to soak for 15 minutes.

Using a food processor or blender, purée the onion, cucumber, garlic, tomatoes and red pepper until they are smooth. Add the sugar and process the mixture again, then slowly work in the olive oil. Add the soaked breadcrumbs with all the juice and blend until smooth.

Add seasoning and a little cayenne pepper, then taste the gazpacho to check the seasoning. Chill well before serving.

Offer the croûtons, olives, green pepper and onion in separate bowls so that they may be sprinkled over individual portions as required.

### OPEN SANDWICHES

Open sandwiches are impressive and appetizing for lunch parties of all sizes. They do need a fair amount of last-minute attention, however, if they are going to look and, more importantly, taste their best. If you want to prepare open sandwiches for more than eight people, to avoid being over-burdened with last-minute garnishes keep the menu simple, serving only the sandwiches and a prepared-ahead dessert.

Trying to set out a stunning array of sandwiches is hopeless if you do not have suitable platters on which to present them. Large meat platters will do but the sandwiches look awkward on wide rims of deep platters. Use large flat cake stands, cheese boards and glass or marble platters.

If you are stuck for serving dishes, buy metal or plastic trays and dress them up by wiring herb sprigs together and taping them around the tray's rim on the outside. Cover the middle of the tray with plain paper doilies or paper napkins to match your table style.

The following is a guide to bases, flavoured butters, spreads and toppings with notes on what to prepare several hours in advance and the essential last-minute additions.

### Bases

**WHITE BREAD** Select an unsliced, square-shaped, sandwich loaf. Cut the crusts off the outside before slicing. This should be sliced fairly thickly and the slices can be cut diagonally to make triangular sandwiches. White bread is good for light seafood toppings and chicken or turkey mixtures.

**LIGHT RYE BREAD** Close-textured light rye bread makes a versatile and firm base for all sorts of toppings, including delicate ingredients such as smoked salmon and caviar-style fish roe. It is not necessary to cut the crusts off.

**DARK OR BLACK RYE BREAD** This tends to have a moister texture than light rye, so it breaks more easily. However, it is more sturdy than ordinary white or wholemeal (whole-wheat) bread, so it can be sliced fairly thinly. The flavour is quite strong and slightly tangy, and the bread usually includes caraway or fennel seeds. Some people like this with smoked salmon, while others prefer the milder light rye. Rye bread is excellent with strong smoked fish, such as mackerel or trout.

**PUMPERNICKEL** Moist, close-textured, tangy and distinctly flavoured, pumpernickel is another candidate for serving with smoked fish and soured cream (fresh sour cream). Herrings are a good topping with chopped dill and sliced raw onion. Full-flavoured meats, such as pastrami and garlic sausages, also go well on pumpernickel.

**ROLLS, CROISSANTS AND BAGELS** Split horizontally, these all make suitable bases but they can look messy if you are not careful and there is more filling than sliced bread. Plain ingredients are the best toppings for rich croissants – smoked ham, finely sliced Emmenthal (Swiss) or Gruyère cheese, thinly sliced smoked turkey – while mixed ingredients with more dominant flavours go well with rolls and bagels. Spicy meats, such as pastrami, mortadella, salami and frankfurters and mixed creamy-dressed salads are also good on thicker bases.

**FRENCH BREAD** This is fine for *al fresco* eating, where delicacy does not feature on the menu! Cut a slim baguette into pieces, then slice them in half lengthways. Use chunky toppings which stay in place well, such as mayonnaise-dressed prawns (shrimp), chicken or rolled ham.

**WHOLE-GRAIN BREAD** Loaves with added whole grains make a pleasing texture for substantial toppings. Avoid the plain, very light wholemeal (whole-wheat) loaves which tend to be slightly dry and uninteresting. Some of the pre-sliced multi-grain loaves make good bases. Halve slices from large loaves with a rounded shape.

### Butters and Spreads

Soften butter before spreading so it does not tear the bread base. Unsalted, lightly salted or salted butter may be used according to taste; consider the delicate flavour of foods such as smoked trout fillets or Parma ham (prosciutto) and you may decide to opt for unsalted butter even if you do not usually use it.

Flavoured butters should be chosen to complement the topping. Here are a few suggestions.

**PARSLEY BUTTER** Chopped fresh parsley adds a refreshing flavour to butter for the majority of toppings, but its flavour is wasted with highly seasoned ingredients, such as curried chicken.

**LEMON BUTTER** Finely grated lemon rind (peel) adds a distinct flavour which is good with fish and seafood, chicken and turkey.

**MIXED HERB BUTTER** Chopped fresh parsley, thyme, basil, tarragon, a hint of sage and rosemary and a little mint combine well. A mixed herb butter is ideal for vegetable-based toppings, such as lettuce and tomatoes, and for yeast pâtés, eggs or cheese.

*A selection of tasty open sandwiches: top tray, Italian Ham with Mango; bottom tray, left, Smoked Mackerel, and right, Smoked Salmon with Dill.*

**ANCHOVY BUTTER** Flavour unsalted butter with anchovy essence (extract) or create a stronger spread by pounding canned anchovies and their oil to a paste before beating into butter. Add a dash of lemon juice and some freshly ground black pepper. Use as a base for roast beef, eggs or salad ingredients, such as cucumbers and tomatoes.

## Toppings

The topping should centre on one or two main ingredients, possibly with a lettuce or tomato base and with a complementary garnish. Unusual cheeses or vegetable pâtés are tasty choices for vegetarians. You can serve almost anything on an open sandwich, so the following are intended only as suggestions to fire your imagination.

**SMOKED SALMON WITH DILL** This is a classic open sandwich topping for lunch, breakfast or brunch. Fold and overlap thin slices of smoked salmon on light rye bread. Parsley butter may

be spread on the bread, if liked. Garnish just before serving, with small dollops of soured cream (fresh sour cream) and a sprinkling of fresh dill, and add a small wedge of lemon. The juice from the lemon is squeezed over the sandwich. A dill sprig may be added for an extra garnish.

**SMOKED MACKEREL** Spread horseradish sauce or creamed horseradish over the base. Top with flaked smoked mackerel or other smoked fish if preferred. Cover at this stage with cling film (plastic wrap) and set aside until ready to serve. Add a garnish of diced, peeled and seeded tomato, diced fresh or dill cucumber and very finely chopped onion or flat leaf parsley just before serving.

**ITALIAN HAM WITH MANGO** Trim the fat from Parma ham (prosciutto) and arrange it in folds on a base of white bread. Cover with cling film (plastic wrap) at this stage and set aside, ready

for last minute garnishing. When ready to serve, add a little radicchio or chicory (endive), a couple of slices of fresh mango and a few shreds of fresh basil. Garnish with basil sprigs at the last minute and trickle a little olive oil over the ham, if liked.

**BACON, LETTUCE AND TOMATO** Spread the bread with anchovy butter, soft cheese flavoured with garlic and herbs or mixed herb butter. Add the rest of the topping no longer than 30 minutes before serving. Top with lettuce leaves and coleslaw or grated carrot. Add some mayonnaise or soured cream (fresh sour cream) and sprinkle with crisp bacon. Garnish with cherry tomatoes, if liked.

**AVOCADO AND PESTO** This is a sandwich to assemble at the last minute. Arrange lettuce leaves on the bread base and top them with sliced avocado. Trickle a little pesto over the avocado and serve.

## Felt Flower Napkin Rings

Choose fine, smooth felt and ribbon in colours to match or harmonize with your table settings.

**YOU WILL NEED:** (for each napkin ring) thin card (posterboard) for template, pencil, scissors, coloured and green felt, needle and thread to match, a few tiny beads; (for each felt flower) 90 cm/1 yd velvet ribbon about 1.5 cm/⅝ in wide, needle and thread to match, 20 cm/8 in plastic-covered tying wire, wire cutters.

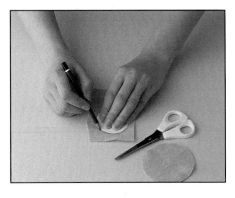

**1** Cut out two circular templates, one 6.5 cm/2½ in in diameter and the other 4 cm/1½ in. Draw the outlines onto the felt and cut out.

**2** Fold each felt circle in quarters and cut a shallow V-shape out of the curved edge to make scalloped 'petals'.

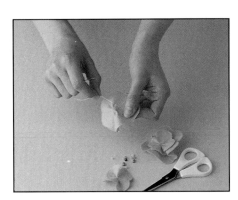

**3** Sew a tiny ring of running stitches around the centre of each flower shape, then pull the thread to pucker the centre slightly.

**4** Stitch the smaller circle on top of the larger one. Sew three or four beads in the centre.

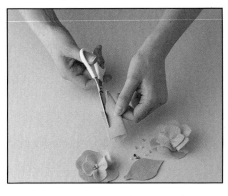

**5** Cut out two leaf shapes from green felt.

**6** Place the leaves on the underside of the flower and stitch.

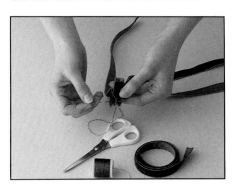

**7** Cut the ribbon into three equal lengths. Stitch the ribbon lengths together at one end with matching thread.

**8** Plait (braid) the ribbon neatly and not too tightly so that it forms an even band.

**9** Secure the end of the plait with a few stitches and trim.

**10** Run a length of plastic-covered tying wire along the back of the plait, securing it in place with a few stitches here and there.

**11** Form the plait into a ring, twisting the ends of the wire together to secure. Trim off the excess wire with wire cutters. Turn the ends of the plait under and stitch together.

**12** Sew the flower to the plait to cover the join.

*continued . . .*

*continued . . .*

A red poppy napkin ring will bring a splash of colour to a summer lunch table. The plaited (braided) ring is made in the same way as before.

**YOU WILL NEED:** (for each poppy) thin card (posterboard) for template, pencil, scissors, red felt, needle and thread to match, black haberdashers' wire for stamens; (for each napkin ring) 90 cm/1 yd velvet ribbon, 20 cm/8 in plastic-covered tying wire, wire cutters.

**13** Make a card template for a three-lobed poppy shape about 7.5 cm/3 in in diameter. Draw the outline onto the felt.

**14** Cut out two poppy shapes for each flower.

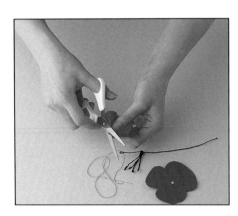

**15** Fold the flower to find the centre and cut a tiny nick with scissors.

**16** Lay the two poppy shapes together with the lobes at different angles. Shape hooked stamens using haberdashers' wire.

**17** Insert the stamens into the centre of the poppy from front to back. Twist the wire around the base of the flower once or twice.

**18** Stitch the wire to the base of the poppy to secure. Attach the poppy to the plaited napkin ring as before (see step 12).

# INVITATION TO TEA

*Tea usually falls into two categories, either an elegant social event taken on the lawn in summer or a heart-warming meeting for fresh toasted buns, lots of steaming hot tea and tall sundaes.*

*Long gone are the days when taking tea meant sitting on best behaviour, making stilted conversation and nibbling the tiniest of sandwiches. Even the most sophisticated events should be relaxed and pleasant, with guests free to move about and catch up with old friends.*

### SENDING OUT INVITATIONS

Depending on the size and type of gathering, invitations may be informal and made by telephone a week or two ahead or they may be written and sent three or four weeks before the event.

Informal invitations imply a homely menu and simple entertainment, perhaps a game of charades or cards. Guests will usually come in smart, casual clothes and this may be an opportunity to meet new members of the family.

Written invitations suggest a grander event. It is up to you to decide whether you want everyone to make a special effort to dress up. For example you may opt for a tea party in the garden and ask all the women to wear hats. One way of making the message unmistakably clear is to cut out novelty invitations in the shape of hats and to dress them up with ribbon, feathers, flowers and bows.

### TABLE DRESSINGS

Lace cloths and fine decorative linens are *de rigueur* for a formal tea party. If there is a buffet arrangement for food, a plain white cloth covered by a lace overcloth looks pretty. Tie the lace cloth in swags and decorate it with posies of roses and ribbon bows.

❖ Tie linen napkins with lace and carefully place a rosebud or a small flower in each. Make a pretty bow by covering a length of satin ribbon with very fine lace. Ribbon of a delicate colour may be used to match a coloured undercloth on the table.

❖ Wire small roses or rosebuds, then trim the stems and wrap them with florists' tape. A small safety pin stuck discreetly through the back of the tape enables the flowers to be worn as buttonholes or they can be pinned to hats.

❖ For a sit-down tea, decorate the table with tulle bonbonnières, or sweet (candy) cups, for each place setting.

## Planning for Large Tea Parties

❖ Some cakes may be made and frozen well ahead.

❖ Sweet pastry cases (pie crusts) can be prepared and cooked for strawberry tarts, then frozen unfilled. Thaw, then warm the cases in the oven briefly before adding a fresh-fruit filling.

❖ Sandwiches should be made on the day of the party; however, fillings that require mixing, such as egg mayonnaise, can be prepared the day before and kept covered in the refrigerator.

❖ Ice cream for sundaes should be scooped out onto baking trays or

into large, shallow containers lined with cling film (plastic wrap) early in the day, then covered and frozen. Glasses for sundaes should be placed on their sides in the refrigerator a few hours ahead if space allows. This makes the process of assembling sundaes quick and easy.

❖ Lay out cups and saucers on a trolley or several trays. Remember to put teaspoons on the saucers. Have small plates and napkins ready.

❖ Have several large teapots ready. If you are entertaining a large crowd, hire (rent) a tea urn from a caterers' or party supply store.

# Bonbonnières

These charming lacy holders for candies or sweets are easy to make and look pretty strewn about the table.

**YOU WILL NEED:** for each holder a circle of tulle or lace about 15 cm/6 in in diameter plus trimming, needle and thread, ribbons, sugared almonds, pastel-coloured mints, cashews, mixed nuts or other confectionery.

**1** Hem the edge of the fabric circle and trim it with lace, if you like.

**2** Place a few sugared almonds or other confectionery in the centre of the circle of fabric. Tie up the bonbonnière into a neat bundle with fine satin ribbon. Attach a small name tag if you like and place the bonbonnières in position on the table.

### Minted Cucumber Sandwiches

Beat a tablespoon of chopped fresh mint into 100 g/4 oz (½ cup) butter. Peel and thinly slice half a cucumber. Spread out the cucumber slices on a dish and sprinkle them with a little salt, then set aside for 20 minutes. Pat dry the cucumber slices with absorbent kitchen paper (paper towels). Season with a little freshly ground black pepper. Spread 16 thin slices of white bread thinly with the minted butter. Arrange a layer of cucumber slices and top with thin slices of white bread. Trim off the crusts and cut into neat triangles. Makes 64.

### DELICATE SANDWICHES

Sandwiches served with afternoon tea should be slim, delicately flavoured and very elegant.
❖ Use bread that is one day old but make sure it is not stale.
❖ Butter must be softened so it spreads easily and thinly.
❖ Fillings should be finely cut or prepared so they form a thin, even layer; at the same time, the flavour of the filling must come through well.
❖ Always cut off the crusts – use a sharp serrated knife and trim each sandwich individually.
❖ Cut the sandwiches diagonally into quarters to make small, neat triangles.
❖ Arrange sandwiches on plates and cover with cling film (plastic wrap), then keep cool until required.

### Watercress Rolls

These add variety to your sandwich platter. Trim and chop a bunch of watercress, then beat it with 100 g/4 oz (½ cup) cream cheese. Add seasoning and a little grated nutmeg to taste. If necessary, stir in a little milk to soften the cheese mixture so it spreads easily. Cut the crusts off 8 slices of white bread. Roll the bread lightly with a rolling pin so it is quite thin. Spread with the watercress mixture, then roll up each slice from the short side. Wrap each roll in cling film (plastic wrap). Use a serrated knife to slice each roll in half before serving. Makes 16.

*Make the most of a leisurely afternoon tea, with piles of freshly made sandwiches and a range of delicious home-made cakes.*

# TRADITIONAL SCONES

—————— MAKES 20 ——————

Served with clotted cream and jam, these traditional scones epitomize the country-style afternoon tea.

*450 g/1lb (4 cups) plain (all-purpose) flour*
*4 teaspoons cream of tartar*
*2 teaspoons bicarbonate of soda (baking soda)*
*½ teaspoon salt*
*100 g/4 oz (½ cup) butter*
*50 g/2 oz (¼ cup) caster (superfine) sugar*
*about 250 ml/8 fl oz (1 cup) milk*
*extra milk to glaze*

*Serve scones with jam and cream.*

Set the oven at 230°C/450°F/Gas 8. Grease 2 baking sheets. Sift the flour, cream of tartar, bicarbonate of soda (baking soda) and salt into a bowl. Rub in (cut in) the butter until it is finely blended with the flour. Stir in the caster (superfine) sugar and add the milk. Mix the dough to a soft but not too sticky consistency, adding a little extra milk if necessary.

Turn out the dough onto a lightly floured surface and roll it out to about 1 cm/½ in thick. Use a fluted cutter to stamp out 20 rounds of dough, lightly re-rolling the trimmings if necessary, but do not over-work the dough. Place them on the prepared baking sheets. Brush the scones with a little milk. Bake for 7–10 minutes, until well risen and lightly browned. Cool the scones on a wire rack.

### PREPARE AHEAD
Scones freeze extremely well and they thaw quickly in a hot oven. They are good for breakfast, with butter and jam or marmalade, as well as for afternoon tea.

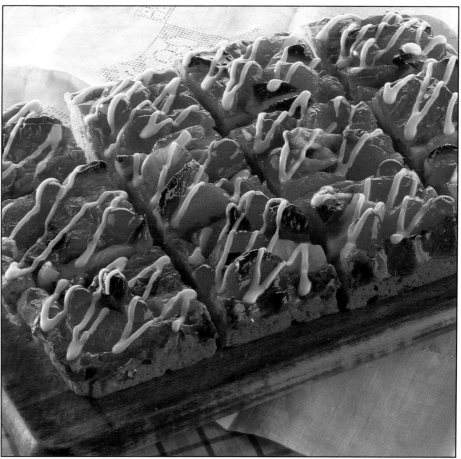

*Dried Fruit Kuchen.*

# DRIED FRUIT KUCHEN

—————— MAKES 16 PIECES ——————

This is a delicious and unusual yeast-based cake, very much in the style of Eastern-European baking.

*175 g/6 oz (1 cup) ready-to-eat dried apricots*
*175 g/6 oz (1 cup) ready-to-eat dried peaches*
*100 g/4 oz (⅔ cup) ready-to-eat dried apple rings*
*300 ml/½ pint (1¼ cups) orange juice*
*350 g/12 oz (3 cups) strong plain (bread) flour*
*1 teaspoon salt*
*100 g/4 oz (½ cup) butter*
*100 g/4 oz (1 cup) finely chopped walnuts*
*50 g/2 oz (½ cup) cut mixed (candied) peel*
*1 sachet (envelope) easy-blend (quick-rising) dried yeast*
*2 tablespoons caster (superfine) sugar*
*175 ml/6 fl oz (¾ cup) lukewarm milk*
*220 g/8 oz marzipan (almond paste)*
*225 g/8 oz (¾ cup) redcurrant jelly*
*100 g/4 oz (⅔ cup) glacé (candied) cherries*
*100 g/4 oz (1 cup) icing (confectioners') sugar*
*a little water*

Place the apricots, peaches and apple rings in a saucepan with the orange juice. Bring to the boil, then reduce the heat and simmer for 15 minutes. Set aside to cool.

Mix together the flour and salt in a bowl. Rub in (cut in) the butter, then stir in the walnuts, peel, yeast and caster (superfine) sugar. Mix in enough milk to form a fairly firm dough. Turn out the dough on to a lightly floured work surface and knead it thoroughly for 10 minutes, until it is smooth and elastic. Grease a large baking sheet or roasting pan. Roll out the dough slightly larger than 30 cm/12 in square and place it on the baking sheet. Turn up the edges slightly to form a neat rim and pinch them into an attractive, narrow border.

Drain the fruit well. Cut the marzipan (almond paste) into small pieces and dot them over the dough base. Arrange the fruit in neat rows on top, overlapping the larger pieces. Cover loosely with cling film (plastic wrap) and leave in a warm place until the dough is risen. Set the oven at 190°C/375°F/Gas 5.

Bake the kuchen for 30–40 minutes, or until the base is cooked. Melt the redcurrant jelly in a small saucepan. Arrange the cherries on the kuchen, then glaze them generously with the jelly and leave to cool. Cut the kuchen into 16 squares, leaving them all in place.

Mix the icing (confectioners') sugar with just a little water to make a thick glacé icing (frosting). Place this in a greaseproof paper (waxed paper) piping (pastry) bag and cut off just the tip of the bag. Drizzle the icing over the top of the kuchen and leave to set before removing the slices from the baking sheet.

## ICE CREAM SUNDAES

These are great fun for adult or children's parties. If you are making sundaes for young children, keep the quantities small to avoid having a lot of waste. Sundaes are not really suitable for large gatherings as they have to be assembled just before they are eaten and assembling more than 12 takes too much time. Have the macerated fruit ready, and any flavoured syrup and toppings in basins with spoons to sprinkle them into glasses. Scoop the required number of dollops of ice cream onto a baking tray lined with cling film (plastic wrap) and return them to the freezer so that you do not have to do battle with this time-consuming stage at the last minute. Also have a chilled piping (pastry) bag of whipped cream ready to add the finishing touches to each sundae.

An adult sundae is a serious concoction, steeped with layers of fruit, ice cream, flavoured syrup or sauce and topped with swirls of cream and a flamboyant decoration. To treat the taste buds as well as create a vision of a feast, buy good-quality ice cream and plan the ingredients carefully.

### Strawberry Sundae

Steep fresh strawberries in a little kirsch or orange-flavoured liqueur (such as Grand Marnier). Empty a jar of apricot jam into a small saucepan and add 8 tablespoons of dry sherry. Gently heat until thoroughly combined, then cool. Spoon 3 strawberries into the base of each tall glass. Top with a scoop of ice cream and trickle some of the apricot sauce over. Add 4 strawberries and some chopped toasted hazelnuts, then a couple of scoops of ice cream. Trickle more apricot sauce over, add a scoop of ice cream and several strawberries. Top with swirls of whipped cream, sprinkle with chopped hazelnuts and top with a whole strawberry.

### Vanilla Sundae

Sundaes for children should be less sophisticated than those for adults. Keep the ingredients simple and top with lots of chocolate sauce. The following sundae is popular with most children.

Make a chocolate sauce: place 225 g/8 oz (8 squares) plain (semi-sweet) chocolate in a heatproof bowl with 50 g/2 oz (¼ cup) unsalted butter and 8 tablespoons of golden syrup. Place the bowl over a saucepan of barely simmering water and stir until the chocolate has completely melted. Leave to cool. Place a small scoop each of vanilla ice cream and strawberry-flavoured ice cream in a glass dish. Add a few slices of canned peaches and seedless green grapes, then top with another scoop of vanilla ice cream. Pour over a little chocolate sauce, and decorate with chocolate caraque, if liked.

### Iced Tea

Make good-quality, fairly weak tea – China or Earl Grey are suitable but avoid stronger Assam or breakfast tea. Take care to ensure that the water is fresh and absolutely boiling. Allow the tea to brew (3 minutes for small-leaf tea; 5 minutes for large-leaf varieties), then strain it into a heatproof jug. Add a thin slice of lemon and a mint sprig for each cup prepared. Sweeten the tea very slightly, if liked, then add ice (one cube for each cup prepared) and leave to cool. Chill the tea before serving in Irish coffee glasses or small, slim, straight glasses. Add a

sprig of lemon balm and an ice cube to each glass, making sure there is a slice of lemon and mint sprig in each portion.

### Orange Tea

Make the tea slightly weaker than you usually do. Pare the rind (peel) from an orange and infuse it with the tea and freshly boiling water, adding a cinnamon stick and 2 cloves. The rind from 1 orange is sufficient to flavour about 8 cups. Leave the tea to brew for 10 minutes (under a tea cosy to keep it hot) before straining it into warmed cups. Add halved, finely cut orange slices to the cups and serve.

### Mocha Sundae

This is a delicious concoction for adults. Place 6 tablespoons of raisins in a basin and sprinkle over 4 tablespoons of brandy. Leave to soak for several hours or overnight. Make a rich chocolate sauce: place 225 g/8 oz (8 squares) plain (semi-sweet) chocolate in a heatproof basin with 50 g/2 oz (¼ cup) unsalted butter, 8 tablespoons of

golden syrup and another 4 tablespoons of brandy. Place the basin over a saucepan of hot water and stir until the chocolate has completely melted. Leave to cool. Place some chocolate sauce in the base of 6 glass dishes. Top each with 4 small scoops of coffee ice cream and sprinkle generously with chopped walnuts. Sprinkle the brandy-soaked raisins over the top, then add a scoop of coffee ice cream to each. Trickle chocolate sauce over each sundae and pipe or spoon a swirl of cream on each. Decorate with chocolate caraque, if liked.

# THE COCKTAIL HOUR

Cocktails have seen something of a renaissance in recent years, and a cocktail party is one option for entertaining in the early part of the evening. If you want to indulge in the delights of dressing up, a cocktail party provides the perfect excuse for introducing a Twenties or Thirties theme, with the women dressed as flappers and the men in black tie or wearing striped blazers.

Carry the theme through with jazz, swing and ragtime music taped as background for the party. Food should be easy to eat with the fingers and there should be plenty of it to quell the effects of strong cocktails. On the subject of drink, make sure there are plenty of alcohol-free alternatives for those who are driving and for quenching raging thirsts before embarking on a cocktail-sampling session.

### COCKTAIL STYLE

The focal point of a cocktail party is the bar. Although the kitchen is an ideal location for this, it is more fun to locate your bar in the main reception room. Here are a few pointers to bear in mind when hosting a cocktail party.

❖ Make sure you have several cocktail shakers. Have a large jug and tall mixing stick for making thirst-quenching cocktails.

❖ Lay out different shapes and sizes of glasses on separate trays ready for different strengths of mixes. Offer mineral water, fruit juices and non-alcoholic alternatives on a separate table.

❖ Place large bowls of nibbles (snacks) around the room, and make sure there are lots of canapés, or very small sandwiches, and finger food such as mini quiches and rolls with pâté.

### Cocktail Checklist

- Nibbles (snacks)
- Ingredients for cocktails
- Alcohol-free drinks
- Cocktail shaker(s)
- Mixing jug
- Cocktail sticks (toothpicks)
- Ice, cubes and crushed
- Decorative cocktail umbrellas
- Cocktail garnishes (cherries, lemons, limes, etc.)
- Olives
- Cocktail glasses
- House cleaning and tidying

*Offer a range of canapés, and pass them round while the guests mix.*

## MUSHROOM SQUARES

──────── MAKES 32 ────────

These can be filled a day ahead and chilled, ready for cooking early on the day they are served. They can, of course, be frozen ahead and they are small enough to be cooked from frozen without requiring a vast increase in cooking time.

*1 tablespoon olive oil*
*1 small onion, finely chopped*
*50 g/2 oz (⅓ cup) pine kernels (nuts)*
*100 g/4 oz (1½ cups) button mushrooms, chopped*
*4 tablespoons chopped fresh parsley*
*1 teaspoon chopped fresh sage*
*salt and freshly ground black pepper*
*squeeze of lemon juice*
*50 g/2 oz (1 cup) fresh breadcrumbs*
*225 g/8 oz puff pastry dough, thawed if frozen*
*beaten egg, to glaze*

Heat the oil in a small saucepan. Add the onion and fry, stirring often, for 10 minutes, until the onion is softened but not browned. Add the pine kernels (nuts) and mushrooms and stir until the mushrooms are reduced slightly in volume and they give up their juice. Continue cooking until all the liquid has evaporated, stirring occasionally to prevent the mixture sticking to the pan. The mushroom mixture will be greatly reduced but it will have a concentrated flavour – if the liquid is not evaporated, the mixture will have a weaker flavour. Off the heat, stir in the parsley, sage, seasoning, lemon juice and breadcrumbs.

Set the oven at 220°C/425°F/Gas 7. Roll out the pastry (dough) into a 40 cm/16 in square. Cut it into 64 squares, each measuring about 5 cm/2 in. Use a teaspoon to put a little mushroom mixture on 32 pastry squares. Brush the remaining squares with a little beaten egg, then use these to cover the mushroom filling, pressing the pastry edges together neatly to seal in the filling. Place the filled pastries on an ungreased baking sheet.

Glaze the pastries with beaten egg. Bake for 12–15 minutes, until well puffed and golden brown. Transfer to a wire rack to cool. Serve hot, warm or cold.

### Non-Alcoholic Cocktails

**FLAMING SUNSET** Half-fill a glass with sweetened cranberry juice drink. Top up with tonic or sparkling mineral water.

**BITTER FRUITS** Shake several dashes of bitters into a glass. Top up with chilled sparkling unsweetened white grape juice. Add a slice of lemon and a maraschino or glacé cherry on a cocktail umbrella.

**MINTY MANIAC** Mix peppermint cordial with a generous squeeze of lime juice and tonic. Serve in a glass with green sugar-frosted rim and float a slice of lime on top.

## Frosting Glasses

The water can be tinted with a few drops of food colouring to make a coloured sugar frosting on the rim of the glass. This is a nice touch for holiday parties such as Christmas or Valentine's Day.

**1** Have a saucer of caster (superfine) or granulated sugar ready. Pour a little water into a saucer. Turn a glass upside down and dip the rim straight down into the water.

**2** Lift the glass cleanly upwards, then dip it straight into the sugar. Hold the glass upside down for a while.

# TRAY CANAPES

#### ———— MAKES ABOUT 48 ————

Baking a large tray canapé base and piping a soft cheese topping is far easier than spending hours fiddling with small bread shapes or tiny individual pastry bases. This is an excellent way of making impressive-looking (and tasting) canapés for a large number of people, as the base can be baked the day before and the prepared topping is quickly added to the whole tray a couple of hours before serving. Choose any garnishing ingredients you like, as long as they are attractive and flavoursome.

*100 g/4 oz (2 cups) fresh white breadcrumbs*
*50 g/2 oz (½ cup) Cheddar cheese, grated*
*4 tablespoons grated Parmesan cheese*
*2 spring onions (green onions), finely chopped*
*salt and freshly ground black pepper*
*4 eggs, separated*
*100 ml/4 fl oz (½ cup) milk*

##### TOPPING
*225 g/8 oz (1 cup) curd (cream) cheese*
*4 tablespoons mayonnaise*

##### GARNISH
*choose from: tiny smoked salmon rolls, tiny ham rolls, sliced stuffed olives, small pieces of blanched green or red pepper (sweet bell pepper), walnut halves, toasted whole blanched almonds, halved cherry tomatoes*

Set the oven at 200°C/400°F/Gas 6. Line a 32.5 × 23 cm/13 × 9 in Swiss roll tin (jelly roll pan) with non-stick greaseproof paper (waxed paper).

Mix together the breadcrumbs, Cheddar, Parmesan, spring onions (green onions) and seasoning. Beat the egg yolks and milk together. In a separate, clean bowl, beat the egg whites until they stand in stiff peaks. Work fairly quickly when mixing the ingredients as the mixture stiffens on standing as the bread absorbs the moisture. Beat the egg yolk mixture into the dry ingredients, then beat in a quarter of the whisked egg whites. Using a large metal spoon, carefully fold in the remaining whites.

Turn the mixture into the lined tin (pan) and spread it out quickly and lightly. Bake at once, for 15–20 minutes, until the mixture is risen and golden.

Have a sheet of greaseproof paper (waxed paper) ready on a wire rack. Turn the baked mixture out onto the rack and carefully remove the lining paper. Leave to cool. When completely cool, return the base to the clean tin in which it was baked.

Use a sharp serrated knife to cut the baked cheese base into 4 cm/1½ in squares. Remove the corner square as this allows for easier removal of the finished canapés without disturbing the toppings.

For the topping, soften the curd (cream) cheese by stirring in the mayonnaise. Place the mixture in a piping (pastry) bag fitted with a star nozzle (tube). Pipe a small swirl of topping on each square. Top each one with a suitable garnish, pressing it gently into the soft cheese mixture. Use a small palette knife or metal spatula to remove the squares from the tray, starting in the open corner.

## A Few Classic Cocktails

**BLOODY MARY** Mix 1 measure vodka, a dash of Worcestershire sauce, a good squeeze lemon juice, 2 measures tomato juice and add seasoning to taste.

**BUCK'S FIZZ (MIMOSA)** Orange juice topped up with champagne (or, for economy, dry sparkling wine) – about 1 part orange juice to 2 parts champagne.

**GIN SLING** Mix 2 measures gin, 1 measure cherry brandy, a squeeze of lemon juice, a twist of lemon rind (peel) and soda to top up.

**MARGARITA** Mix 3 measures tequila to 1 measure Cointreau. Frost the rim of the glass with lime juice and salt before pouring in the cocktail.

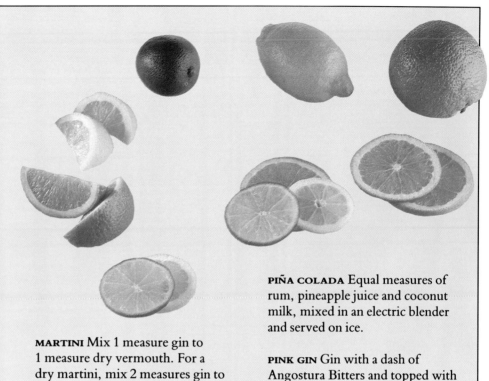

**MARTINI** Mix 1 measure gin to 1 measure dry vermouth. For a dry martini, mix 2 measures gin to 1 measure vermouth.

**PIÑA COLADA** Equal measures of rum, pineapple juice and coconut milk, mixed in an electric blender and served on ice.

**PINK GIN** Gin with a dash of Angostura Bitters and topped with tonic to taste.

## Different Drink Ideas

**APPLE AND BRANDY** Top up brandy with unsweetened apple juice to taste. Serve with ice and a slice of lime.

**CITRUS GIN** Mix 2 measures gin, 2 measures orange juice, 1 measure grapefruit juice.

**DAIRY MAID'S DELIGHT** Mix 2 measures crème de cacao, 1 measure rum, 3 measures milk.

**PASSION JUICE** Mix 1 measure vodka to 3 measures passion fruit juice.

**TROPICAL SUNSET** Mix 1 measure vodka to 2 measures tropical fruit juice. Add a piece of pineapple, a cherry and a twist of lime on a cocktail stick or toothpick.

### Not So Strong . . .

**CIDER REFRESHER** Mix 2 measures dry (hard) cider to 1 measure orange juice.

**SPRITZER** Half white wine to half sparkling mineral water (seltzer).

## Cocktail Tray

Give a plain or scratched old tray a face-lift with a cut-out paper design. The instructions here show a sophisticated geometric pattern for an oval tray, but the principle can be adapted to any shape of tray. You can trim the tray just to fit it in with a particular party theme, but using strong glue and two coats of clear polyurethane varnish will effect a permanent transformation.

**YOU WILL NEED:** tray, paper for templates, pencil, scissors, ruler, gold and silver good-quality stiff paper, glue, black good-quality stiff paper or tape, paper or polyurethane varnish (optional).

**1** For the first template, take a sheet of paper large enough to cover the base of the tray. Stand the tray on the paper and draw around the base.

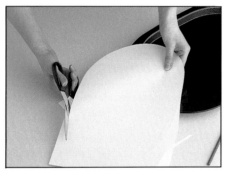

**2** Cut out the tray shape. Check that it fits the tray bottom accurately.

**3** Fold the template in half lengthways, then open it out again. Make folds across both ends of the paper as shown, then open them out.

**4** Fold the template in half again along the first fold. Fold the curved ends of the paper back towards the centre, using the second fold as a guide, then pleat the folded ends as shown to make three wedge-shaped creases at each end of the template.

**5** Open out the template. Use a ruler and sharp pencil to draw lines along each of the fold marks. Draw the diamond shape and triangles in the middle of the tray. Make a second identical template.

**6** Turn one template over and spread glue evenly on the unmarked side. Stick it down smoothly onto the tray so that the pencil marks are on top.

**7** Fold and then cut the second template in half. You will need this quantity of gold and of silver paper, but do not yet cut out the individual segments.

**8** Mark on both templates which segments are to be gold and which are to be silver: the two colours alternate.

**9** Cut apart the sections of the second template, then cut out the corresponding pieces of gold and silver paper.

**10** Lay the pieces of gold and silver paper in position on the tray, following the marks on the template. Check that they all fit before applying any glue.

**11** Glue the pieces of paper in position on the tray. (The kind of glue depends on how lasting you want the decoration to be.)

**12** Cut narrow strips of black paper or tape to cover the joins between the different papers. Remember to cut the ends at angles where they join other black strips and to fit the edges of the tray neatly. Carefully glue the strips over the joins.

**13** Coat the finished tray with paper varnish or two coats of clear polyurethane varnish, allowing the varnish to dry thoroughly between coats and before use.

# FRIENDS FOR SUPPER

*Informal suppers with people you know well are opportunities for trying new recipe ideas. Serve-yourself suppers are popular, for example, and allow guests to experiment with different flavours and textures. Table decorations can be fun, too. Experiment with different fabrics, colours and alternative centrepieces. Dispense with standard setting arrangements and give vent to individual layouts or set a completely different dining scene to reflect the chosen food.*

*I*nviting friends around for an informal supper is probably one of the easiest ways of entertaining. Simple should not mean disorganized, however – it is still important to plan ahead.

### SERVE-YOURSELF SUPPER

This is an easy and fun way of sharing a kitchen supper with people you know well. The numbers you can invite depends on the size of your kitchen, but you really need at least six people to make the idea worthwhile and to warrant preparing a range of foods.

### Planning

The idea is to have the majority of the food prepared but to leave all the last-minute assembly to your guests. It is important to select sauces, fillings and toppings which do not deteriorate quickly on standing and to pick foods that are easy to handle. Pizza, pancakes (crêpes), baked potatoes, pasta and fritter meals are all suitable. Here are a few thoughts on planning in each case.

PIZZA Make lots of small pie bases, about 7.5 cm/3 in across so that everyone has to make up at least two or three toppings. Bake the bases in advance until they are just cooked but not browned. These may be frozen and then defrosted on the day. Lay out a

**Supper Checklist**

- First course
- Main course
- Dessert
- Wine
- Alcohol-free drinks
- Coffee
- Any special dietary needs?
- Table linen
- Cutlery (flatware), china and glassware
- House cleaning and tidying

wide variety of toppings and stack the pizza discs. Heat the oven and make sure you have enough baking sheets.

Prepare dips and crudités, and serve drinks while people wait for their pizza to cook. Have a salad to go with the cooked pizza.

BAKED POTATOES Bake lots of small potatoes and let guests help themselves to the toppings and fillings.

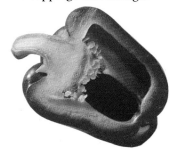

PASTA Have prepared sauces and toppings, then cook fresh pasta in front of your guests and let them help themselves to different combinations of pasta and sauces. Small bowls are best so that everyone tries a variety.

FRITTERS These can be fun: prepare a variety of suitable ingredients for making fritters, such as vegetables, seafood, cooked meat and fruit. A flour and water batter can be made in advance and whisked egg whites should be folded in at the last minute. Guests dip food into the batter, then deep-fry the pieces on fondue forks. Put out plenty of absorbent kitchen paper (paper towels) for draining the fritters and serve dipping sauces or condiments for dressing them.

*Offer two or three hot fillings with a serve-yourself supper of pancakes (crêpes), such as a Light Chicken Filling (above).*

**PANCAKES OR CRÊPES** Pancakes (crêpes) are ideal for a serve-yourself supper where a range of fillings is on offer. The pancakes can be frozen up to a couple of months ahead or they can be chilled for up to 3 days before the party. They should be well wrapped so that they don't dry out and each separated with absorbent kitchen paper (paper towels) during storage.

Stack the pancakes in ovenproof serving dishes, brush each one very lightly with a little melted butter, and cover with foil. Set the oven at 180°C/350°F/Gas 4. Reheat the pancakes about 15 minutes before everyone is ready to eat. The hot fillings should be placed on warmers or burners.

The idea is that diners serve themselves with pancakes and a little filling, then fold or roll and eat them. As well as the prepared fillings, it is a good idea to offer grated cheese, soft cheese with herbs, finely grated carrot dressed with a little French dressing, shredded cooked ham, chopped tomato and other suitable savoury ingredients so that a range of fillings can be created. Remember syrups, chocolate spread, chopped nuts and diced fresh fruit for dessert. Children love foods like frankfurters and peanut butter too!

If you want to keep the party really informal, and encourage guests to eat with their fingers, make sure all the ingredients are finely chopped so that they stay in the pancakes when wrapped, and pile stacks of good-quality paper napkins to clean sticky fingers.

## LIGHT CHICKEN FILLING

——— ENOUGH TO FILL 16 PANCAKES ———
(CRÊPES) LIGHTLY

2 tablespoons oil
3 boneless chicken breasts (chicken breast
halves), skinned and cut into fine strips
salt and freshly ground black pepper
2 tablespoons chopped fresh sage
2 leeks, finely sliced
4 tablespoons flaked almonds
2 courgettes (zucchini), peeled and sliced
2 tablespoons plain (all-purpose) flour
4 tablespoons dry sherry
250 ml/8 fl oz (1 cup) chicken stock

Heat the oil in a flameproof casserole or heavy-bottomed saucepan. Add the chicken, then season well and brown the pieces all over. Sprinkle in the sage, add the leeks and almonds and continue to cook, stirring often, until the leeks are softened: about 15 minutes.

Stir in the courgettes (zucchini) and cook for 2 minutes before stirring in the flour, then pour in the sherry and stock. Bring to the boil, stirring, and reduce the heat. Simmer the mixture for 10 minutes and taste for seasoning before serving.

## BASIC BATTER

——— MAKES 14—16 ———

The pancake (crêpe) batter will thicken slightly if it is left to stand for any length of time. Add a little extra water before pouring into the pan if this is the case.

100 g/4 oz (1 cup) plain (all-purpose) flour
2 eggs
300 ml/½ pint (1¼ cups) milk
1 tablespoon oil, plus extra for frying
2 tablespoons water
oil for cooking

Place the flour in a bowl and make a well in the middle. Add the eggs and a little of the milk. Gradually beat the eggs and milk together, incorporating some of the flour to make a smooth, thick batter. Gradually pour in the remaining milk until all the flour is incorporated in a smooth batter. Beat in 1 tablespoon oil and water. Leave the batter to stand for 30 minutes before cooking.

Brush a little oil over a non-stick or heavy-based flat pancake pan or frying pan (skillet). A 15—17.5 cm/6—7 in pan is best, as this makes small pancakes (crêpes) which are easy to fill and hold, and allows guests to sample all the fillings. Pour a thin layer of batter into the pan, tilting the pan to spread it evenly. Cook over a medium heat until the batter is set and the underneath lightly browned. Use a spatula or palette knife to turn the pancake and cook the second side until lightly browned. Transfer to a warm plate, cover with absorbent kitchen paper (paper towel) and continue until all the batter is used up.

*Pancakes (crêpes), with Pineapple with Maple Syrup filling.*

### Dessert Fillings

Here are two delicious fillings for dessert pancakes (crêpes).

PINEAPPLE WITH MAPLE SYRUP Cut the base off a ripe fresh pineapple. Cut off the leafy top and the peel, making sure to remove all the spines. Cut the fruit in half and cut out the hard core in a wedge shape. Cut the fruit into small pieces and place in a bowl. Trickle pure maple syrup over. Cover and chill for at least 2 hours. Toss the pineapple in the syrup before serving. Serve with a bowl of yogurt to spoon over.

CHOCOLATE CREAM Spoon half a pot of chocolate hazelnut spread into a basin and add 2 tablespoons of brandy. Stand the basin over a saucepan of hot water and stir the chocolate mixture until it is just runny. Remove from the pan and cool slightly. Whip 300 ml/½ pint (1¼ cups) double (heavy) cream and fold it into the chocolate. Cool.

**Serve-yourself Pasta**

An alternative to pancakes (crêpes) – allow 100–175 g/4–6 oz (¾–1¼ cups) pasta shapes per person. Serve pasta shapes rather than noodles, which can be difficult to serve in small portions, when diners want to take several helpings to sample different toppings rather than one larger serving. Shapes are also far easier to eat with only a fork, so this is ideal for a fairly large gathering where everyone stands and chats.

❖ Dried pasta can be cooked a little ahead, tossed with a small amount of olive oil and butter, then placed in an ovenproof serving dish and covered with foil. Reheat in the oven just before serving. Cover with a lid or suitable plate to reheat in the microwave instead of the oven.

❖ Fresh pasta has to be cooked just before serving for best results but it is ready after 3 minutes' boiling. Check the manufacturers' recommended times for ready-filled pasta shapes, as they usually take a little longer.

❖ Serve some cold pasta with a variety of suitable salad vegetables and dressings. For example, offer cooked diced carrot, sweetcorn, cut green beans, green or red pepper (sweet bell pepper), diced ham, shredded salami and so on.

❖ Creamy salad dressings include yogurt with blue cheese and chives, soured cream with chopped parsley and shredded basil or fromage frais with chopped herbs and spring onions (green onions). Oil and vinegar dressing should also be included.

❖ Make fresh pesto by puréeing the leaves from a punnet of basil with pine kernels (pine nuts), freshly grated Parmesan, a couple of garlic cloves and olive oil. You need about 50 g/2 oz (⅓ cup) pine kernels, 100 g/4 oz piece of Parmesan and 250 ml/8 fl oz (1 cup) olive oil to a punnet of basil. Add seasoning to taste.

❖ Cook several chopped garlic cloves in olive oil, add plenty of freshly ground black pepper and lots of chopped parsley. Keep this warm so that it can be spooned over the pasta – it is good alone or great as a base for adding other ingredients.

---

**Dessert Ideas for Pasta Parties**

❖ Make a nutty caramelized orange salad by layering sliced fresh oranges with chopped walnuts in a heatproof dish. Coat generously with freshly made caramel and leave to cool, then chill overnight.

❖ Mix lots of diced prepared fresh and dried fruit with plain yogurt (thicker Greek-style yogurt is wonderful!). Turn it into a bowl. Roast some sesame seeds, sunflower

seeds and chopped walnuts in a heavy-bottomed saucepan over low heat. Cool, then sprinkle the nut mixture and some grated chocolate

over the fruit yogurt. Serve with honey, preferably the runny variety.

❖ Make a large chocolate trifle. Use chocolate cake as the base, sprinkling it with rum or brandy. Top with strawberries or raspberries and cover with custard (custard sauce). Top with a layer of whipped cream and sprinkle generously with grated chocolate. Decorate with white chocolate shapes or leaves and fresh strawberries or raspberries.

*Apple Pie.*

## POTLUCK SUPPERS

A potluck supper where everyone brings a dish is a good idea among friends who often dine together. The host or hostess usually prepares the main course, then friends bring the first course and one or two desserts. The arrangement works well for everyone, but it is never a good idea to suggest that friends you rarely see bring some form of dish. Even a polite offer of help should not provide the excuse for off-loading your cooking onto someone else.

### Quick Custard Sauce

This custard sauce is best freshly made but if you do have to make it in advance, cover the surface directly with a piece of dampened greaseproof paper (waxed paper) or cling film (plastic wrap) to prevent a skin forming.

Mix 3 tablespoons of cornflour (cornstarch) and 3 tablespoons of sugar to a paste with a little milk taken from 600 ml/1 pint (2½ cups). Stir in 3 egg yolks and a teaspoon of natural vanilla essence (extract). Carefully heat the remaining milk to just below boiling point. Remove from the heat, then gradually pour it over the cornflour mixture, stirring all the time.

Pour the custard back into the saucepan and bring to the boil, stirring all the time. Simmer for 2 minutes, then serve.

# APPLE PIE

### ———— SERVES 8 ————

Serve ice cream or Quick Custard Sauce with this pie.

*225 g/8 oz (2 cups) plain (all-purpose) flour*
*75 g/3 oz (5 tablespoons) butter*
*50 g/2 oz (¼ cup) white vegetable fat (shortening)*
*2 tablespoons water*
*450 g/1 lb cooking apples, peeled, cored and sliced*
*50 g/2 oz (⅓ cup) raisins*
*6 cloves*
*1 teaspoon ground cinnamon*
*75 g/3 oz (⅓ cup) caster (superfine) sugar*
*milk, to glaze*
*caster (superfine) sugar, to sprinkle*

Set the oven at 190°C/375°F/Gas 5. Place the flour in a bowl, then rub in (cut in) the butter and vegetable fat (shortening). Mix in the water to bind the pastry (dough). Divide the pastry in half. Roll out half on a lightly floured surface and use to line a 23 cm/9 in tart (pie) plate.

Pile the apples in the middle of the plate, leaving the pastry on the rim uncovered. Sprinkle the raisins, cloves, cinnamon and sugar between the apple slices. Roll out the remaining pastry large enough to cover the pie completely. Dampen the pastry rim on the base of the pie, then cover it with the rolled-out pastry. Gently tuck the pastry in around the apples. Press the edges to seal them well, then trim off the excess pastry.

Knock up the pastry edges with the back of a knife, then make a small scalloped edge. Cut leaves from the pastry trimmings and arrange them on the tart. Make a small hole in the middle to allow steam to escape, then brush the pastry with milk. Bake the tart for 50–60 minutes, until the pastry is golden and the apples are well cooked.

Sprinkle caster (superfine) sugar over the tart as soon as it is removed from the oven. Serve hot or warm.

## FONDUES

A fondue makes a fun, one-course feast. Even though it does not seem to be a vast quantity, do not underestimate this rich dish. Day-old French bread is best for cutting into chunks and the fondue clings to it well. A couple of light salads are always appreciated, providing guests with a palate-cleansing break between dipping sessions. Prepare a bowl of fresh

*End the meal with chocolates and coffee.*

fruit instead of a dessert (remember to lay out small plates and knives) or simply offer some chocolate truffles or petits fours with coffee.

### Fondue Etiquette

Each diner spears the dippers on a special long-handled fondue fork and coats the food in the rich cheese dip. Regulate the burner so that the fondue is kept hot, bubbling occasionally, but not boiling.

Hidden at the bottom of the pot is the traditional delicacy which many consider to be the highlight of the meal – the golden cheese crust! Some heavy-based metal pots yield a delicious crust which comes away easily with the help of a flexible spatula.

Remember that diners who drop their dippers in the fondue have to make a forfeit – traditionally it is an occasion for kissing all the guests of the opposite sex.

*A fondue is an excellent way to enjoy an informal meal with friends.*

## Paper Flowers Centrepiece

Choosing tissue paper in closely graded colours for these flowers achieves the vibrant, glowing quality of real live peonies or roses. You can vary the diameter of your paper circles, with 7.5 cm/3 in being about the smallest workable size.

**YOU WILL NEED:** tissue paper in various colours, scissors, florists' wire, darning needle (optional), green crêpe paper.

**1** Cut circles of tissue paper. Fold them into quarters and flute the edges using scissors.

**2** Stack four or six circles of tissue paper together. Bend a small loop in one end of a length of florists' wire. Use a needle to make a hole in the centre of the paper circles, then thread the straight end of the wire through from front to back.

**3** Turn the paper over and gently bunch the circles up around the wire loop. Wind the wire around the base of the flower at the back to secure. Gently ease the tissue paper into attractive 'petal' shapes at the front.

**4** Cut leaf shapes from crêpe paper in proportion to the flower heads. Although crêpe paper is stiffer than tissue, do not make them too large, or they will flop.

**5** Bend small loops at one end of lengths of florists' wire and attach the leaves singly or in pairs. Arrange the finished flowers and leaves in a bowl.

## SWISS CHEESE FONDUE

—————— SERVES 4 ——————

Most fondue pans will take up to double this quantity, so you can easily multiply the recipe ingredients if you want to serve 6–8 guests. If you have a couple of spirit burners or a candle-heated table warmer which holds several candles, fondue also works well for larger numbers, particularly if you sit your guests on large cushions and arrange a couple of fondue burners on low coffee tables. Remember to ensure that the tables are sturdy to avoid accidents.

Prepare bowls of bread, thickly sliced celery, small chunks of courgette (zucchini) and small cauliflower florets (flowerets) in advance. The fondue has to be made just before it is served, so make sure all the diners are comfortable with drinks and nibbles, then warn them that you are doing to disappear to the kitchen for a little while.

450 g/1 lb (4 cups) grated Gruyère cheese
1 tablespoon plain (all-purpose) flour
salt and freshly ground black pepper
3 tablespoons freshly grated Parmesan cheese (optional)
1 small garlic clove, crushed
150 ml/¼ pint (⅔ cup) dry white wine
2 tablespoons kirsch
grated nutmeg

Mix the Gruyère with the flour, seasoning and the Parmesan, if using. Do this well ahead and set it aside in a covered bowl.

Place the garlic in a flameproof fondue pan. For a less pronounced garlic flavour, simply rub a cut clove of garlic around the inside of the pan but do not add it to the fondue. Add the wine and heat gently until it is steaming but not boiling. Add about one-third of the cheese mixture and stir over low to medium heat until the cheese is more or less melted. Add a little more cheese and stir until it melts: continue adding the cheese in this way. Each addition should be three-quarters melted before the next batch is added. Stir the fondue all the time and regulate the heat so the cheese melts fairly quickly but the mixture does not begin to simmer.

Once all the cheese has been added, bring the fondue just to simmering point, so that it bubbles a few times, then remove the pan from the heat. Stir in the kirsch and nutmeg to taste. Transfer the fondue pot to a spirit burner.

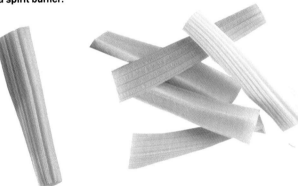

### Side Dishes for Fondue

**BASIL–DRESSED TOMATO SALAD**
The combination of tomato and fresh basil is a particularly delicious one, and it is excellent to go with a cheese dish. Peel ripe tomatoes, remove their cores and cut them into eighths, which are easier to eat using just a fork than when sliced. Sprinkle with a little caster

(superfine) sugar and seasoning. Dress with plenty of shredded basil leaves and trickle a little olive oil over. Add a squeeze of lemon juice and sprinkle with snipped chives. Leave to marinate for at least 1 hour before serving. the salad will last for 2–3 hours in the marinade without becoming too soggy.

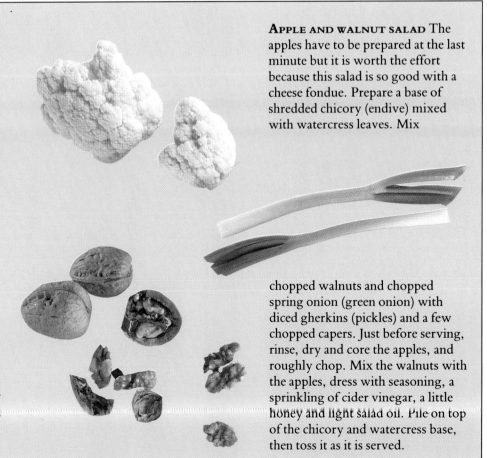

**APPLE AND WALNUT SALAD** The apples have to be prepared at the last minute but it is worth the effort because this salad is so good with a cheese fondue. Prepare a base of shredded chicory (endive) mixed with watercress leaves. Mix

chopped walnuts and chopped spring onion (green onion) with diced gherkins (pickles) and a few chopped capers. Just before serving, rinse, dry and core the apples, and roughly chop. Mix the walnuts with the apples, dress with seasoning, a sprinkling of cider vinegar, a little honey and light salad oil. Pile on top of the chicory and watercress base, then toss it as it is served.

## Bowl of Candles

Make a bowl of candles for the centrepiece of an informal supper party. Use a bowl which has a lovely rim or highly decorated exterior. Colourful stones or coloured glass pebbles could also be used to cover the sand.

**YOU WILL NEED:** a suitable bowl, sand, coloured candles in different sizes, a range of sea shells.

**1** Fill the bowl two-thirds full with clean sand. The sand must be deep enough to support the candles. Place a tall candle securely in the middle of the bowl.

**2** Place shorter candles around the central candle. Depending on the size of the bowl, you may have room for several rows of candles, with each row getting smaller towards the edge of the bowl.

**3** Once the candles are in position, arrange a variety of pretty shells around them to cover the sand completely.

# Winter Candles

This seasonal arrangement of pine cones and nuts can be transformed into a Christmas centrepiece with a coating of gold or silver spray paint. Tie a gold or silver ribbon around the outer rim of the bowl and finish with a bow.

**YOU WILL NEED:** a suitable bowl, sand, candles of different sizes, pine cones, selection of nuts.

**NOTE:** Never leave candles unattended and make sure they do not burn down too close to any decorative arrangements.

**1** Fill the bowl two-thirds full with clean sand. The sand must be deep enough to support the candles. Place a tall candle in the middle of the bowl, and arrange smaller ones around it.

**2** Once the candles are in position, arrange the pine cones on the sand.

**0** Fill any gaps left by the pine cones on the sand with nuts.

# DINING IN STYLE

*P*roper dinner parties can be fun, as well as formal, especially if you know your guests well. This is an opportunity to lay the table with your best table linen and chinaware, and to prepare dishes that are special and out of the ordinary. Plan to have all the cooking calmly under control and to allow yourself a period of all-important relaxation before your guests arrive so you are on sparkling form and can enjoy the occasion.

### GIVING A DINNER PARTY

This is an occasion when you will probably want to impress your guests – especially if the boss or important business contacts are coming for dinner. To ensure everything goes smoothly, draw up a checklist of things that need to be done, starting with jobs that can easily be completed a few days before the event, such as the shopping and cleaning. Try to prepare as much as possible in advance: make and freeze suitable dishes – dishes that can't be frozen can be made the day before and stored in the refrigerator. Leave only the finishing touches to be done on the day. One word of warning – as a general rule don't be tempted to try out a dish you've never cooked before and avoid preparing anything too complicated, particularly when you don't know your guests well and it's important that the evening is a success. You'll feel more confident offering a tried-and-tested favourite – remember, it will be new to your dinner guests – than possibly struggling with an unknown dish that is not turning out as expected. And you certainly don't want to spend most of the evening in the kitchen!

---

### Menu Reminders

Menus for dinner parties are best kept simple, and cook-ahead dishes are ideal, as most will not spoil if your guests linger over pre-dinner drinks.
❖ Simple first courses often make the most memorable appetizers – opt for prime-quality ingredients and serve them with style. You might try avocados and chopped walnuts with a oil and vinegar dressing, melon with Parma ham (*prosciutto*) or fresh figs (serve with a twist of freshly ground black pepper), or juicy melon balls with ginger and a little mint.

❖ Classic casseroles such as Coq au Vin, Boeuf Bourguignon or a rich Hungarian goulash are practical and versatile dinner party fare. Lightly spiced curries are also most acceptable and they often benefit from being cooked a day ahead.
❖ Even if you plan an elaborate dessert, it is a good idea to offer a simple alternative. Do not dismiss fresh fruit – turn out a salad of exotic fruit or a platter of prepared mango slices, pineapple slices, halved passion fruit and sliced figs. Sorbets (water ice), meringues with whipped cream or a rich chocolate mousse are all favourites.

---

*Opposite: a dinner party table set for a special occasion. An arrangement of fresh flowers completes the picture.*

---

### Dinner Party Checklist

- Pre-dinner drinks
- Pre-dinner nibbles (snacks)
- First course
- Main course
- Dessert
- Cheese and biscuits (crackers), fruit
- Coffee
- Brandy and liqueurs
- Any special dietary needs?
- Table linen
- Cutlery (flatware), china and glassware
- Flowers
- House cleaning and tidying

# CHICKEN KORMA

———— SERVES 4 ————

A lightly spiced creamy dish which is ideal for serving at a dinner party. It is an ideal dish to cook ahead.

75 g/3 oz (⅓ cup) ghee or clarified butter
2 onions
2 garlic cloves, crushed
3 tablespoons grated fresh root ginger
1 tablespoon ground coriander
1 teaspoon ground cumin
2 cloves
4 green cardamom pods
1 cinnamon stick
1 bay leaf
6 boneless chicken breasts (chicken breast halves), skinned and cut into chunks
250 ml/8 fl oz (1 cup) plain yogurt
2 tablespoons ground almonds
1 tablespoon rose water
100 ml/4 fl oz (½ cup) water
salt and freshly ground black pepper
50 g/2 oz (½ cup) slivered almonds
250 ml/8 fl oz (1 cup) single (light) cream
chopped fresh coriander leaves (cilantro), to garnish

Heat a third of the ghee or butter in a frying pan (skillet). Chop 1 onion finely and add it to the ghee with the garlic and ginger. Cook, stirring often, for 10 minutes, then stir in the coriander, cumin, cloves, cardamom pods, cinnamon and bay leaf. Cook the spices for about 5 minutes, stirring all the time. Remove from the heat and cool slightly. Place the chicken in a basin and pour the cooked onion mixture over. Add the yogurt, mix well, cover and chill overnight.

Heat half the remaining ghee or butter in a flameproof casserole. Use a slotted spoon to lift the chicken from the yogurt marinade, draining off as much of the yogurt as possible, then add the pieces to the pan and brown them lightly. Stir in the ground almonds and cook for

2 minutes, then add the yogurt marinade, scraping all the spices from the basin, and the rose water. Pour in the water and add plenty of seasoning. Stir until the mixture begins to simmer, then cover the pan and leave the chicken to cook gently for 45 minutes.

Meanwhile, roast the slivered almonds in a heavy-based frying pan (skillet), stirring them virtually all the time, until they are golden brown. Tip the almonds out of the pan, add the remaining ghee or butter to the pan, thinly slice the remaining onion and brown the slices.

Stir the cream into the korma, then heat gently without boiling and taste for seasoning. Serve topped with the browned onions, roasted almonds and a sprinkling of chopped coriander leaves (cilantro).

*Opposite: Chicken Korma with Saffron Pilau Rice, Spiced Spinach and Mushroom Bhaji.*

## CHICKEN KORMA: SIDE DISHES

### Saffron Pilau Rice
This savoury rice is the perfect accompaniment to Chicken Korma. Cook a chopped onion, 3 green cardamom pods, a bay leaf, a cinnamon stick and 4 cloves in 25 g/1 oz (2 tablespoons) butter. Wash 225 g/8 oz (1½ cups) basmati rice in cold water and drain before adding to the pan. Pour in 600 ml/1 pint (2½ cups) cold water and add seasoning. Bring to the boil, stir once, then cover the pan tightly and reduce the heat to the minimum. Leave to simmer for 20 minutes. Meanwhile, pound a teaspoon of saffron strands to a powder in a mortar, using a pestle. Add 2 tablespoons of boiling water and

stir well. Cook a sliced onion in some butter until browned, add a tablespoon of cumin seeds and cook for 2 minutes. Sprinkle the saffron over the rice, cover the pan quickly and leave for 5 minutes. Fork the rice into a serving dish and top with the browned onions and cumin.

### Spiced Spinach
Spiced spinach is a typical side dish for many curried main courses. Trim and thoroughly wash 1 kg/2 lb fresh spinach. Cook a chopped onion, a crushed garlic clove, a teaspoon of turmeric and 2 tablespoons of cumin seeds in a little ghee, butter or oil. Add the spinach and cover the pan tightly, then cook for 5 minutes, shaking the

pan often. Uncover and continue to cook for another 5 minutes, or until the liquid has evaporated and the spinach is tender. Season to taste.

### Mushroom Bhaji
Cook a chopped onion in 25 g/1 oz (2 tablespoons) butter until soft. Add a bay leaf, 2 teaspoons of ground coriander, a quarter teaspoon of grated nutmeg, a pinch of chilli powder and 450 g/1 lb sliced mushrooms. Cook, stirring occasionally, for 30 minutes, until the liquor from the mushrooms has evaporated. Stir in a 400 g/14 oz can of chopped tomatoes and season to taste, then simmer for 10 minutes. Sprinkle with chopped fresh coriander leaves (cilantro) before serving.

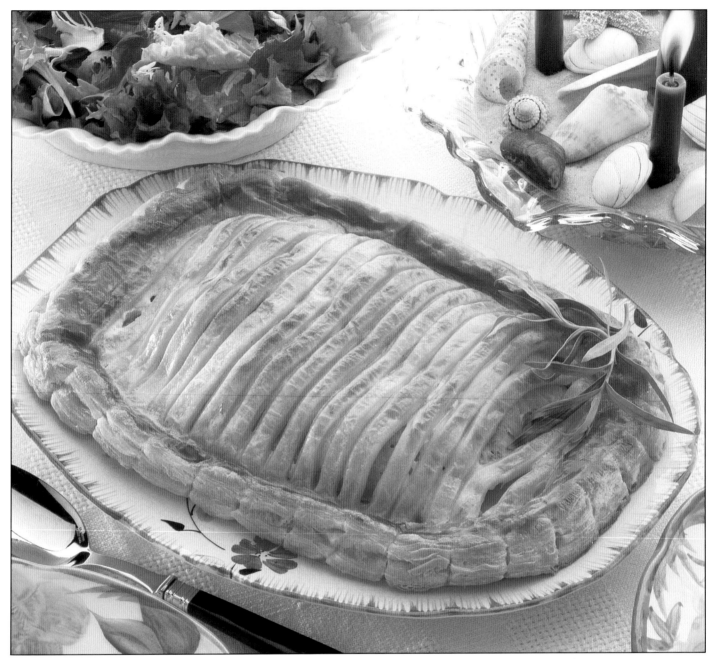

*Seafood Surprise.*

# SEAFOOD SURPRISE

### ———— SERVES 6 ————

The simple filling in this pastry seafood dish makes for quick and easy preparation.

*175 g/6 oz peeled cooked prawns (shrimp)*
*150 g/5 oz packet soft cheese with herbs and garlic*
*1 tablespoon chopped fresh tarragon (optional)*
*1 × 175 g/6 oz can crab meat, drained*
*225 g/8 oz puff pastry dough, thawed if frozen*
*8 small trout fillets, or 4 large trout fillets, skinned*
*salt and freshly ground black pepper*
*beaten egg, to glaze*
*sprig of fresh tarragon, to garnish*

Set the oven at 220°C/425°F/Gas 7. Grease a baking sheet. Mix the prawns (shrimp) with the soft cheese and tarragon, if using. Lightly mix in the crab meat. The seasoning from the cheese should be sufficient to flavour the mixture.

Cut the pastry (dough) in half, one portion slightly larger than the other. Roll out the smaller portion into an oblong measuring 30 × 12.5 cm/12 × 5 in. Place on the baking sheet. Top with the trout fillets, leaving a border around the edge of the pastry and overlapping the fillets as necessary. Season the fillets lightly, then top with the prawn and crab mixture.

Roll out the second sheet of pastry slightly larger, so it will cover the filling. Fold the pastry in half lengthways, then use a sharp serrated knife to make cuts into the folded edge. Start 5 cm/2 in away from the end and make the cuts at 2.5 cm/1 in intervals, leaving the last

5 cm/2 in without cuts. Cut about two-thirds of the way across the pastry.

Brush the pastry border around the fish with a little beaten egg. Lift the folded pastry over the filling, so the fold runs down the middle of the filling, then open out the pastry to cover the filling completely. The cuts should appear as slits down the length of the pastry lid. Press the edges of the pastry together well to seal in the filling. Use the blunt side of a knife to knock up the pastry edges, then flute them into an attractive border. Brush the pastry with beaten egg. Bake for 15 minutes. Reduce the oven temperature to 200°C/400°F/Gas 6 without opening the oven door and continue baking for a further 15–20 minutes, until the pastry is well puffed and golden and the filling cooked through. Garnish with a sprig of tarragon and serve at once.

# PINEAPPLE AND LIME CHEESECAKE

## SERVES 6

An unusual method that turns out a perfect cheesecake with zesty, exotic flavours.

100 g/4 oz chocolate digestive biscuits, crushed
50 g/2 oz (¼ cup) unsalted butter, melted
50 g/2 oz (½ cup) cornflour (cornstarch)
grated rind (peel) of ½ lime
50 ml/2 fl oz (¼ cup) lime juice
50 g/2 oz (¼ cup) caster (superfine) sugar
1 × 200 g/7 oz can crushed pineapple
1 egg, separated
225 g/8 oz (1 cup) cream cheese
225 g/8 oz (1 cup) curd (cream) cheese or low-fat soft cheese

### DECORATION
strips of lemon rind (peel)
strips of lime rind (peel)
2 teaspoons caster (superfine) sugar
150 ml/¼ pint (⅔ cup) double (heavy) cream

*Pineapple and Lime Cheesecake.*

Mix the biscuits with the butter and press the mixture into the base of a 25 cm/10 in round, loose-bottomed cake tin (pan). Chill the biscuit mixture until firm.

In a heavy-bottomed or non-stick saucepan, mix the cornflour (cornstarch) with the lime rind (peel), juice and sugar to make a smooth paste. Stir in the can of pineapple with all its juice. Stir the mixture over low to medium heat until it boils, then simmer for 3 minutes. The mixture makes a thick fruit sauce which must be stirred all the time to prevent lumps forming. Remove the pan from the heat and stir in the egg yolk, then quickly beat in the cream cheese until it is evenly distributed. Beat in the curd (cream) cheese, making sure it is evenly distributed. The mixture must not have any lumps of cheese in it.

Whisk the egg white until it stands in stiff but not dry peaks, then fold it into the cheese mixture. Pour the cheese mixture over the biscuit base, spreading it evenly. Chill the cheesecake overnight.

Whip the cream until it stands in soft peaks, then spoon it into a piping (pastry) bag fitted with a star nozzle (tube). Remove the cheesecake from the tin and place it on a flat platter – a large cake stand is ideal. Pipe cream around the edge of the cheesecake. Toss the strips of rind (peel) in the sugar and decorate the piped cream.

### Chocolate Mint Hearts

These Chocolate Mint Hearts are excellent for serving at the end of special meals. Mix 100 g/4 oz (½ cup) cream cheese with 2 tablespoons of icing (confectioners') sugar and a few drops of peppermint essence (extract). You can add a hint of green food colouring if you like. Melt 225 g/ 8 oz plain (semi-sweet) chocolate in a bowl placed over a pan of hot water. Lay a sheet of baking parchment on a baking sheet.

Spread half the chocolate on the paper into a square measuring about 17.5 cm/7 in. Chill the chocolate quickly in the freezer so it sets, then spread the cream cheese mixture over it and chill for 10 minutes longer. Do not leave the remaining chocolate over hot water while you do this or it will overheat and separate. Instead, warm the chocolate again just before you are ready to use it. Spread the remaining chocolate over the cheese mixture. Leave at room temperature until only just set – do not chill.

Use a heart-shaped aspic cutter to stamp out hearts in the mixture. Dip the cutter in hot water and wipe it with kitchen paper (paper towel) after each cut. Now chill the hearts without removing them from the paper. When thoroughly set, invert on to the work surface, carefully peel back the paper away from the mints and trim off the spare scraps to free the hearts. The underside, on the paper, will be shiny – lift the chocolate hearts carefully with a palette knife (metal spatula) to avoid handling and marking them.

## Ribbon Candle Holder Trims

Simple and quick to conjure up, these pretty ribbon trims can be made to echo a special colour scheme. Remember: lit candles should never be left unattended, and make sure they do not burn to within reach of the candle holder trims.

**YOU WILL NEED:** wide-topped candle holders, fine garden or florists' wire, ribbon, scissors, candles, herbs or other greenery (optional).

**1** Wind two or three thicknesses of wire into a ring just large enough to fit neatly inside the top of each candle holder. Twist the ends of the wire around the ring to secure.

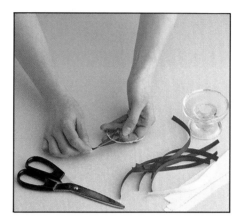

**2** Cut the ribbon into pieces about 15 cm/6 in long. Double a length of ribbon and insert the loop under the wire.

**3** Pass the ends of the ribbon through the loop and tighten to knot it on the wire.

**4** Continue knotting ribbon around the wire ring until the wire is completely covered.

**5** Trim the ends of the ribbon to neaten, then repeat for the second ring. Place the wire rings in the candle holders. Decorate with herbs or other greenery if wished.

# Valentine's Heart

Set hearts a-flutter with this red and white ribbon-covered decoration. Choose ribbons in pattern variations on your chosen colour scheme. Alternatively, use patterned and plain fabric, carefully cut into ribbon strips.

**YOU WILL NEED:** 50–60 cm/20–24 in thick plastic-covered garden wire, piece of florists' wire, about 7.5 m/8 yd ribbon 2.5 cm/1 in wide, about 0.5 m/½ yd ribbon 5 cm/2 in wide, scissors, needle and thread.

**1** Twist the thick wire into a heart shape and bind the two ends together securely in the centre with florists' wire. Cut the narrower ribbon into approximately 15 cm/6 in lengths.

**2** Double a length of ribbon and knot it over the wire. Repeat with more ribbon knots until the wire is completely covered.

**3** Fold a 20 cm/8 in length of wider ribbon to make a bow loop and hold it together with a couple of stitches.

**4** Loop the rest of the wider ribbon around the middle of the bow loop and shape into a pair of tails. Secure with a stitch or two.

**5** Attach the bow at the centre of the heart to cover the florists' wire. Trim the ends of the ribbon into swallowtail shapes.

### Valentine's Day Dinner Party

❖ Cut heart-shaped invitations and send them to good friends who will want to share Valentine's Day night as a foursome.

❖ The menu is light and pink champagne is the perfect drink!
❖ The idea of the menu is that it can be romantic for two, or something of a fun occasion for four. Take the "pink heart" theme to extremes by

fixing a pink cocktail before dinner – a mixture of Angostura Bitters, gin and tonic. It can be fun to go completely over the top by preparing heart-shaped cheese biscuits (crackers) too!

# STYLISH BUFFETS

*planning with a few hints on pitfalls to avoid. The food really does command attention at a buffet, but to complement a glorious spread make sure you dress up the table with swags or garlands and generous bows of ribbon. Flowers may form the backdrop or centrepiece, or a fantastic pyramid arrangement of exotic fruit will definitely steal the show.*

*Preparing a buffet is the practical answer to most types of home entertaining when more than eight people are invited. The buffet can, of course, be equally as impressive as a sit-down menu, as this section highlights.*

*There are a few brief reminders on the important points of*

*Lastly, don't hide your buffet away, let guests absorb the beauty of your art before the meal — throw open the dining room doors and allow a sense of anticipation to prevail.*

## BUFFET BANQUETS

❖ Site the buffet in a cool, well ventilated place: away from radiators and out of the sun.

❖ Cover the table with a protective cloth before adding the decorative linen as there are always spills when guests serve themselves.

❖ The buffet should be set with savoury food for the main part of the meal. If a starter (appetizer) is served it can be brought to the buffet at the beginning of the meal where the hostess should assist the guests with it. Alternatively, and the better arrangement, the first course should be served from a side table.

❖ Desserts and cheese may be served from the buffet if the main dishes are removed. If, at large gatherings, the desserts and cheese are set out before the main course is cleared, then a side table should be prepared for them.

❖ If port or red wine is served with cheese at small gatherings, then it may be served from the buffet rather than the bar.

❖ Always make arrangements for receiving used dishes and cutlery (flatware) when preparing a buffet. At a large gathering some guests may not feel inclined to bring their dishes out to the kitchen, therefore it is a good idea to set up a trolley (cart) where these may be placed if you have not hired a waitress or waiter to remove them.

### Buffet Checklist

- Invitations
- Contact caterers, if using
- Organize serving staff, if using
- Pre-buffet nibbles (snacks)
- First course
- Main course
- Dessert
- Cheese and biscuits (crackers), fruit
- Wines
- Alcohol-free drinks
- Ice
- Coffee
- Brandy and liqueurs
- Any special dietary needs?
- Table linen
- Cutlery (flatware) — in napkin or separate
- China and glassware
- Flowers
- House cleaning and tidying

### Avoiding Buffet Pitfalls

❖ Have dishes which are easy to serve – complicated dishes may make guests feel inhibited about attempting to help themselves.

❖ Avoid offering foods which really must be cut with a knife for easy eating.

❖ Avoid putting a first course on the buffet with all the main dishes so that everyone advances on all the food at once: if you want to keep a dish as a first course, then make sure you serve it yourself, otherwise guests will pile on the salads and other food, too.

❖ Arrange savoury and sweet foods on dishes at different levels, rather than in flat dishes and two or three rows deep on the table. Use cake stands and stemmed dishes to full advantage so the food creates a splendid display.

❖ Serve salad dressing separately for guests to help themselves, otherwise you may have lots of dressed salad which has to be thrown out.

*A fine selection of cheeses for the buffet table is always welcome.*

## COUSCOUS WITH PEPPERS

──────── SERVES 8–10 ────────

This is an excellent side dish for a buffet.

6 tablespoons olive oil
2 garlic cloves, crushed
2 large onions, chopped
1 teaspoon dried oregano
2 green peppers (sweet bell peppers), seeded
and diced
2 red peppers (sweet bell peppers), seeded
and diced
2 yellow peppers (sweet bell peppers), seeded
and diced
450 g/1 lb tomatoes, peeled, quartered
and seeded
salt and freshly ground black pepper
450 g/1 lb couscous
75 g/3 oz (5 tablespoons) butter
100 g/4 oz (¾ cup) black (ripe) olives, stoned
(pitted) and thinly sliced
4 tablespoons chopped fresh parsley,
(optional)
fresh sprigs of parsley, to garnish

Heat the oil in a heavy-based saucepan. Add the garlic, onions and oregano, then cook, stirring often, for 20 minutes, until the onions are softened but not browned. Add all the peppers and cook, stirring often, for a further 15 minutes. Stir in the tomatoes and seasoning, cover and simmer for 15 minutes.

Meanwhile, place the couscous in a large heatproof bowl. Pour boiling water over it to cover the grains by about 2.5cm/1 in. Cover the bowl with a plate and leave to stand for 15–20

minutes by which time the couscous will be fluffy and hot, ready to serve. The couscous may be prepared in advance by covering with cold water, then heated briefly in the microwave at the last minute.

Melt the butter in a saucepan, then pour it over the couscous and fork it into the grains. Tip the couscous into a serving bowl. Add the olives and chopped parsley, if liked, to the pepper mixture, then pour it over the couscous. Garnish with fresh sprigs of parsley and serve.

## GALANTINE OF CHICKEN

──────── SERVES 8–12 ────────

A galantine of chicken can be prepared and frozen up to one month ahead of the party, ready for thawing and roasting the day before it is served. Alternatively, simply prepare and roast it the day before, cooling it quickly and chilling it overnight. A butcher or supermarket poultry counter will bone out the bird, as long as you order it in advance.

1.6 kg/3½ lb chicken, boned

STUFFING
450 g/1 lb (2 cups) medium-fat soft cheese,
such as Philadelphia Light
100 g/4 oz (2 cups) fresh white breadcrumbs
1 tablespoon chopped fresh sage
4 large spring onions (green onions), finely
chopped
salt and freshly ground black pepper
100 g/4 oz (¾ cup) shelled and roughly
chopped lightly salted pistachio nuts
4–6 large slices good-quality cooked ham,
trimmed of fat

GARNISH
salad ingredients
herb sprigs

Set the oven at 180°C/350°F/Gas 4. Mix the soft cheese with the breadcrumbs, sage, spring onions (green onions) and plenty of seasoning. Add the nuts and pound the ingredients together well. This stuffing must not be too soft but it should be of a suitable consistency for pressing evenly on to the chicken.

Lay the chicken on a board, with the skin down. Spread one-third of the filling over the middle of the bird, then top with half the cooked ham, overlapping the slices neatly. Distribute half the remaining stuffing over the top without disrupting the base layers. Top with the remaining ham, then add the rest of the stuffing. Fold the sides of the chicken over and sew it up to enclose the filling completely.

Turn the chicken over and place it on a sheet of well-greased foil. Plump up the chicken into a neat shape, then close the foil around it, sealing the edges well. Place in a roasting pan and cook for 1½ hours. Open the foil and cook for a further 15–20 minutes to brown the top of the bird. Close the foil again and leave the chicken to cool in the baking juices, then chill it for at least 2 hours before slicing the galantine.

Use a sharp serrated knife to slice the chicken and arrange the slices on a serving platter. Garnish with salad ingredients and/or fresh herbs. Alternatively, the chicken may be coated with a classic chaudfroid sauce.

COOK'S TIP
As for most other buffet foods, the number of servings you can expect a recipe to yield depends on the number of guests and size of the buffet. If this size galantine is served as the only main dish, with a small selection of side salads, then it will comfortably serve 8 persons. Two or more galantines will serve at least 12, if not 15.

### Stuffings for Galantines

The type of stuffing you use to stuff a boned bird influences the number of portions which the galantine will yield. The soft cheese and ham stuffing in the main recipe gives a plump galantine which slices well when cold, so each slice is a generous portion. Richer stuffings may be used in smaller quantities and the bird rolled rather than plumped up, which will result in smaller slices and fewer portions. A rich pâté, for example, makes an excellent filling, either on its own or spread over slices of cooked ham, which are then rolled before being placed in the boned bird. Alternatively, try a sage and onion stuffing with sausage meat.

*Opposite: Couscous with Peppers.*

# Ribbon Rosette

This simply made old-fashioned idea is a classic trim for swathes of filmy fabric.

**YOU WILL NEED:** firm satin ribbon about 2.5 cm/1 in wide in two toning shades: about 1.8 m/2 yd in deeper tone and about 90 cm/1 yd in paler tone, scissors, needle and thread.

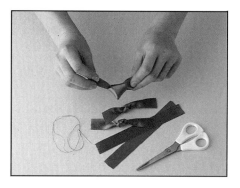

**1** Cut seven 17.5 cm/7 in lengths of deeper-toned ribbon and tie a single knot fairly loosely in the middle of each.

**2** Twist the ends of one of the knotted pieces of ribbon so that they lie on top of one another.

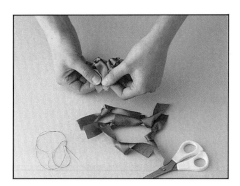

**3** Twist a second piece of ribbon in the same way and hold the ends together, with the knots lying side by side.

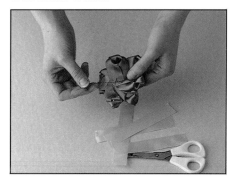

**4** Continue to arrange all seven pieces of ribbon into an overlapping circle, knots evenly spaced around the edge and ends gathered in the centre. Secure the ends with a few stitches.

**5** Cut five 17.5 cm/7 in lengths of paler-toned ribbon and tie in knots as before. Arrange them in the centre of the rosette and stitch in place.

**6** Make a small loop of darker ribbon. Sew this in the centre of the rosette to conceal the ends and stitching, puckering it gently to make an attractive shape. Sew two long tail pieces of ribbon to the back of the rosette.

## PHYLLO PASTRIES

Phyllo pastry (dough) is sold prepared in thin sheets, either chilled or frozen. It can be used to make a wide variety of sweet and savoury pastries; small savoury pastries are especially well suited to buffet presentation as they are easy to eat. Follow these simple rules for using phyllo.

### Buying Phyllo

Various package sizes are available, and as a rule of thumb the smaller boxes contain small sheets, not fewer of them. The larger sheets are most versatile, suitable for preparing dozens of individual pastries or for lining a large tin (pan). Avoid damaged packages and always keep frozen phyllo well frozen until you are ready to thaw it – if it part thaws on the way home from the supermarket, the sheets can stick together or be damaged.

### Using Phyllo

Prepare a clean, dry surface. Dampness makes the pastry sticky, causing it to stick to the surface and break. Always keep phyllo pastry covered except for the specific sheet you are working with. Lay out the required number of sheets and wrap the rest of the pastry in cling film (plastic wrap), otherwise it will dry out, become brittle and break up. For crisp results and flaky layers, lightly brush the pastry with fat – melted butter or oil, or a mixture of both – however, the fat does not have to be used lavishly and lighter results are achieved with a sparse "greasing" applied between layers, with the main brushing used on the surface of the filled and shaped pastries. It is this surface brushing that prevents the pastry from becoming too brittle and breaking during baking. Do not glaze with milk or egg.

### Making Triangular Pastries

Lightly brush a sheet of phyllo pastry (dough) with melted butter or oil. Cut into 7.5 cm/3 in wide strips. Place a little filling at one end, then fold the corner of the pastry over the filling. Fold the filling and pastry across at an angle in the opposite direction. Continue folding the pastry until all the strip of phyllo is used and the filling is enclosed in several layers. Brush again with melted butter or oil.

### Making Phyllo Bundles

Sandwich 2 sheets of phyllo pastry (dough) with a little melted butter or oil. Cut the pastry into 10 cm/4 in squares. Place a little filling in the middle and brush around it with a little melted butter or oil. Gather the pastry around the filling to enclose it completely, pinching the pastry together over the filling to make a bundle.

### Phyllo Filling Ideas

TUNA An economical filling that tastes extra special. Mash a well-drained 200 g/7 oz can of tuna with 2 finely chopped spring onions (green onions) and the grated rind (peel) of a lemon. Add a crushed garlic clove, if you like, and 4 tablespoons of grated Cheddar cheese. Season with pepper and add a squeeze of lemon juice.

SPICED VEGETABLES Vegetarians will welcome this mildly spiced filling. Cook half a chopped onion, a crushed garlic clove, a tablespoon of cumin seeds, a tablespoon of mustard seeds and 2 teaspoons of ground cumin in a little melted butter for 5 minutes. Add a diced cooked potato, 4 tablespoons of well-drained canned sweetcorn and 4 tablespoons of cooked peas. Season to taste and serve.

## FROZEN CHOCOLATE TERRINE

———— SERVES 12 ————

Frozen Chocolate Terrine keeps for up to one month in the freezer if the tin (pan) is well wrapped in a plastic freezer bag once the chocolate mixture has frozen solid.

450 g/1 lb (16 squares) plain (semi-sweet) chocolate
175 g/6 oz (³⁄₄ cup) unsalted butter
4 tablespoons brandy
6 eggs
225 g/8 oz (8 squares) white chocolate
150 ml/¹⁄₄ pint (²⁄₃ cup) whipping (heavy) cream

DECORATION
50 g/2 oz (2 squares) white chocolate
frosted decorations such as crystallized violets
small frosted mint leaves

Line the base of a 1.8 litre/3 pint (7½ cup) loaf tin (pan) with non-stick baking parchment. Place the plain (semi-sweet) chocolate, three-quarters of the butter, the brandy and 4 egg yolks in a heatproof bowl. Place the bowl over a saucepan of hot but not boiling water – the pan should be smaller than the base of the bowl to prevent any moisture reaching the chocolate mixture. Stir the chocolate mixture until melted and smooth.

Remove the bowl of chocolate from the saucepan. Beat 4 egg whites until they stand in stiff peaks but are not dry in texture. Stir 1 spoonful of the whites into the chocolate, then use a large metal spoon to fold in the remaining whites. Spoon the mixture into the tin and place it in the freezer for 40 minutes.

Meanwhile, place the white chocolate and remaining butter and egg yolks in a heatproof bowl and melt like the dark chocolate mixture. Whip the cream until it holds its shape in soft peaks. Stir 1 spoonful of the cream into the chocolate, then use a large metal spoon to fold in the rest of the cream. Beat the remaining egg whites until still stiff but not dry and fold them into the white chocolate mixture. Turn the white chocolate mixture into the tin on top of the dark chocolate. Freeze until firm. Seal in a freezerproof plastic bag; return to the freezer.

To serve the terrine, select a large, flat freezerproof platter. Dip the base of the tin in a bowl of very hot water and dry the outside quickly with a towel. Slide a knife around the inside of the tin to loosen the mixture, cover with the platter and invert both, giving a firm shake. Lift the tin off and remove the lining paper. Return to the freezer.

Melt the white chocolate for decoration as above. Spoon it into a small greaseproof paper (waxed paper) piping (pastry) bag and fold the ends over to seal in the chocolate. When you are ready to pipe the chocolate, snip off just the tip of the paper bag. Pipe chocolate from side to side across the top of the terrine, creating a zig-zag pattern along the whole length. Return the terrine to the freezer until it is to be taken to the buffet table. Add crystallized violets and tiny sugar-frosted mint leaves to complete the decoration just before serving the terrine. Use a sharp serrated knife, dipped in a jug (pitcher) of very hot water, to slice the terrine. Wipe the knife after cutting each slice.

*For a more substantial cheeseboard, offer bunches of grapes and bowls of nuts and olives.*

### THE ULTIMATE CHEESEBOARD

Whether the cheese course is an adjunct to the meal or an important feature of the buffet is entirely up to you. Some of the finest buffet parties are those that rely totally on cheese – a really good cheese and wine party is not to be dismissed; however, avoid the Sixties-style approach of having tiny cubes of anonymous cheese speared on cocktail sticks (toothpicks). Here are some thoughts on the types of cheeses to offer and on the various ways that they can be presented.

### Selection for the Cheese Course

A European practice is to serve a limited variety of cheeses as a first course, a course before dessert or as an alternative to dessert or at the end of the meal. Decide on three to six types of cheese, including hard cheeses, blue

*Offer a separate cheeseboard of soft cheeses.*

cheeses and soft-rind cheeses. Because this cheese selection is intended to complement the other foods on the buffet – or after a formal meal – it is best to avoid the heavily seasoned cheeses, such as those with strong herbs, garlic, nuts or chutneys blended into them. Present the soft cheese on one platter, the hard types on another, or use the same platter with separate knives for both types. Grapes or fresh dates are usually offered together with plain biscuits (crackers).

## A Special Cheese Dish
This replaces the cheeseboard and it is served as a course before or after dessert, again in the European style. It is an ideal dish to replace dessert. Potted cheese is suitable. For example, pound blue Stilton to a paste with a little unsalted butter and some port, then press it into a pot and chill lightly. Cheddar can be potted the same way with a little butter, mustard and cider (hard cider).

For a more sophisticated and lighter-flavoured alternative, try a brandied Brie. Scrape the rind from 225 g/8 oz ripe brie and cut the cheese into pieces. Soak in 2 tablespoons of brandy for several hours, then mash well. Mix with 75 g/3 oz (1½ cups) fresh white breadcrumbs and 3–4 tablespoons of single (light) cream. Place the mixture in a serving dish and chill well before serving with biscuits (crackers).

## Wide Variety of Cheese
Cheese may be included as part of a mixed buffet to be eaten at any stage, rather than as a separate course. For example, cheese may be eaten with a salad accompaniment. In this case,

offer several different types of cheese and group them on platters. Arrange semi-soft and soft cheeses, such as Brie and Camembert, together with soft-rinded goats' cheese and pots of cream cheese flavoured with herbs. Garnish the cheeses with grapes, dates and figs.
❖ Arrange a selection of hard cheeses on a board, such as Cheddar, Jarlsberg, Gruyère and so on. Blue cheeses may be included on this platter, or simply offer one excellent piece of blue cheese on a dish by itself. Use plenty of crisp celery sticks and leaves to garnish the hard cheeseboard.
❖ A third platter may include flavoured cheeses – hard cheeses to which chives, garlic, nuts, onion or herbs have been added. Pepper-coated cheeses and flavoured soft cheeses may also be included.

## Serving a Single Cheese
Offering one popular cheese in prime condition is an economical and sophisticated option. A small whole Brie or slice of a whole Stilton are both ideal. To do this well you must check the quality and ripeness of the cheese before buying it. A specialist cheese

*Wrap eating utensils prettily in a napkin.*

merchant or good delicatessen is the ideal place to order the cheese a couple of weeks in advance. Alternatively, speak to the delicatessen manager at the supermarket a week before the party to check the availability of whole cheeses and their ripeness.

## A Cheese and Wine Party
If you are going to do this, do it well! Do not be tempted to let lots of alternative side dishes and salads creep into the menu: stick to an excellent selection of cheeses, with one cheese recipe, such as a brandied Brie, fruit and a single salad.
❖ Arrange different types of cheeses on separate platters.
❖ Offer a good choice of plain biscuits (crackers) and crispbreads, crusty bread, wholemeal (whole-wheat) and rye breads.
❖ Serve marinated cheeses in attractive, colourful bowls to indicate their colourful flavours. For example, marinate feta cheese cubes in olive oil, garlic and chopped herbs. Or marinate small whole cheeses, such as goats' cheeses, in a mixture of salad oil and walnut oil, with basil, chopped black (ripe) olives and sun-dried tomatoes.
❖ Serve a platter of different goats' cheeses with fresh figs and dates.
❖ Bowls of olives, small pickles or silverskin onions and gherkins (pickles) should be arranged around the table.
❖ A simple, green salad, with dressing offered separately, is excellent for refreshing the palate. Do not make mixed salads and creamy dressings which confuse the menu.
❖ Include bowls of fruit, positioning them near the cheeses they complement; for example, have a deep dish of polished apples near the hard cheese and a basket of pears on tissue paper for the soft cheeses.
❖ Make a vegetable arrangement from celery, radishes, carrot sticks, cauliflower florets (flowerets) and chicory (endive) leaves as a centrepiece for the table. Include fresh vine (grape) leaves if available and herb sprigs.
❖ Include a selection of nuts. A bowl of nuts in their shells looks attractive – remember the nut crackers – but an arrangement of shelled nuts on a large platter is more practical. Have both – a shallow dish of shelled nuts on a huge flat basket looks brilliant surrounded with an arrangement of nuts in shells.

# THE YOUNGER CROWD

*P*arties for young adults are not always centred on music, dancing and a whirl of socializing – there are times when all young people share events with their family as well as friends. Whether the celebration is a coming of age, graduation, bar or bat mitzvah or another significant point in the transformation from youth to adulthood, it is a good idea to avoid organizing two completely separate events by planning an afternoon gathering for older members of the family, leading into an evening party for friends and the young at heart.

**A PARTY FOR YOUNG AND OLD**

Successfully mixing youth and age at the same gathering needs a little forethought. It can be all too easy for the party to split into a room full of the older generations, with the occasional visit from younger members only when nudged into social action by their parents. Avoid this problem by allocating "introduction duties" to selected

## Menu Reminders

With all the family and friends gathered together for a special celebration, and probably staying all day, catering for everyone can be a problem. Make life easier for yourself with easy-to-make eats and drinks to suit all tastes.

❖ Savoury dishes might include mini quiches, tray bakes and bite-sized spicy meatballs.

❖ Old favourites, such as cocktail sausages or chunks of full-flavoured cheese, are excellent standbys for afternoon buffets. Pep up the table with small bowls of cherry tomatoes, cucumber and carrot sticks and small rolls of salami.

❖ A special celebration cake is often the order of the day – add to the sweet side of the buffet by including various tray bakes – for example chocolate brownies – cut into bite-sized squares and topped with a swirl of freshly whipped cream.

❖ Later in the day – or evening – top up with bowls of savoury nibbles (snacks), such as nuts, vegetable crudites and crispy breadsticks.

❖ Remember that many young people prefer a meat-free diet, so always include vegetarian alternatives.

young guests, who are then responsible for making sure that their friends circulate. Do not leave all the work up to the teenagers, however – ask one or two adults to reciprocate by introducing the older generation to the youngsters. A couple of hours in the afternoon will keep everyone happy, then the party can be allowed to develop in its own way.

## Dips and Dunkers

A must for teenage parties!

*Hummus.*

**HUMMUS** This dip is a speciality from the Mediterranean. Drain two 425 g/15 oz cans chickpeas (garbanzo beans) and purée or mash them with a garlic clove, 2 tablespoons of tahini (sesame seed paste), 2 tablespoons of chopped onion, a tablespoon of ground coriander and 2 tablespoons lemon juice. Gradually beat in 175–250 ml/ 6–8 fl oz (¾ cup) olive oil. Add the oil very slowly so it mixes with the chickpeas to make a creamy paste. A food processor is ideal for this. Add seasoning and extra lemon juice to taste. Serve with sesame breadsticks, celery sticks, warmed pitta bread fingers and thin Melba toast.

**TOMATO DIP** Peel, seed and chop 4 ripe tomatoes. Mix with 2 finely chopped spring onions (green onions). Beat 4 tablespoons of grated Parmesan cheese into 350 g/ 12 oz (1½ cups) cream cheese, then gradually mix in the tomatoes and all their juice. Stir in seasoning to taste. Shred 4 basil sprigs quite finely, then mix them into the dip. Serve with breadsticks, plain crackers, crisps (potato chips) and courgette (zucchini) fingers.

**ONION DIP** Finely chop 2 large onions and cook them in 2 tablespoons of olive oil with half a teaspoon of dried oregano, a quarter teaspoon of dried thyme and a garlic clove for 20 minutes, until soft but not browned. Cool. Gradually work the onions into 450 g/1 lb curd cheese. Add seasoning to taste. Serve with cauliflower florets (flowerets), celery sticks, carrot sticks, crisps (potato chips) tortilla chips and corn chips.

# HAMBURGER BAKES

——————— MAKES 64 PIECES ———————

These savoury party snacks are popular with young and old.

450 g/1 lb (4 cups) strong plain (bread) flour
1 teaspoon salt
25 g/1 oz (2 tablespoons) butter
1 sachet (envelope) easy-blend (quick-rising) dried yeast
1 teaspoon sugar
250 ml/8 fl oz (1 cup) water
2 onions, very finely chopped
450 g/1 lb lean minced (ground) steak
2 eggs, beaten
salt and freshly ground black pepper
2 tablespoons tomato purée (paste)
1 teaspoon dried oregano
2 tablespoons chopped fresh parsley
1 tablespoon Worcestershire sauce
100 g/4 oz (1½ cups) mushrooms, finely chopped
50 g/2 oz (1 cup) fresh breadcrumbs
sesame seeds

GARNISH
8 ripe tomatoes
sliced gherkins (pickles)
cocktail onions

Grease a large baking sheet or roasting pan. Mix the flour and salt, then rub in (cut in) the butter and stir in the yeast and sugar. Mix in the water to make a firm dough. Turn out the dough onto a lightly floured surface and knead it thoroughly for 10 minutes, until smooth and elastic. Cut the dough in half.

Roll out half the dough to a 30 cm/12 in square and place it on the prepared baking sheet. Wrap the rest of the dough in cling film (plastic wrap). Cover the rolled-out dough with cling film and set aside while you prepare the hamburger mixture.

Combine the onions with the meat and eggs. Add plenty of seasoning, the tomato purée (paste), oregano, parsley, Worcestershire sauce and mushrooms. Mix together the ingredients until the meat is thoroughly combined with the vegetables and seasoning in a fairly moist mixture. Add the breadcrumbs and mix them in thoroughly. Distribute this meat mixture evenly over the rolled-out dough base. It is best to do this with your fingertips, avoiding pressing down on the base and flattening it.

Roll out the remaining dough to cover the meat. Press it neatly in place, using your fingers, pinching the edges together. Cover loosely with cling film and leave in a warm place until the dough is well risen, about an hour. Meanwhile, set the oven at 180°C/350°F/ Gas 4. Brush the top of the dough with water and sprinkle with sesame seeds. Bake for

45–50 minutes, until baked through and well browned. Leave until cool.

Use a sharp serrated knife to cut the hamburger bake into 3.5 cm/1½ in squares. These may be heated in the oven for about 5 minutes before serving, if liked, or they may be served cold. For the garnish, halve the tomatoes and scoop out their seeds, then cut each half into quarters. Thread a piece of tomato, slice of gherkin (pickle) and cocktail onion onto each of 64 cocktail sticks (toothpicks). Stick these into each square just before serving.

# CELEBRATION CAKE

—— MAKES ABOUT 26 PORTIONS ——

An important stage in a young person's life —
graduation or coming of age, for example —
calls for a special celebration cake.

225 g/8 oz (1 cup) butter
225 g/8 oz (1¼ cups) caster (superfine) sugar
½ teaspoon natural almond essence (extract)
4 eggs
350 g/12 oz (3 cups) self-raising (self-rising)
flour
100 g/4 oz (1¼ cups) ground almonds
3 tablespoons brandy

COVERING AND DECORATION
100 g/4 oz (⅓ cup) apricot jam, warmed and
sieved (strained)
1 kg/2 lb marzipan (almond paste)
icing (confectioners') sugar
1.25 kg/2½ lb ready-made sugarpaste (rolled
fondant)
a little vodka or light gin
ready-made royal icing mix (decorators' white
icing mix)
apricot food colouring
ready-to-make pastillage (gum paste) mix
apricot dusting powder
confectioners' glaze (a varnish
available from specialist suppliers)

Set the oven at 180°C/350°F/Gas 4. Line and
grease a 23 cm/9 in round cake tin (pan).
Cream the butter, sugar and almond essence
(extract) until soft, pale and creamy. Gradually
beat in the eggs, adding a little of the flour to
prevent the mixture (batter) curdling. Use a
metal spoon to fold in the flour. Fold in the
ground almonds and brandy, then turn the
mixture into the tin and smooth the top, making
a slight indentation in the middle.

Bake the cake for about 1¼–1½ hours, or
until a metal skewer inserted into the middle
comes out clean. Leave to cool in the tin for 15
minutes, then turn out onto a wire rack and
leave to cool completely.

If necessary to trim the top level, freeze the
cake for 1 hour; the cake crumbles less when
part frozen. Use a serrated knife. Once
trimmed, return the cake to the freezer. Roll
out the almond paste on a surface lightly
dusted with icing (confectioners') sugar into a
circle measuring about 30 cm/12 in in
diameter.

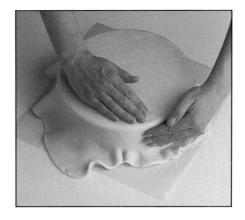

**1** Place the cake on a sheet of greaseproof
paper (waxed paper) and brush the top
and sides with apricot jam. Lift the marzipan
(almond paste) over the cake and smooth it
gently in place with your hands. The marzipan
stretches slightly as you smooth it over the
cake so it will completely cover the sides. Ease
out all the creases in the marzipan as you apply
it to the cake. This base covering of marzipan is
important because any uneven patches show
through the sugarpaste. Use smoothers to
gently rub down the marzipan.

Roll out 1 kg/2 lb of the sugarpaste (rolled
fondant) as for the marzipan, on a surface
lightly dusted with icing (confectioners') sugar.
Brush the marzipan with a little vodka or gin,
then cover with sugarpaste and gently smooth
it into place with your hands.

Gently smooth the sugarpaste over the cake
to reach the base, carefully easing out any
folds and creases and allowing the paste to
overhang the cake onto the paper. Trim excess
paste with a small sharp knife, leaving just a
little extra.

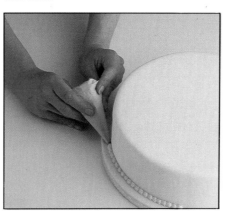

**3** Colour the rest of the icing a pale apricot to
match the flowers and ribbon. Fit the star tube
in a piping (pastry) bag and fill it with icing.
Pipe a shell border around the bottom edge of
the cake to cover the join with the board.
Squeeze out the rest of the icing and reserve it
in a covered container.

**2** Roll out the remaining sugarpaste and use
to cover a 27.5 cm/11 in round cake board,
dampening the board slightly with water first.
Trim the excess neatly.

Make up a small amount of royal icing mix
(decorators' white icing mix). Place a little in
the middle of the board, then put the cake on
top, carefully peeling away the paper from
underneath. Smooth the bottom edge of the
cake and lightly rub out any marks on the
sugarpaste. The bottom edge of the cake will
be covered by piping so do not worry about any
small gaps.

**4** Position the prepared pastillage (gum paste)
plaque on top of the cake without fixing it. Roll
a small piece of pastillage or sugarpaste into a
ball, flatten it slightly and use this as a base for
the flower arrangement. Place it on a small
piece of greaseproof paper and rest it on top of
the cake. Push the stems of the flowers into
the lump of paste. When you are happy with
your flower arrangement, carefully remove the
paper from underneath and fix the lump of
paste in place on top of the cake by dampening
it slightly underneath or by putting a tiny dot of
royal icing under it.

**5** Once the flowers are in place, fit a piping bag with a fine plain tube and fill with apricot icing. Squeeze a little icing to fix the plaque in place and press it down gently. Pipe the tiny picot edge border all around the plaque. Finish the cake by attaching ribbon around the base, just above the piped border, keeping it in place with a tiny squeeze of royal icing on the underneath side.

**6** Attach the ribbon around the board edge and fix it with a little icing.

### DECORATIVE PLAQUE

Roll out the pastillage thinly on a surface lightly dusted with icing (confectioners') sugar. Stamp a plaque cutter in icing sugar, then stamp out the shape in pastillage. It is a good idea to cut out a few plaques in case you break or spoil one when you are adding the decoration. Stamp out the required numerals, again cutting at least one spare set. Leave the pastillage pieces to dry overnight. Meanwhile, make up a little royal icing, and keep well covered until ready to use.

Brush the numerals with apricot dusting powder. Glaze the plaque and the numerals with confectioners' glaze and leave to dry. Attach the numerals to the plaque with a little royal icing, pressing them down gently.

The numerals are finished by outlining them with apricot-coloured royal icing. This is done after the edging is piped on the cake (see above). Thin a little of the apricot icing very

slightly with a drop of water so that it flows only slightly more easily than when piping the shell border. This gives a smoother straight line. Practice outlining one of the spare pastillage numerals if you like, then outline the numerals on the plaque and leave to dry before attaching the plaque to the cake.

### COOK'S TIPS

Pastillage (gum paste) is a tough paste which is used for modelling and making flowers in sugarcraft. It is available in powder form from cake decorating suppliers and should be mixed according to packet (package) instructions. Mix only a small amount as the paste should be rolled out thinly.

Unless you are adept at covering cakes with marzipan (almond paste) and sugarpaste, it is easier to use more paste than many experts recommend even at the risk of wasting some excess.

## Stars and Moons Mobile

Add a sparkle to a party with this glittering mobile. Suspend it from a central position in the party area, or make a series of mobiles that can be distributed around the room.

**YOU WILL NEED:** thin card (posterboard), pencil, card for template (optional), scissors, gold and silver spray paint, gold and silver glitter, plastic-covered florists' wire or model-makers' wire, pliers, fishing line or similar nylon cord.

**1** Draw four stars and five moons on the card. It may be easier to make a template of the star and moon shapes first and trace them onto the card. Carefully cut out the shapes with a pair of sharp scissors.

**2** To assemble the mobile, cut two long pieces of wire of equal length and two shorter pieces of wire of equal length. Tie the shorter lengths together with fishing line or similar nylon cord where they meet in the centre. Curve the wires down to form an umbrella shape. At the end of each wire, use a pair of pliers to form a small loop. Repeat with the shorter lengths of wire. Suspend the smaller mobile from the centre of the larger using fishing line or similar cord.

**3** Spray the stars with gold spray paint and the moons with silver spray paint. Make sure the surface you are working on is protected and that the area is well ventilated.

**4** When the spray paint has dried, cover one side of a star with a thin layer of glue. Sprinkle a little gold glitter onto a sheet of paper, then press the glued side of the star into the glitter. Repeat on the other side. Cover all the stars and moons with glitter in the same way. Use silver glitter for the moons.

**5** Use a large needle to pierce a hole through one point of each star, and the tip of each half moon shape.

**6** Attach the shapes to the wires using short lengths of nylon cord tied through the holes. Attach a length of cord to the middle of the top of the wire and hang the mobile in place.

# ENGAGEMENT ANNOUNCEMENT

*T*his is another occasion on which family and friends of all ages gather to celebrate, but often without the clear rules and rituals which apply to weddings.

Although less common than it once was, the traditional way in which engagements are conducted is that the couple make the parents aware of their intentions before any formal announcement. It is customary for the man to consult the woman's father on the subject, if not to ask for permission to marry, then at least to make clear that his intentions are honourable and that he is in a suitable position to marry. Nowadays, less weight is given to such formalities.

Normally, relatives and close friends are told of the engagement before any public announcement is made in the newspaper. The bridegroom's parents write to the bride's parents to express their joy and to arrange a meeting, if the parents do not already know each other.

Celebrations may take many forms: the bride's parents may host a large party for both families and for friends; there may be a small gathering for relatives on both sides; the engaged couple often host their own party for a wider circle of friends. This section includes recipes for a buffet which would do justice to a formal family celebration.

## CELEBRATION IDEAS

❖ A formal dinner or lunch party is a good way to introduce the two sets of parents and immediate relatives. It is a good idea for the parents to meet beforehand, at least to make acquaintance, otherwise the dinner can be extremely stilted.

❖ If one set of parents travels a long distance and anticipates staying with the other set or weekending in a nearby hotel, then an informal lunch or afternoon tea breaks the ice before both families spend a larger celebration evening together.

❖ An engagement can be an excuse for several parties. Most parents will be eager to invite family and friends to a dinner or lunch party. The engaged couple may arrange a drinks or cocktail party for friends.

### Engagement Buffet Checklist

- Invitations
- Contact caterers, if using
- Organize serving staff if using
- Pre-buffet nibbles (snacks)
- Starter
- Main course
- Dessert
- Cheese and biscuits (crackers), fruit
- Wines
- Alcohol-free drinks
- Ice
- Coffee
- Brandy and liqueurs
- Any special dietary needs?
- Table linen
- Cutlery (flatware) – in napkin or separate
- China and glassware
- Flowers
- General house clean and tidy

### Menu Reminders

An engagement party is the perfect opportunity to flaunt the theme of heart and flowers.

❖ Heart-shaped cheese biscuits (crackers), heart-shaped vols-au-vents, and heart-shaped croûtons to garnish savoury dishes establish the theme.

❖ For a small engagement party, a simple but splendid buffet might consist of smoked salmon with soured cream (fresh sour cream), platters of cold meats and cheeses.

❖ Cheesecakes or sponge cakes (plain or chocolate) can easily be made in heart-shaped baking tins (pans). Strawberries and cream make a delicious filling for sponge cakes.

❖ If your budget does not cover the cost of champagne, consider sparkling wine instead. Alternatively, you might offer a sparkling punch served from large jugs. These punches usually consist of a combination of inexpensive wine and sparkling mineral water – the proportion of wine to water can be adjusted to taste – to which a selection of sliced soft fruits such as peaches, strawberries and/or raspberries have been added. Top the punch bowl or individual glasses with mint leaves.

*Salmon Mousse.*

# SALMON MOUSSE

———— SERVES 8–10 ————

If you are nervous about unmoulding the mousses just before the buffet, or have space problems in the refrigerator, then set the mousse in one glass bowl and garnish it with whole prawns (shrimp) and slim cucumber slices, slit so they sit attractively on the rim of the dish. This way you can double up the quantities if liked.

*3 salmon steaks (about 450 g/1 lb in weight)*
*4 tablespoons dry white wine*
*2 tablespoons melted butter*
*oil for greasing ramekins*
*4 tablespoons water*
*2 tablespoons unflavoured powder gelatine*
*300 ml/½ pint (1¼ cups) soured cream*
*300 ml/½ pint (1¼ cups) mayonnaise*
*2 tablespoons tomato purée (paste)*
*2 tablespoons finely snipped fresh chives*
*4 tablespoons chopped fresh dill or parsley*
*salt and freshly ground white pepper*
*3 egg whites*
*450 g/1 lb peeled cooked prawns (shrimp)*
*1 teaspoon grated lemon rind (peel)*
*1 tablespoon lemon juice*
*2 tablespoons light salad oil*

GARNISH (OPTIONAL)
*fresh dill sprigs*
*cucumber slices*
*a little aspic, for brushing*
*whole cooked prawns (shrimp)*

Remove the skin from the salmon steaks, then place them on a double-thick piece of foil. Fold the edges of the foil up, then sprinkle the wine and melted butter over the fish and close the foil around it to seal in all the juices. Place in a steamer and cook over boiling water for 15 minutes, then leave to cool until just warm. Allow 20 minutes if the steaks are very thick.

Lightly oil 8 ramekins with a very light salad oil. Drain the juices from the steaks and mix with the water in a heatproof bowl. Sprinkle the gelatine over the liquid and set aside without stirring for about 15 minutes or until the gelatine has swollen and become spongy.

Remove all the salmon flesh from the bones and blend it to a purée in a food processor or blender, adding the soured cream and mayonnaise. Alternatively, thoroughly mash the fish with a fork. Stir in the tomato purée (paste), chives, half the dill or parsley and seasoning to taste.

Set the gelatine bowl in a saucepan of simmering water and stir until it has dissolved. Remove from the pan and cool slightly, then stir in a few spoonfuls of the salmon mixture.

Pour the gelatine mixture into the main batch and mix well. Beat the egg whites until they stand in stiff but not dry peaks. Use a large metal spoon to fold them into the salmon mixture. Divide the mixture evenly between the ramekins and chill until set, or overnight.

Meanwhile, mix the prawns (shrimp) with the remaining dill or parsley, seasoning, lemon rind (peel), lemon juice and oil. Cover and leave to marinate in the refrigerator for 2–4 hours before serving.

Just before you are ready to unmould the mousses, blanch the cucumber slices for 30 seconds in boiling water. Drain and cool quickly under cold running water.

Quickly dip the base of each ramekin into a bowl of hot water and mop it with a tea-towel. Unmould the mousse onto a wetted flat plate, sliding it carefully into place before lifting off the ramekin. Mop the damp plate around the mousse. Surround the top and sides of each mousse with thin overlapping slices of cucumber and brush with aspic. Place the prawns (shrimp) around the mousse and garnish with dill sprigs.

# CELEBRATION CREAM GATEAU

—— MAKES 2; SERVES ABOUT 30 IN TOTAL ——

This luscious gâteau makes the perfect centrepiece for an engagement buffet, or any other joyous celebration.

450 g/1 lb (2 cups) unsalted butter, softened
4 teaspoons natural vanilla essence (extract)
grated rind (peel) of 2 oranges
450 g/1 lb (2¼ cups) caster (superfine) sugar
8 eggs
450 g/1 lb (4 cups) self-raising (self-rising)
flour
450 g/1 lb (4 cups) walnuts, finely chopped

FILLING AND DECORATION
1.12 litres/2 pints (5 cups) double (heavy)
cream
6 tablespoons icing (confectioners') sugar,
sifted
6 tablespoons orange liqueur
350 g/12 oz (3 cups) walnuts, chopped
frosted flowers and leaves

COOK AHEAD
The cakes can be made and frozen up to a couple of months in advance. It is a good idea to assemble them in their frozen state early on the day of the party as the cold of the cake will keep the cream decoration cool. Leave them in a clean, cold place, tented with foil. If you are preparing them on a warm day in summer, then place the cakes separately on heart-shaped cake boards so they can be kept in the refrigerator, then place them on their boards in position with the flowers and ribbons just before serving.

**5** Spread the rest around the sides of the cakes and place them on sheets of greaseproof paper (waxed paper). Coat the sides of the cakes with chopped walnuts, pressing them on with a palette knife (metal spatula). When the cakes are neatly coated, transfer them to a cake board before completing the decoration.

**1** Make the cakes in 2 batches unless you have 4 heart-shaped tins (pans). Set the oven at 170°C/325°F/Gas 3. Base line and grease 2 23 cm/9 in heart-shaped tins: measure the tins from the bottom of the point to the top of the heart.
　　Cream half the butter with half the vanilla essence (extract), the rind (peel) of 1 orange and half the sugar until very soft and pale. Beat together 4 eggs, then gradually beat them into the creamed mixture, adding a little of the flour to prevent curdling.

**3** Divide the mixture between the tins and spread it evenly. Bake the cakes for 30–40 minutes, until risen, springy to the touch and lightly browned. Turn out to cool on a wire rack, removing the lining paper. Make 2 more cakes in the same way.

**6** Whip the remaining cream with the remaining icing sugar and liqueur. Fit a star nozzle (tube) into a large piping (pastry) bag and fill with the flavoured whipped cream. Spread the remaining cream over the top of the cakes, marking it into neat lines with a small palette knife or round-bladed knife. Do not overwork the cream or it will separate slightly and become buttery or curdled. Take care around the top edges of the gâteaux as these should be kept neat without pushing the walnut coating outwards. If the cream does not quite reach the edge it does not matter. Pipe a border of swirls around the tops of the cakes.

**2** Use a large metal spoon to fold in half the majority of the flour and half the walnuts.

**4** To make the filling, whip half the cream with half the icing (confectioners') sugar and liqueur until it stands in soft peaks. Sandwich the cakes together in pairs with some of the cream.

**7** Frosted flowers and floral decorations on the board are added at the last minute but they should be organized in advance. Prepare a curved spray of fresh flowers, using dry florists' foam (styro foam) as a base. Attach 2 pieces of satin ribbon under the flower spray to link it with the heart cakes. Use a palette knife to carefully lift the edge of each cake in turn and tuck the ribbon ends under the dipped centre at the top of each heart.
　　Place the frosted flowers on top of the cakes, adding some leaves to balance the decoration. Arrange small groups or individual blooms of frosted flowers on the board.

### Frosted Flowers

Although some flowers are edible, most cooks never suggest eating frosted flowers, reserving them only for decorative purposes. If you do want to eat the flowers, then be absolutely certain that the ones you prepare are edible because many flowers, particularly those derived from bulbs, are poisonous.

Primroses, rosebuds, miniature roses and violets make the perfect decoration for the top of the Celebration Gâteaux.

❖ In a screw-topped jar, gradually stir 2 tablespoons gum arabic with 3 tablespoons of water. Cover the jar tightly and shake it well, then set it aside for 2 hours. Stir the gum mixture, which should now be slightly syrupy in consistency.
❖ Select only perfect blooms which are clean and dry. Pour some caster (superfine) sugar into a small bowl and have a teaspoon ready. Use a fine paintbrush to brush the gum arabic solution over the flowers, working right down to the base of each petal, inside and out.

❖ When the flower is well coated in gum, rest it on top of the sugar. Use a teaspoon to sprinkle sugar all over the flower, between the petals, outside and inside. Shake off the excess sugar, then lay the flowers on a piece of greaseproof paper (waxed paper) until the gum has dried and the flowers are crisp.

Leaves, such as those from mint, roses and primroses, can also be frosted. Pick out small leaves which will complement the dainty appearance of the frosted flowers you have chosen.

## Woven Heart Bonbon Holder

The symbolic interlacing in this pretty heart-shaped pouch makes it appropriate as a Valentine's Day gift as well as for an engagement announcement. Two colours underline this theme, but the result is attractive when card (posterboard) of just one colour is used.

**YOU WILL NEED:** card, pencil, ruler, scissors, glue, ribbon, shredded tissue paper, bonbons.

**1** Measure and draw a 23 × 15 cm/9 × 6 in oblong shape on two different coloured pieces of card (posterboard).

**2** Cut out the oblongs.

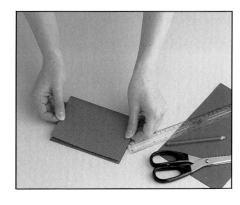

**3** Fold each piece of card in half widthways.

**4** Lay the two pieces of card together in an L-shape, with folded sides facing away from you, to form a square where they overlap, and lightly mark in pencil the central point at the top edge where they meet.

**5** Along one short edge of each piece of folded card, measure and mark in pencil two equally spaced 11.5 cm/4½ in lines.

**6** Cut along the marked lines through both layers of card.

**7** Mark smooth curves at each end of the uncut short side of each folded piece of card and cut off the corners to make the rounded top edges of the heart.

**8** Place the two pieces of card side by side, with the folds at right angles to each other and facing outwards. Weave the first strip from the right-hand piece over the nearest strip from the left-hand piece, through the second strip and over the third.

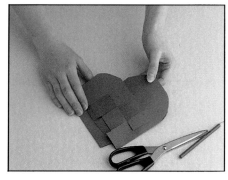

**9** Weave the second strip in the same way as the first, alternating the over and under sequence. Weave the third strip in the same way as the first.

**10** Turn the heart over and weave the strips on the underside in the same way to make a pouch shape at the top of the heart.

**11** Dab a little glue under the ends of the strips and stick each one down.

**12** Stick lengths of ribbon to the centre back and centre front of the heart, on the inside.

**13** Pack some shredded tissue paper into the heart before loosely filling with bonbons.

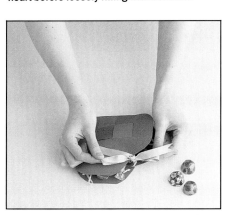

**14** Tie the ribbons in a bow to close the packet and hold the bonbons inside.

# WEDDING CELEBRATIONS

*H*osting and being involved in the practical preparations for a wedding reception must be the ultimate test of anyone's capabilities for organizing parties. This section offers ideas, pointers and recipes which will be helpful; the decision to take on all the work or to involve professional help for any part must be yours – only you know how much you can cope with.

With copious list-writing, careful planning and a hand-picked group of helpers, any confident hostess can make the arrangements for a small wedding reception for between twenty and forty guests. With the right back-up and a less formal approach, parties for up to a hundred can be arranged with a slightly modified approach to the catering.

## PLANNING WEDDING BUFFETS

If you intend taking on the catering for your own wedding or you are the mother of the bride, then arranging the marriage ceremony for mid afternoon is a practical solution which leaves the morning, at least until noon, free for paying last-minute attention to the details of the food. This also provides a suitable time – late afternoon – for guests to be greeted at the house. This is a practical way of ensuring that the work can be finished completely and allow time for a relaxing bathe or rest before setting off for the church.

Here are a few essential points to plan.

❖ You will definitely need help with adding the finishing touches from someone who is not directly involved in the ceremony.

❖ It is sensible to hire a couple of servers to hand out drinks and to help with placing dishes on the table at the last minute, leaving you free to socialize with guests. You should also seek the assistance of a good friend who knows the layout of your kitchen well enough to direct helpers if need be.

You should brief them thoroughly beforehand. It is best to ask them to visit the day before or early on the day to familiarize themselves with the house. Asking them to set out cutlery (flatware) and china is also a good idea.

❖ Do not be over ambitious – it is better to under-estimate your kitchen's capacity and your own capabilities as a cook than to land yourself with a catering problem.

### Wedding Buffet Checklist

- Invitations
- Organize outside caterers, if using
- Organize serving staff, if using
- Or organize extra kitchen help
- Order ready-made food if using
- Pre-buffet nibbles (snacks)
- First course
- Main course
- Dessert
- Cheese and biscuits (crackers), fruit
- Wines
- Alcohol-free drinks
- Ice
- Coffee
- Brandy and liqueurs
- Any special dietary needs?
- Table linen
- Cutlery (flatware) – in napkin or separate
- China and glassware
- Flowers
- House cleaning and tidying

*Ribbons and flowers add a decorative touch.*

*A wedding arrangement of white lilies, delicate cream roses, exotic Singapore orchids and pale yellow mimosa.*

❖ Remember, elegant finger food is preferable to a disastrous second-rate three-course buffet.

❖ Plan ahead for freezer and refrigerator space.

❖ Select dishes which need the minimum of last-minute attention, or concentrate on one item which needs a certain amount of finishing touches and select other foods which can be more or less completed the day before.

❖ Make sure you have help the day before to get the majority of the preparation finished with ease.

❖ Delegate responsibility for drinks, coats and seating to a trusty helper.

❖ Make lists of everything that has to be done and tick off each item as it is completed.

❖ Think about getting ready-made food and using caterers if this is easier and more practical. Have the food deli-

vered on the morning to avoid the problem of refrigerator space; however, DO double-check a couple of days before that all is in order and specify the delivery time.

❖ Lastly, make sure you have help after the reception as well as before. It is a good idea to arrange for dishwashing and to organize for someone to be in attendance when the reception is in progress.

**Portion Guide for Ham**

To be absolutely practical when serving an impressive ham as a centrepiece, think in terms of having some left over rather than on calculating the exact weight for the number of guests. Remember that estimating portions for self-service buffets is extremely difficult, because some guests will take small portions, while others will have several generous helpings if available. As a guide, a small whole ham on the bone weighs at least 4.5 kg/10 lb and will serve 20–25 people generously. A ham weighing about 6.8 kg/15 lb will serve up to 40 guests.

When buying a boned ham, allow about 350 g/12 oz wastage at the end, unless you are hiring a waitress or waiter to carve for the guests. Think in terms of portions of about 100–175 g/4–6 oz; if the ham is on the bone, then calculate a portion size at 225 g/8 oz.

In fact, a boned ham is not as good a buy as one on the bone: the smaller the boned ham becomes as guests serve themselves, the more difficult it is to carve and the less palatable it looks. Also, towards the end of the joint the slices tend to get cut in chunks and people are apt to take more than they intend. Conversely, it is easy to carve thin pieces of meat off a bone-in joint.

# BAKED HAM

A whole baked ham makes an impressive centrepiece for a wedding buffet, allowing generous portions and providing useful leftovers for sandwiches for an evening party or house guests. The ham may be cooked on the bone or boned; in fact, meat on the bone is more practical as it is easier for guests to carve off portions as required simply by grasping the bone end than it is to use both carving fork and knife which some find awkward.

There are two options: buy a raw ham and soak and bake it, or buy a cooked ham from a good butcher or the delicatessen or gourmet counter of a supermarket, then glaze and bake it at home. However, it is also worth assessing the quality of cooked hams in the supermarket, then ordering a whole joint in advance.

**1** You will need to cook the ham first, by either boiling or baking it. For both cooking methods, allow 20 minutes per 450 g/1 lb plus an extra 20 minutes cooking time. If you are boiling a large ham, you can hire (rent) a catering pan. Add 2 sliced onions, a sliced carrot, 2 sliced celery sticks, 2 bay leaves, 1 blade of mace, 1 cinnamon stick, 1 tablespoon black peppercorns and 6 cloves to the cooking water.

**2** Alternatively, soak the ham for 3 hours, then wrap it tightly in double-thick foil with the vegetables (*see* step 1) and bake it in the oven at 180°C/350°F/Gas 4. Skim the scum from the surface of the water.

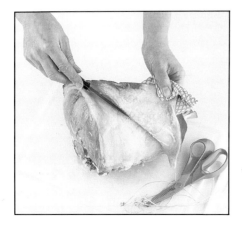

**3** To glaze the ham, use a sharp knife to cut off the rind – this is easiest when the ham is freshly cooked and hot.

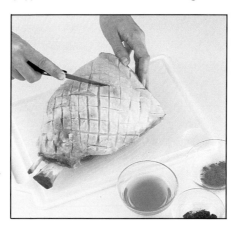

**4** Score the fat into diamond shapes.

**5** Brush the surface of the fat lightly with warmed clear honey and sprinkle with a little ground cinnamon and a pinch of ground cloves. Bake at 180°C/350°F/Gas 4 for a further 40–50 minutes, brushing the fat with more honey to build up a glossy, well-browned crust.

**6** Place a ham frill on the bone end and rest the ham on a ham stand or large flat platter.

**NOTE**
Sprinkling the ham with a little ground cinnamon and cloves before baking it gives an excellent flavour; the crust is easier to eat at a buffet than when studded with whole cloves, another traditional way to prepare ham.

# Ham Frill

Covering the bone end of a whole ham with a frill is not only decorative; it makes it easier and cleaner to hold the meat for carving. Have the end of the bone trimmed neatly and make the frill to measure. Smaller versions can be made for individual servings of chicken drumsticks and lamb cutlets.

**YOU WILL NEED:** white fine paper (about 40 × 15 cm/16 × 6 in), scissors, paper clip, sticky (transparent) tape or stapler.

**1** Fold the strip of paper in half lengthways.

**2** Make regular narrow cuts inward from the folded edge about two-thirds of the way across the paper.

**3** Open out the paper and then fold it in half in the opposite direction, allowing the folds to billow out rather than pressing them flat.

**4** Wrap the paper around the fingers of one hand and secure the layers with a paper clip. Adjust the overlap until the frill fits the bone. Secure the frill with sticky tape or a staple, and remove the paper clip.

# PASTA SALAD

SERVES 8–10

Try to avoid making salads which are overcrowded with ingredients when preparing a classic buffet. It is better to make a careful choice of classic, flavoursome ingredients which will allow the salad to complement other foods as well as stand on its own as an option for those who are following a vegetarian diet. Make a bowl of pesto which may be spooned over the pasta salad, if liked. Although bought pesto is handy in an emergency, it is very inferior to the true sauce and the salad will not be anywhere near as delicious.

450 g/1 lb pasta shapes
salt and freshly ground black pepper
8 sun-dried tomatoes, chopped
100 ml/4 fl oz (½ cup) dry white wine
100 ml/4 fl oz (½ cup) olive oil
2 tablespoons lemon juice
4 tablespoons chopped parsley
6 spring onions (green onions), chopped
2 tablespoons chopped tarragon
ground nutmeg
4 tablespoons pine kernels, (pine nuts) lightly toasted

Cook the pasta in plenty of boiling salted water for about 12 minutes, until tender but not too soft. Drain well. Meanwhile, place the sun-dried tomatoes in a small saucepan with the wine, olive oil and lemon juice. Heat gently until simmering, cover the pan and simmer for 5 minutes, then remove from the heat and allow to stand for at least 1 hour. The dressing is best made a day ahead. The pasta can be cooked the day before, tossed with a little olive oil and covered, then chilled.

Add the parsley, spring onions (green onions) and tarragon to the dressing with seasoning to taste. Toss the dressing into the pasta and season with a little nutmeg. Sprinkle with the pine kernels (pine nuts).

## SALAD WITH CROUTONS

A simple salad provides a palate-refreshing lift to the buffet. Here are a few guidelines for successful buffet salads.

❖ Some vegetables may be cut and allowed to soak in iced water overnight, giving them an excellent crunchy texture and cutting out a lot of last-minute work. Cut celery, carrots, spring onions (green onions) and green peppers (sweet bell peppers) into short, fine strips about the size of matchsticks. Place in one or more large bowls with plenty of ice cubes and pour in water to just cover the vegetables. Cover and leave in a cool place overnight. Drain well next day.

❖ Finely shred an iceberg lettuce as a base or break a head of chicory (endive) into small pieces.

❖ Mix but do not dress the salad. Provide a jug of salad dressing for moistening individual portions. This means that any leftover salad may be used for sandwiches or it may be turned into a summer soup.

❖ Make a large bowl of croûtons flavoured with garlic. Cut the crusts off thinly sliced bread, then dice the bread. Fry in a mixture of olive oil and butter, with a crushed garlic clove added, until crisp and golden. Drain on absorbent kitchen paper (paper towels). Place the croûtons next to the salad or sprinkle them over it at the last minute.

### Portion Guide for Salad

One iceberg lettuce, half a head of celery, a bunch of spring onions (green onions), 2 green peppers (sweet bell peppers), 2–3 carrots and a peeled and diced cucumber will make a bowl of salad to serve up to 40 guests if there are plenty of other dishes on the buffet. This type of salad is not usually eaten in large portions at a buffet meal.

# SACHERTORTE

SERVES 12

A rich chocolate sponge which can be made well ahead and frozen. Serve a large jug of cream for pouring over portions of cake. The classic method of decorating the cake is to pipe 'Sacher' across the top in milk chocolate.

100 g/4 oz (4 squares) plain (semi-sweet) chocolate
6 large eggs, separated
175 g/6 oz (¾ cup) caster (superfine) sugar
2 teaspoons natural vanilla essence (extract)
50 g/2 oz (¼ cup) unsalted butter, melted
100 g/4 oz (1 cup) self-raising (self-rising) flour

ICING AND DECORATION
225 g/8 oz (¾ cup) redcurrant jelly
225 g/8 oz (8 squares) plain (semi-sweet) chocolate
1 teaspoon sunflower or grapeseed oil
75 g/3 oz (3 squares) milk or white chocolate (optional)
crystallized flowers or rose petals

**1** Set the oven at 180°C/350°F/Gas 4. Line and grease a 23 cm/9 in round loose-bottomed cake tin (pan). Place the chocolate in a heatproof basin and set this over a small saucepan of hot water. Stir occasionally, until the chocolate melts but do not overheat the chocolate or it will separate.

**2** Meanwhile, whisk the egg yolks, caster (superfine) sugar and vanilla until very pale, thick and creamy.

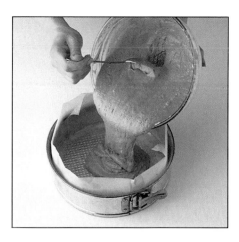

**3** You have to complete the next stage quickly, otherwise the chocolate begins to set and the flour stiffens the mixture so that you will not be able to fold in the egg whites. Whisk the egg whites until stiff but not dry. Beat the chocolate and melted butter into the yolk mixture.

**4** Immediately fold in the flour, then quickly fold in the egg whites and turn the mixture into the prepared tin. Spread the mixture lightly and bake the cake for 45–50 minutes, until risen and firm to the touch. Cool on a wire rack.

**5** To decorate the Sachertorte, melt the redcurrant jelly and let it cool slightly, then brush it all over the cake in an even glaze. Leave to set.

**6** Melt the plain (semi-sweet) chocolate with the oil. Stand the cake on a rack over a piece of cooking foil. Pour the chocolate over the cake, teasing it down the sides in an even coating. Leave to set.

**7** If you feel confident about piping chocolate, melt the milk chocolate and spoon it into a small greaseproof paper (waxed paper) piping (pastry) bag. Snip off just the tip of the bag and pipe "Sacher" on the cake. Add crystallized flowers or petals to the cake at the last minute.

## Silk Posy

The flowers for this posy should include one outstanding 'star', such as a full-blown rose, and a selection of smaller blooms and buds. Leaves and fine composite flower heads provide a delicate background and infilling to the composition.

**YOU WILL NEED:** florists' paper ribbon, silk and/or dried flowers and leaves, fine florists' wire, florists' tape, scissors.

**1** Carefully tear off a narrow strip of ribbon.

**2** Loop the wide length of ribbon once to form a bow shape. Pinch the ribbon together in the centre gently without creasing it too much.

**3** Loop the ribbon again to make a double bow. One end of the ribbon will be in the centre front: loop this end around into a small, neat circle to finish off the bow. Hold it in place with the thumb.

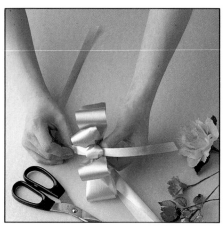

**4** Still holding the bow with one hand, thread the narrow strip of ribbon through the central loop of the bow.

**5** Turn the bow over and tie the narrow ribbon firmly to secure the bow. Don't trim the ends.

**6** Attach individual flowers to fine florists' wire. Wire the smaller flowers and buds together in clusters. Tape the wired stems and add leaves.

**7** Tie on a strip of ribbon for the tails of the bow. Measure the flowers against the bow when forming the posy. Make the posy almost as wide as the bow at the top, tapering gracefully below. When the shape is right, wire the flowers together firmly and use the ends of narrow ribbon to tie them firmly at the back of the bow. Make a hanging loop from the narrow ribbon, then trim off any excess.

# A CHRISTENING IN THE FAMILY

*C*hristenings are informal gatherings for family and close friends and they are usually held on a Sunday. The ceremony may be performed immediately after the morning service or separately in the afternoon.

*A simple buffet lunch or afternoon tea is usually prepared for guests. The immediate relatives and godparents may be the only guests present at a christening held after the morning service and the company may well book a table for family lunch at a nearby hotel or grandparents who live close by may host lunch. Then an informal late afternoon tea party may be arranged to include other close friends.*

**A CHRISTENING PARTY**

Christenings usually bring together a wide range of age groups, all of whom will need some looking after. Remember to take care of godparents and close relatives such as grandparents and favourite aunts, providing them with somewhere special to sit, and making sure generally that they are well catered for. It is usual at christenings for friends and relatives to bring gifts for the baby. It is also a nice idea to give the godparents small gifts which will remind them of the occasion.

It is a good idea to be well prepared with suitable activities for children, given that parents might not want to pack lots of toys for their children. Provide large colouring books, crayons, and other inexpensive but quiet pastimes, such as jigsaw puzzles and board games.

In summer youngsters tend to be less of a problem as they can run around in the garden (yard).

### Christening Tea Checklist

- Invitations
- Sandwiches
- Cakes
- Tea
- Coffee
- Drinks for children
- Table linen
- China
- Flowers
- House cleaning and tidying

## Ribbon Rosebuds

Tiny ribbon rosebuds make charming decorations for all sorts of occasions, from weddings to christenings. They also look good as trimmings for table linen and in guest rooms.

**YOU WILL NEED:** green and yellow satin ribbon, needle and matching thread, scissors, florists' wire.

**1** Curl the end of a long piece of ribbon into a tight roll.

**2** Secure one end of the roll with a small stitch of matching thread.

**3** Make tiny running stitches along the edge of the ribbon to gather it slightly.

**4** Roll the ribbon up, tightly at first and then more loosely until the rosebud is the required size. Trim away surplus ribbon, then turn the raw edge under to prevent fraying and secure with a tiny stitch.

**5** Stitch the roses in small clusters to lengths of florists' wire.

**6** Using green thread, stitch a few loops of green ribbon around the base of the rosebuds. Wind the ribbon around the wire and secure with a stitch.

*Strawberry Tarts (centre) and Citrus Meringues (top left).*

## CHICKEN CHOUX BUNS

——— MAKES 20 ———

*100 ml/4 fl oz (½ cup) water*
*50 g/2 oz (¼ cup) butter*
*65 g/2½ oz (⅔ cup) plain (all-purpose) flour*
*2 eggs, beaten*
*50 g/2 oz (½ cup) mature Cheddar cheese,*
*grated*
*½ teaspoon dried thyme*

FILLING
*225 g/8 oz (1½ cups) cooked chicken, finely*
*diced*
*1 celery stick, finely diced*
*2 tablespoons chopped walnuts*
*1 spring onion (green onion), finely chopped*
*1 no-need-to-soak dried peach, finely diced*
*150 ml/¼ pint (⅔ cup) mayonnaise*
*150 ml/¼ pint (⅔ cup) Greek-style yogurt*
*salt and freshly ground black pepper*
*fresh herb sprigs to garnish (optional)*

**1**  Set the oven at 220°C/425°F/Gas 7. Grease 2 baking sheets. Place the water and butter in a medium saucepan. Heat gently until the butter melts, without allowing the liquid to simmer. Then bring the liquid to a rapid boil.

**2**  Tip all the flour into the pan, stir immediately and remove from the heat.

**3**  The ingredients form a paste which will leave the sides of the pan clean. Do not beat.

## STRAWBERRY TARTS

——— MAKES 24 ———

*225 g/8 oz (2 cups) plain (all-purpose) flour*
*175 g/6 oz (¾ cup) butter*
*3 tablespoons caster (superfine) sugar*
*2 tablespoons cold water*

FILLING
*450 g/1 lb strawberries*
*225 g/8 oz (¾ cup) good-quality*
*strawberry jam*
*2 tablespoons kirsch*

Place the flour in a bowl and rub in (cut in) the butter. Mix in the caster (superfine) sugar and stir in the water to bind the pastry. Roll out thinly on a lightly floured surface. Cut out circles of pastry large enough to line patty tins (shallow muffin pans) and gently ease them into the tins. Re-roll pastry trimmings and cut out more circles. Prick all over and chill the pastry cases (pie crusts).

Meanwhile, set the oven at 190°C/375°F/Gas 5. Cook the pastry cases for about 20 minutes, until cooked and lightly browned. Leave in the tins for 5 minutes, then transfer to a wire rack and leave to cool.

Halve medium strawberries and cut larger fruit into quarters. Divide the strawberries between the pastry cases. Heat the jam in a small saucepan until just runny, then stir in the kirsch. Glaze the strawberries generously with the jam. Cool before serving.

**4** Stir in the grated cheese and thyme. Leave to cool for 10 minutes.

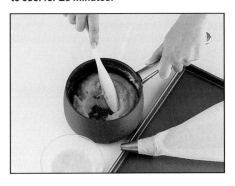

**5** Gradually beat the eggs into the paste, then continue to beat until the paste is very smooth and glossy.

**6** Place in a piping (pastry) bag fitted with a large plain nozzle (tube) and pipe small buns on the baking sheets. Alternatively, the paste may be dropped on the tray from a teaspoon.

**7** Bake the buns for 10 minutes, then reduce the oven temperature to 190°C/375°F/Gas 5 and cook for a further 10–15 minutes, until crisp and golden. Make a slit in each of the buns as soon as they are removed from the oven and leave them to cool on a wire rack. If the buns are not slit they will become soggy. The buns may be frozen, then crisped briefly in a hot oven.

**8** For the filling, mix together the chicken, celery, walnuts, spring onion (green onion) and dried peach. Stir in the mayonnaise and yogurt. Add seasoning to taste.

**9** Use a teaspoon to fill the buns with chicken mixture and pile them in a serving dish. Garnish with fresh herbs, if liked.

*Chicken Choux Buns.*

## CITRUS MERINGUES

— MAKES 24 —

*4 egg whites*
*225 g/8 oz (1¼ cups) caster (superfine) sugar*
*grated rind (peel) of 1 lemon*
*175 g/6 oz (6 squares) plain (semi-sweet)*
*chocolate, melted*
*225 g/8 oz (1 cup) cream cheese*
*4 tablespoons ready-made lemon curd*

Set the oven at 110°C/225°F/Gas ¼. Line two baking sheets with non-stick baking paper.

Whisk the egg whites until they are stiff and dry. Gradually whisk in the sugar, a little at a time, then continue whisking until the meringue is very glossy and stiff. Finally, whisk in the lemon rind (peel) very quickly. Spoon the meringue into a piping (pastry) bag fitted with a plain nozzle (tube). Pipe 48 very small meringues on the prepared baking sheets.

Turn the oven to the lowest possible setting before putting in the meringues. Dry out the meringues for 3–4 hours, or until they feel firm and crisp. If possible keep the oven door slightly ajar by propping it open with a wooden spoon; however, some ovens will not operate unless the door is shut.

Leave the meringues to cool. Brush the flat side of each meringue with melted chocolate to coat it evenly and leave to set. Mix the cream cheese with the lemon curd. Spread a little on a meringue and sandwich a second one on top. Continue sandwiching the meringues with the lemon cheese mixture. Place them in paper cases, if liked.

# SHARING WEDDING ANNIVERSARIES

*The major anniversaries to mark twenty-five, forty and fifty years of marriage are usually occasions for great celebration with friends and acquaintances. Lunch or supper parties, buffet-style, are often planned at home or the responsibility may be handed over to a hotel or restaurant. Close relatives of the couple often host the party.*

*In addition to a large gathering, a relaxed meal offers more scope for reflecting and for sharing the occasion more fully with immediate family. This may well be prepared on the anniversary day itself, with the larger party following on at the first weekend; or this could be a Friday or Saturday evening dinner before a party on the following day. This is a good time for the couple to open gifts over drinks before the meal and to indulge in a spot of nostalgia with brandy later!*

### AN ANNUAL CELEBRATION

Although family and friends usually join in with the celebrations for the important anniversaries – twenty-five years, forty and fifty years – there is no reason why a romantic or fun time cannot be had every year. This needn't involve anything lavish – perhaps exchanging simple but fun gifts and taking the opportunity to share a relaxed meal together at home or in a restaurant. One way to mark the passing years is to investigate the meaning of every year of marriage and to take this as your theme annually. For the first year of marriage for example – paper – you could exchange paper gifts, or make a tissue paper flower arrangement for the table. For the second year – cotton – a cotton lace tablecloth would be a pretty way to indicate the anniversary on a celebration table, and so on.

## Wedding Anniversaries

One year – paper
Five years – wood
Ten years – tin or aluminium
Fifteen years – crystal
Twenty years – china
Twenty-five years – silver
Thirty years – pearl
Thirty-five years – coral
Forty years – ruby
Forty-five years – sapphire
Fifty years – gold
Fifty-five years – emerald
Sixty years – diamond

## Menu Reminders

If you are planning a large gathering, select simple dishes that are easy to eat with a fork. This form of food is especially appropriate if a number of elderly couples will be present.
❖ The following would be suitable buffet fare for a large wedding anniversary: a substantial salad, for example diced cooked ham and chicken with a mayonnaise dressing; a fish mousse, such as salmon mousse; and a jellied seafood or meat mould. If you are planning a sit-down meal, start with a delicate soup, such as watercress soup or even an economical leek and onion soup (also known as Vichyssoise). Opt for some form of casserole for the main course if you have a large gathering to feed. A smaller get-together makes something more sumptuous manageable – beef or pork in pastry, for example, or even a roast with all the trimmings.
❖ When it's two for company, celebrate with a simple treat . . . and champagne – of course! Here are some romantic food ideas: grilled oysters, smoked salmon served with a dollop of soured cream (fresh sour cream) and chopped dill, fresh figs with goats' cheese, pastrami with warmed pitta bread, avocado salad, Parma ham (*prosciutto*) with an olive oil and lime dressing and some freshly ground black pepper.

# WATERCRESS AND ALMOND SOUP

―――――― SERVES 6 ――――――

This light, delicately flavoured soup is the perfect appetizer to a special meal.

*25 g/1 oz (2 tablespoons) butter*
*1 onion, chopped*
*1 bay leaf*
*1 bunch watercress, trimmed*
*2 tablespoons plain (all-purpose) flour*
*100 g/4 oz (1 cup) ground blanched almonds*
*1.1 litres/2 pints (5 cups) chicken stock*
*blade of mace*
*100 ml/4 fl oz (½ cup) milk*
*150 ml/¼ pint (⅔ cup) single (light) cream*
*salt and freshly ground black pepper*
*about 4 tablespoons flaked (slivered) almonds, toasted*

Melt the butter in a saucepan. Add the onion and bay leaf and cook for 15 minutes, stirring occasionally, until the onion is softened but not browned. Stir in the watercress and cook for 2–3 minutes, then stir in the flour and ground almonds. Stirring all the time, gradually pour in the stock. Add the blade of mace and bring to the boil. Reduce the heat, cover the pan and simmer for 20 minutes.

Discard the bay leaf and mace, then purée the soup in a blender or food processor and return it to the pan. Stir in the milk and cream, then heat gently without boiling. Season to taste. Serve topped with toasted flaked (slivered) almonds.

## Wedding Anniversary Lunch Checklist

- Invitations
- Pre-lunch drinks
- Pre-lunch nibbles (snacks)
- First course
- Main course
- Dessert
- Cheese and biscuits (crackers), grapes
- Any special dietary needs?
- Wine
- Alcohol-free drinks
- Ice
- Brandy and liqueurs
- Coffee
- Table linen
- Cutlery (flatware), china and glassware
- Flowers
- House cleaning and tidying

*Watercress and Almond Soup.*

# ROSE MOUSSE

### SERVES 6

Serve the mousse in dainty glasses on doily-topped saucers and arrange one or two crisp dessert biscuits (cookies) beside each glass. Brandy (ginger) snaps are suitable, but some of the delicate rolled — cigarette — biscuits are more fun.

*8 tablespoons rose water*
*4 teaspoons unflavoured powdered gelatine*
*3 eggs, separated*
*75 g/3 oz (⅓ cup) caster (superfine) sugar*
*1½ teaspoons natural vanilla essence (extract)*
*450 ml/¾ pint (2 cups) whipping (heavy) cream*
*frosted miniature roses or rose petals to decorate*

**1** Place the rose water in a small heatproof bowl. Sprinkle the gelatine over and set aside for 15 minutes, until the gelatine is spongy. Stand the bowl in hot water and stir until the gelatine has completely dissolved.

**2** Place the egg yolks, caster (superfine) sugar and vanilla essence (extract) in a bowl over a saucepan of hot water and beat until thick and very pale.

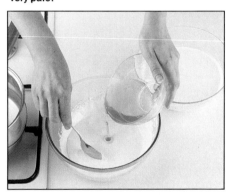

**3** Remove the bowl from the pan, beat until cooled slightly, then stir in the gelatine. Stir in colouring, if liked.

**4** Whip the cream until it stands in soft peaks, then fold it into the mousse mixture.

# PORK IN PASTRY

### SERVES 6

Soaking the prunes in port first gives a marvellously rich stuffing for the pork.

*225 g/8 oz no-need-to-soak prunes, stoned (pitted) and roughly chopped*
*150 ml/¼ pint (⅔ cup) port*
*grated rind (peel) and juice of 1 orange*
*25 g/1 oz (2 tablespoons) butter*
*1 onion, finely chopped*
*225 g/8 oz (1½ cups) lean cooked ham, diced*
*175 g/6 oz (3 cups) fresh breadcrumbs*
*salt and freshly ground black pepper*
*350 g/12 oz puff pastry dough, thawed if frozen*
*1 pork tenderloin, weighing about 675 g/1½ lb*
*1 egg, beaten*

Mix together the prunes, port and orange rind (peel) and juice. Cover and soak overnight.

Melt the butter in a small saucepan. Add the onion and cook for 5 minutes, stirring occasionally, until slightly softened. Stir the onion into the prunes, then add the ham, breadcrumbs and seasoning to taste.

Set the oven at 220°C/425°F/Gas 7. Reserve one-quarter of the pastry (dough) for garnishing, then roll out the rest into an oblong which is slightly longer than the pork and about 20 cm/8 in wide. Spread half the stuffing down the middle of the pastry, then lay the pork tenderloin on top. Carefully spoon the remaining stuffing over the pork, pressing it neatly in place around the meat.

Fold one side of the pastry over the filling and brush with a little beaten egg along the edge. Then fold the other side of the pastry over to enclose the pork and stuffing completely. Trim some of the top pastry away at the ends, if necessary, then fold the bottom flap up and seal the ends with beaten egg. Roll the complete pastry package onto a baking sheet, so the join (seam) of the pastry is underneath.

Roll out the reserved pastry and any trimmings, then cut out a long, narrow strip. Brush the top of the pastry package with beaten egg. Arrange the long strip of pastry, trailing decoratively along the top of the package. Cut out leaves and mark veins in them using the point of a knife. An ivy leaf cutter used by cake decorators makes an excellent cutter for these leaves. Arrange the leaves on the pastry. Glaze the pastry decoration with beaten egg.

Bake the pork for 20 minutes, then reduce the oven temperature to 190°C/375°F/Gas 5 and bake for a further 30 minutes, until the pastry is golden and the filling cooked through. Serve on a large platter. Use a sharp serrated knife to gently slice through the pastry crust, then down through the filling to cut neat slices.

### COOK'S TIP

Serve a wine sauce to accompany the Pork in Pastry. Cook 1 small onion, 1 bay leaf and 100 g/4 oz finely diced lean, rindless bacon in a little butter until the onion is soft, then stir in 25 g/1 oz (¼ cup) plain (all-purpose) flour. Gradually stir in 500 ml/16 fl oz (2 cups) chicken stock and 300 ml/½ pint (1¼ cups) dry red wine. Bring to the boil, reduce the heat, then simmer, covered, for 40 minutes. Taste for seasoning before serving.

**5** Whisk the egg whites until they stand in stiff peaks, and fold into the mousse.

**6** Pour the mixture into 6 glasses or glass dishes and chill for several hours.

**7** Serve the mousses decorated with frosted roses or rose petals.

## Hanging Dried-flower Posy

An elegant bow in timeless silk sets the keynote of this dome-shaped arrangement designed to be hung or carried. Choose flowers in rich tapestry tones to harmonize with the bow.

**YOU WILL NEED:** silk fabric, needle and matching thread, hemisphere of florists' dry foam (styro foam), florists' wire, about 12 main dried flowers, other smaller flowers and sprays, dried reindeer moss.

**3** Stand back and consider the arrangement before adding final blossoms all around to balance and soften the shape.

**1** Make a large bow of silk fabric and sew a narrow hanging loop to the back. Thread a length of florists' wire through the back of the bow, twist the ends together and stick it into the foam. Begin the arrangement from the bow by inserting some smaller blossoms and moss.

**2** Build up the arrangement around the edges of the foam. Anchor tufts of moss with loops of wire. Distribute the main deep-coloured blooms evenly around the hemisphere. Gradually work in towards the centre, interspersing the main blooms and moss with smaller flowers and sprays.

*A ruby red table setting provides an appropriate back drop for a fortieth wedding anniversary dinner.*

## TABLE STYLE

Silver (twenty-five years), ruby red (forty years) and gold (fifty years) are the colours to highlight for these key occasions. A central table decoration of dried flowers and foliage sprayed with silver or gold may be echoed by trimming plain napkin rings with the gold or silver leaves and flowers. Use gold and silver glass bells sold for Christmas decorations to trim the tablecloth. Hold them together with satin ribbons tied into bows and pin in place. And as well as flowers and foliage, wire small silver, gold and ruby-coloured glass balls to fill in spaces in the central arrangement. For a formal table, try gathering the edges of a long cloth into scallops so that they sit just above the floor and trim them with bows of the appropriate ribbon.

### Wedding Anniversary Wreath

Small wreaths of dried flowers and foliage, shaped in the appropriate number for the wedding anniversary, make a beautiful and long-term reminder of the happy occasion. They may be used on the table, hung in the hallway or even displayed on the front door, weather permitting. The raffia plait (braid) can be made quite thick, then tinged with gold or silver spray paint before being decorated.

Bind three strands of raffia securely to tying wire to make three strands: wiring each strand instead of the finished plait (braid) makes the arrangement more secure and durable.

Wire dried autumn leaves with fine floral wire and spray them with gold or silver paint. Use a variety of dried flowers, seed heads and grasses on the wreaths, threading their stems into the raffia and securing them, where necessary, with small loops of bent wire.

Silk and feather flowers or small rosebuds made from satin ribbon should be included to enliven the arrangement. Select blues and mauves for the silver arrangements; oranges and gold colours for the golden arrangement and deep ruby flowers for the red wreath. Use lush green trimmings with the red flowers.

# RETIREMENT GATHERINGS

*R̲etirement is an important life event, and one of the best ways to mark it is to give a party, whether it's an office party with colleagues or a family get-together, or both.*

*Whatever the occasion, such a party will be laden with a variety of messages, ranging from congratulations and thanks for work done to good luck and sadness.*

**OFFICE RETIREMENT PARTY**

Although a formal party may be arranged by a senior member of staff, in many companies it is the person who is leaving or retiring who prepares

an informal celebration for colleagues. This usually takes the form of wine and finger food.

❖ Prepare food which is easily packed and transported and which may be prepared in advance without deteriorating in quality, such as cocktail sausages on sticks, vol-au-vents filled with a selection of cold fillings, small slices of quiche, and of course a range

---

> **Office Retirement Party Checklist**
>
> - **Finger food**
> - **Wine and/or beer**
> - **Alcohol-free drinks**
> - **Ice**
> - **Plastic plates/bowls**
> - **Plastic cups**
> - **Paper table cover**
> - **Balloons and streamers, if using**
> - **Absorbent kitchen paper (paper towels)**

of ready-made snacks.

❖ Pack lots of paper plates and napkins. These now come with a range of decorative designs on them. Plastic plates or bowls are useful for holding snacks, as they are easier to hand round.

❖ Take a paper table cover to drape over a desk or table. To introduce more of a party atmosphere, and if this is appropriate, also bring some balloons and streamers to create a decorative centrepiece.

❖ Plastic cups, possibly matching the paper plates and napkins, may be used, or buy inexpensive plastic wine cups from a catering supplier. The company may have wine glasses already – if this

is the case, check whether you can use these for the party.

❖ Wine cases are the most practical containers to transport and they allow a variety of inexpensive but drinkable wines to be offered. Dry and medium-dry white, and red wine are the usual choices to offer.

❖ Non-alcoholic refreshments should also be offered. Take large plastic bottles of mineral water and screw-top cartons of orange juice.

*Colourful napkins and matching paper plates and cups always look festive, even when the party setting is in the office.*

## INFORMAL FAMILY LUNCH

An informal lunch is a good way to celebrate a retirement with a small group of friends and relatives. A Saturday or Sunday is often the most convenient day for people and the family party may be extended to offer an evening buffet spread for a wider group of friends without increasing the workload too much.

❖ Prepare a tureen of soup in winter – something substantial like minestrone or winter vegetable.

❖ Serve French bread, a variety of rolls, cheese and a platter of cold meats for lunch.

❖ Include a meat and a fish pâté.

❖ Serve red and white wine, and include non-alcoholic refreshments.

❖ Have a beautiful basket of fresh fruit both as decoration and for dessert.

❖ For the evening party, trim leftover cheese and arrange it on a cheeseboard. Any remaining pâté can be spread on crackers to hand around with drinks. Tidy the fruit basket, and use it to decorate a cheeseboard. Leftover French bread can be sliced and spread with garlic butter, then wrapped in foil and heated.

### BASKET CAKE

This can be adapted to suit your requirements for the cake and to delight both male and female recipients. The cake base can be Madeira or a pound cake, or a rich fruit cake. Use a buttercream icing (frosting) for a light cake, and coat the top of the cake with buttercream first before piping on a basketweave pattern. Cover a rich fruit cake with marzipan (almond paste) and coat with sugar paste (rolled fondant) or royal icing (decorators' white icing) first before piping with royal icing. The basketweave piping technique is easy and the same for buttercream and royal icing.

❖ The cake may be round, or an oval cake may be cut from a large square cake using an oval-shaped template.

❖ Before applying any coating to the cake, cut a template the same size as the top of the cake, then fold it in half and cut along the fold. Roll out pastillage (gum paste) fairly thinly and cut out two pieces the shape of half the cake top – they will form the lid. Leave to dry.

❖ Fill the open area under the basket lid with chocolates and sweets (candies), flowers, moulded marzipan fruit or vegetables. Or other novelty decorations can include moulded spools of sewing threads or D.I.Y. tools for the handyman.

**1** You need 2 greaseproof paper (waxed paper) piping (pastry) bags: one fitted with a small plain tube, the other fitted with a basketweave tube, which has a flat, serrated end. Pipe a plain vertical line, then pipe short lengths of basketweave across the line.

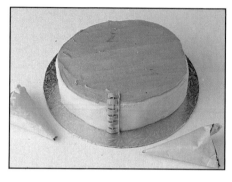

**2** Then pipe another plain line along the ends of the basketweave strips.

**3** Pipe the next row of basketweave strips in the spaces left between the existing strips and over the new plain line. Continue building up the basketweave until the whole area is covered.

**4** Brush the underside of the pastillage (gum paste) lid with an appropriate powder food colour, then pipe a basketweave on top.

**5** Divide the top of the cake in half and pipe a line of basketweave along this central line.

**6** Use 2 or 3 lumps of pastillage to support each lid half in an open position on the cake. Fill the area under each lid with chocolates and/or sweets (candies). If using royal icing (decorators' white icing), the join between each open lid and the cake should be edged with piped shells, both on top and underneath.

# LET'S PARTY!

*T*his is the real business of party-giving, with fun being the key objective. Throw caution and convention to the wind, forget stuffy rules of etiquette and invite everyone to join in with a light-hearted spirit and good nature.

How much food you make is up to you, but there should be sufficient refreshments to balance the alcohol intake. Preparing canapés, hors d'oeuvre and delicious nibbles *(snacks) for drinks parties and cocktail parties is, in fact, extremely time consuming, so the better option can be to make a large potful of something wholesome and serve it with a great bowl of rice or a stack of baked potatoes.*

*Since most guests will find themselves a seat on the floor if the atmosphere is informal enough, presenting food which has to be eaten with the assistance of a knife is rarely a problem. Bread, cheese and pâté are all quick, easy and satisfying. Do not dismiss platters of sandwiches which can be reserved for later in the evening. Keep sandwich fillings neat and avoid the likes of cress (sprouts) or lettuce which escape from the clutches of the bread too easily.*

## PARTY PREPARATIONS

Here are some suggestions and ideas to make your party a success:

❖ Clear the floor in one room to allow space for dancing. Set chairs aside but make sure that there are some comfortable areas where less lively guests can congregate and talk.

❖ Subdued lighting always casts a flattering glow, so arrange table lamps and standard lamps around the room. The buffet table and bar should be well illuminated.

❖ The bar may be set up in the kitchen or towards one end of a large room. If you are entertaining a large number and have two rooms or a very spacious area, then it can be a good idea to have two bars. Do not use too small a table as there is a danger of glasses getting knocked off. Have a thick cloth on the table and pile plenty of clean towels and rolls of absorbent kitchen paper (paper towels) near. Place waste bags under the table.

❖ Order ice in advance from a local wine merchant or buy it from a convenience store. Buy white and red wine and beer, and the necessary spirits and mixers for the punch, if serving.

❖ If you are short of chilling space, particularly for beers, then use a clean dustbin (trash can) and tip a couple of large bags of ice into it. Pour in a couple of buckets of cold water. Stand this conveniently outside the back door and place all the unopened bottles and cans in it. Knot a few towels on the dustbin handles for wiping off chilled bottles and cans.

❖ Always have plenty of alcohol-free drinks: mineral water, soda water, lemonade, tonic, fruit juices, alcohol-free beer and low-alcohol wine.

❖ Make large chunks of ice for chilling punches: they do not melt as quickly as small cubes, therefore they dilute the punch more slowly. Use margarine tubs or similar containers.

❖ Make colourful ice cubes for mixed drinks and cocktails by freezing cherries, green olives, pieces of orange or lemon in water in ice cube trays.

❖ Open-freeze orange and lemon slices by spreading them out on baking sheets lined with cling film (plastic wrap). Adding lots of frozen fruit to punch helps to chill the drink.

❖ Frozen strawberries are colourful and they add flavour to a wine punch.

*Opposite: paper streamers are inexpensive and quickly establish the party mood.*

**Summer Fruit Cup**

A fruit cup always goes down well at any party gathering. Served in a large glass or punch bowl it also looks wonderfully festive. Slice an orange, a lemon, 8 strawberries, a dessert apple and a 2.5 cm/1 in length of cucumber into the bowl and add 4 mint sprigs, and 4 lemon balm sprigs, if liked. Pour over 150 ml/¼ pt (⅔ cup) of sweet sherry and leave the fruit and herbs to stand for between 2 and 4 hours. This will impart a full, fruity flavour to the punch. Just before you serve the punch, pour in a chilled bottle of red wine, and top up with sparkling mineral water (seltzer) to taste (about 600 ml/1 pint). Add lots of ice and stir well before ladling the punch into glasses. Makes about 10 glasses.

## PARTY THEMES

Here are a few suggestions to set your own ideas in motion for a fancy dress (costume) party. Remember that the invitations, decorations and food should fit in with the chosen theme.

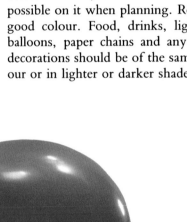

### Sportswear Party

An easy and inexpensive theme for any guest. Everyone dresses in some form of sportswear, from tennis dresses to jogging clothes. Invitations can be cut in the shape of a piece of sports equipment such as a tennis racquet.

### Nightwear

Another favourite theme for dressing up, allowing shy guests to attire themselves in sensible robes over ample pyjamas while others opt for less covered up nightwear.

### Colour

Select a colour, then base as much as possible on it when planning. Red is a good colour. Food, drinks, lighting, balloons, paper chains and any other decorations should be of the same colour or in lighter or darker shades.

### Roman Party

Even the least enthusiastic guests will be able to clothe themselves in white sheets and manage to tie a long strand of ivy into a wreath for head or shoulders! Slaves, emperors, soothsayers and Roman guards are all welcome; someone may even come as the lion. Set out ample provisions of grapes and have large floor cushions spread around for lounging.

### Space Party

Send out flying-saucer invitations and dress the table in a space blanket (foil survival blanket from camping shops). Costume design can be as simple or sophisticated as guests please, ranging from black or lurex tights (spandex) and T-shirts to hired (rented) outfits from science fiction film or play productions. Plastic bubble wrap material can be used to make simple T-shaped garments and applying foil tape in close stripes to the outside disguises the identity of the material. Body paints and hair gels allow for fantastic transformations in personal appearance and can be part of the fun.

### Vagabonds and Thieves

This offers plenty of scope for dressing up as specific characters from history, as well as simply dressing the part. Historic dress, jailbird outfits and pirates are all suitable.

### Goodies and Baddies

Another excellent way of channelling thoughts for a fancy dress (costume) party. Superman, the Christmas fairy, Cinderella, Santa Claus, Robin Hood and Maid Marion are a few goodies; the ugly sisters, a vampire, a Mafia figure, a highwayman or a *Batman* villain are a few baddies.

### Explorers and Voyagers

A theme for those who prefer to spend a little time researching their costumes. Of course, guests do not have to dress up as a particular figure from history, they can simply adopt the mode of attire worn by sailors, space travellers, deep-sea divers, Vikings, mountain climbers and so on.

## CHEESE CROQUETTES

———— MAKES 24 ————

*350 g/12 oz (3 cups) grated mature Cheddar cheese*
*225 g/8 oz (4 cups) fresh white breadcrumbs*
*2 tablespoons chopped fresh parsley*
*1 tablespoon chopped fresh sage*
*1 teaspoon dried thyme*
*1 tablespoon whole-grain mustard*
*4 tablespoons milk or beer*
*salt and freshly ground black pepper*
*2 eggs, beaten*
*175 g/6 oz (1½ cups) dry white breadcrumbs*
*oil for deep-frying*

Mix the cheese with the fresh breadcrumbs, parsley, sage, thyme, mustard and milk or beer. Add seasoning to taste, then mix well. Shape the mixture into 24 small balls. Coat these in beaten egg, then in the dry breadcrumbs. The mixture must be thoroughly and evenly coated.

Heat the oil for deep-frying to 190°C/375°F. Fry the croquettes briefly, until golden brown, working in batches if necessary. Drain well on absorbent kitchen paper (paper towels). These croquettes are good served warm or cold, and they can be made in advance and re-heated briefly in the oven before serving.

## SPICED TURKEY AND POTATO SALAD

———— SERVES 12 ————

This is a practical dish to prepare for party gatherings, not least because the quantities can be increased both easily and comparatively economically by buying a whole boned turkey breast, or by roasting a whole bird. It is also worth tasting the roasted turkey breast which is sold at delicatessen counters, because some supplies have a good flavour. Although not the cheapest way of buying turkey, it can be convenient to have a large portion cut ready for dicing at home.

*2 tablespoons oil*
*1 garlic clove, crushed*
*1 large onion, finely chopped*
*2 tablespoons finely chopped fresh root ginger*
*1 tablespoon ground coriander*
*½ teaspoon ground turmeric*
*1 tablespoon ground cumin*
*600 ml/1 pint (2½ cups) mayonnaise*
*300 ml/½ pint (1¼ cups) Greek yogurt or fromage frais*
*salt and freshly ground black pepper*
*1 kg/2 lb (8 cups) cooked skinless turkey, cubed*
*6 celery sticks, diced*
*1.4 kg/3 lb small new potatoes, cooked*
*4 tablespoons chopped fresh parsley*

GARNISH
*chopped fresh coriander leaves (cilantro)*
*1 red pepper (sweet bell pepper), seeded and diced*

Heat the oil in a small saucepan. Add the garlic, onion and ginger and cook, stirring, for 15 minutes without allowing the onion to brown. The onion should be fairly well softened if not completely cooked. Add the coriander, turmeric and cumin, then continue to cook for 3 minutes, stirring and taking care that the spices do not overcook.

Remove from the heat and cool slightly before stirring the spice mixture into the mayonnaise. Add the yogurt and seasoning.

Mix together the turkey, celery, potatoes and parsley in a large bowl. Add the dressing and toss well to coat all the ingredients. Turn the mixture into a large serving dish and garnish with chopped coriander (cilantro) and the red pepper.

# Paper Hats

Make these hats as glamorous or as bizarre as you like. You can go to town decorating them with exuberant paper flowers and extravagant bows. Before you begin, take a rough measurement for size. Place a ruler flat on the top of the wearer's head and hold the hands underneath it on either side of the head with the thumbs vertical to give an indication of the diameter of the crown.

**YOU WILL NEED:** coloured card (posterboard) or stiff paper, pair of compasses, pencil, scissors, glue, sticky (transparent) tape, paper flowers, twisted paper, etc for decoration.

**1** Use a pair of compasses to draw a circle on coloured card (posterboard) or paper the diameter of the crown of the hat plus 5 cm/2 in. Draw a second circle 2.5 cm/1 in inside the first one.

**2** Cut out the paper around the outer circle.

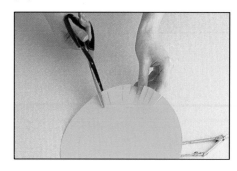

**3** Make even cuts 2.5 cm/1 in deep from the edge of the paper to the pencilled inner circle.

**4** Fold the cut flaps of paper up at right angles.

**5** For the sides of the hat, cut a strip of paper 7.5 cm/3 in wide and long enough to fit around the folded-up edge of the paper circle. Then draw a line lengthways down the middle of the paper.

**6** Make even cuts in as far as the drawn line on the paper strip. Spread glue along the other, uncut side.

**7** Stick the glued side of the paper band around the edge of the paper circle, ensuring that all the cut strips are neatly attached to it.

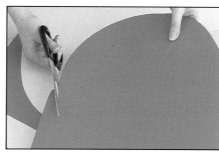

**8** Cut a large circle of contrasting card for the brim, about 7.5 cm/3 in wider all around than the crown.

**9** Cut out a circle from the centre of the brim that measures the same diameter as the crown. Place the crown right way up on a surface, with the cut strips around the sides of the hat folded outwards. Then slide the brim into position. When you know it fits neatly, turn the hat over and glue the cut strips in place on the brim. Secure them with sticky (transparent) tape and leave to dry.

**10** Add finishing touches such as wide ribbons, bows and flowers.

## Venetian Masks

Give rein to your fantasy and artistic flair when making these masks. Sequins, diamanté strips, coloured beads, fun fur and feathers will all add to the glamour and glitter of the occasion.

**YOU WILL NEED:** card (posterboard) for template, coloured card, scissors, craft knife, adhesive stars, crêpe paper, glue, sticky (transparent) tape, 30 cm/12 in lengths of fine bamboo cane, ribbons.

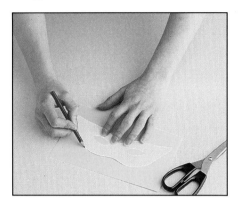

**1** Draw your own mask shape, fitting it against your face. Cut out the shape in white card (posterboard), then lay this on coloured card and draw around the outline to make an identical shape.

**2** Cut out the mask shape drawn on the coloured card.

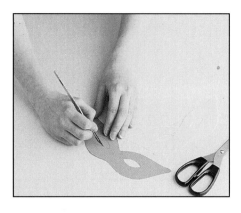

**3** Use a craft knife to cut out the peep-holes for the eyes.

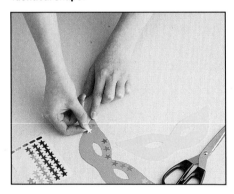

**4** Stick coloured paper stars around the upper and outer edges of the masks.

**5** Cut two strips of crêpe paper about 7.5 cm/ 3 in deep for each mask. Pleat each piece until it is the right length to fit along one half of the top edge of the mask. Secure the pleats with glue.

**6** Stick the pleated crepe paper to the back of the mask with glue. Secure it with sticky (transparent) tape for extra support. Repeat with the second piece of crêpe paper.

**7** Cover the piece of cane with ribbon, gluing it in place at one end before winding it up around the cane. Add other ribbons of different colours and widths if you like.

**8** Curl the ends of the ribbon by pulling them sharply and tightly across the blade of an open pair of scissors. Then stick the ribbon firmly in place at the end of the cane, with the curls dangling down. Stick the cane behind the mask with glue, and secure it with sticky tape.

# BARBECUES FOR ALL

*B*arbecues are fun occasions to share with family and friends, young and old alike. This section includes ideas for food with notes on planning and safety. If you are thinking about buying a barbecue, there are also a few points worth considering before making a final purchase.

## BARBECUE PLANNING

Here are some important points to consider when planning a barbecue:

❖ Place the barbecue grill away from fences or other combustible material. Do not light up right next to your neighbour's back door as the fumes may cause offence!

❖ The barbecue should be on a stable, level surface in a place where it is not likely to get knocked over and safely positioned to avoid any accidents caused by children running past.

❖ If you are using charcoal, this should be fresh and dry: old material from a previous season may have absorbed damp, making it difficult to light easily.

❖ Use firelighters or a commercial barbecue lighting fuel for charcoal. DO NOT pour petrol (gasoline), paraffin or methylated spirits onto a smouldering bonfire.

❖ Make sure you have a grill, or grills, large enough to cook sufficient food for the number of guests invited. Check that you have enough propane gas or fuel such as wood or charcoal.

❖ If you have a vegetarian contingent as well as meat-eating guests, then you should grill the vegetarian food separately so that the juices do not mix.

### Barbecue Checklist

- Charcoal, if using
- Firelighters or commercial barbecue lighting fuel, if using charcoal
- Gas, if using
- Nibbles (snacks)
- First course
- Main course
- Dessert
- Wine and/or beer
- Alcohol-free drinks
- Ice
- Any special dietary needs?
- Skewers
- Table linen
- Cutlery (flatware)
- China and glassware or paper plates and cups

## TYPES OF BARBECUE

### Kettle Barbecue

This is a domed-shaped container with a base rack for burning fuel, a grill above that, then a domed lid which may be closed during cooking. Large kettle barbecues cope with an impressive quantity of food. Their real plus is for cooking large joints of meat and whole poultry, and for imparting a strong smoky flavour to food.

### Brick-built Barbecue

You can construct a brick-built barbecue to your own requirements, buying all the racks and base grids you need. There should be a solid layer for catching ash; a perforated metal sheet sits a couple of bricks height above this to hold the burning fuel; the cooking grill should have several positions, ranging from 17.5 cm/7 in above the burning plate upwards. It should be easy to raise or lower once the fire is lit.

### Hibachi Grill

Small- or medium-sized open grill which holds a limited amount of fuel. You can keep the coals burning for several hours by adding to one side at a time. It has the advantage of being portable, which makes it useful for beach barbecues or picnics in the park.

### Disposable Barbecue

This is a small foil container filled with charcoal, and is ideal for supplementing a picnic menu.

### Gas or Electric Barbecue

A gas barbecue is the most popular and they are fed from bottled gas. These are fairly large and the most elaborate are ideal for sophisticated entertaining.

### Barbecue Safety

❖ An awareness of safety is vital, especially when there are lots of children around: *never* leave the barbecue unattended for children to play nearby, and always make sure children are aware of the danger. Keep pets well away.

❖ Pay special attention to food safety and hygiene. Keep ingredients chilled before cooking and never leave food to stand out in the sun where flies and insects can contaminate it before or after cooking. Foods with eggs or mayonnaise must be kept cool to avoid food poisoning.

## Menu Reminders

❖ Fix a large bowl of refreshing punch for everyone to sip and keep lots of cold beer and sodas in a clean dustbin (trash can) or cooler full of ice and water.
❖ Make sure there are lots of nibbles (snacks), dips and dunkers (chips) for guests to munch while the main food is grilling.
❖ Involve everyone in the cooking as well as in the eating, this way the burden is distributed and everyone has a chance to display their barbecue skills.
❖ Marinate meats and dry foods to moisten and flavour them.

## AMUSEMENTS

Most people are happy to sit around and chat at a barbecue, but it can be fun to join with children in a few light activities at a lunchtime barbecue or before an evening meal. Have a few small prizes ready for the winners.

### Hoop-la

Fix a small piece of garden cane (bamboo stake) in the lawn and stand all the contestants behind a fixed point. Throw hoops at the cane, allowing about six throws for each go. Look in the hardware store for suitable hoops which have various gardening uses. Make the throwing line nearer the stick for small hoops.

### Three-legged Races

Take a partner and stand side by side. Use a short piece of fabric or a scarf to tie the two ankles nearest each other together. Practice walking, then running when tied together. If the garden (yard) is not big enough for straightforward races, then plan a course for each couple with some task to be completed and time them doing it. For example, they may have to carry an armload of oranges and deposit them in six containers around a set course or tie a bunch of balloons around a washing line (clothes line).

# BRUSCHETTA

—— MAKES ABOUT 20 ——

1 French loaf, sliced fairly thickly
2 garlic cloves, crushed
150 ml/¼ pint (⅔ cup) olive oil
1 teaspoon dried oregano
salt and freshly ground black pepper
8 ripe tomatoes, peeled and diced
4 large fresh basil sprigs, shredded
2 tablespoons chopped fresh parsley

## CRUDITES WITH DIPS

Crudités are the pieces of vegetables or other ingredients for dunking into dips. Some may be bought, some prepared well ahead and others should be cut the day before or on the same day.
❖ Cauliflower florets (flowerets), carrot sticks and celery sticks can be cut the day before and soaked in iced water overnight. Drain well on absorbent kitchen paper (paper towels).
❖ Radishes, chicory (endive) and cherry tomatoes are also good for dipping.
❖ Dips are also nice with breadsticks, crisps (chips) and mini melba toasts.

## Mini Melba Toasts

Make these a few days in advance. Toast medium-thick bread, cut off the crusts and slice each piece in half horizontally. Cut into quarters and cook away from heat under a low grill (broiler) until golden and crisp. Cool before storing in an air-tight container.

Lightly toast 1 side of the bread, then lay the slices on a large baking sheet or in the grill (broiler) pan. Mix together the garlic, olive oil, oregano and seasoning. Use a teaspoon to trickle this mixture evenly over the bread, then leave the slices to stand and absorb the oil for 10 minutes. Cook well away from the heat under the grill until the bread is lightly toasted and thoroughly heated.

Meanwhile, mix together the tomatoes, basil and parsley. Transfer the hot bread to a serving platter and top with the tomato mixture. Serve at once.

*Fresh Herb Dip.*

### Fresh Herb Dip

Mix 2 tablespoons of finely chopped fresh parsley, a tablespoon of chopped fresh mint, a tablespoon of chopped fresh lemon balm (if available), a teaspoon of chopped fresh thyme and 2–3 shredded basil sprigs into 100 g/4 oz (½ cup) cream cheese. Gradually work in 250 ml/8 fl oz (1 cup) Greek-style yogurt. Season to taste. Cover and chill until ready to serve. Serves 6.

### Cheese and Walnut Dip

Mix 100 g/4 oz (1 cup) finely grated mature Cheddar with 100 ml/4 fl oz (½ cup) mayonnaise. Stir in 100 g/4 oz (1 cup) very finely chopped walnuts and 2 tablespoons of snipped fresh chives. Stir in 250 ml/8 fl oz (1 cup) soured cream (fresh sour cream). Season to taste. Cover and chill. Serves 6.

## Table Weights

Prevent the tablecloth from blowing in the breeze by weighing it down with corner pockets. To make, cut triangles of fabric, hem one edge and sew the others into the hem of the tablecloth.
❖ The pockets may be fairly small and sewn into the back of the cloth, which is ideal if you want to sew them on an existing cloth because the fabric does not have to match, or they may be slightly larger and sewn on the front of the cloth.
❖ Place a pebble in each pocket to weight down the cloth. Fill front pockets with posies.

### FISH FOR THE BARBECUE

Many types of fish cook extremely well on the barbecue, notably the oily varieties, such as salmon and mackerel, and the firm-fleshed fish, such as cod or haddock. Fish cooks quickly, so take care not to overcook it, or it will rapidly fall apart or completely dry out depending on type. Fish racks are useful for grilling small whole fish, such as sardines or mackerel.

### Sardines and Mackerel

If you can get hold of fresh sardines and mackerel, they are both excellent grilled whole. Have the fish gutted but with heads and tails on, because this helps to keep them together during grilling. Season very well all over and sprinkle with lemon or lime juice.

Herbs such as oregano and rosemary both go well with these full-flavoured fish. Brush the outside of the skin with oil and use 2 fish slices (pancake turners) to turn the fish over if they are not on a fish rack.

### Tuna and Swordfish Steaks

These are also ideal for barbecuing because they are meaty and firm. They can be dry, however, so they benefit from being marinated before grilling. Olive oil, garlic, chopped thyme, lemon rind (peel) and juice, crushed coriander seeds and seasoning are all suitable marinade ingredients. Leave the fish to marinate for at least a couple of hours or overnight. Brush with the leftover marinade during grilling.

### Salmon

Salmon steaks barbecue well. The fish oils they contain keep the flesh moist and flavoursome during grilling. Plain seasoning and a brush with light cooking oil is sufficient, but the fish can take very pronounced seasoning, such as crushed coriander seeds, cardamom and bay leaves.

### Fish Skewers

Select firm-fleshed fish, such as swordfish, tuna, monkfish or thick cod fillets. Because barbecue cooking is more rough and ready than indoor grilling (broiling), there is a greater risk of the fish breaking up on the skewers. An excellent method of avoiding this is to wrap the chunks of fish in rindless streaky bacon rashers (slices) before skewering them. The bacon imparts a wonderful flavour to the fish, its fat bastes the chunks while they cook and the kebabs stay in shape. Smoked bacon goes well with some fish.

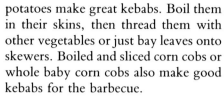

### Other Seafood

Large raw prawns (shrimp) are terrific barbecued in their shells, particularly if they have been marinated with lots of chopped garlic, soy sauce and a little sesame oil beforehand. Prawns may also be skewered along with other ingredients to make kebabs. Scallops, mussels and oysters can be grilled in their shells too. Place the cleaned seafood on a deep shell and season lightly, then sprinkle with a little lemon juice and melted butter. Wrap them loosely in foil or cook in a covered barbecue. They cook in a few minutes over hot coals, so watch them carefully and serve the seafood as soon as the flesh is just firm.

### BARBECUING VEGETABLES

### Skewers

Raw and cooked vegetables can be skewered for grilling on the barbecue. Either marinate the vegetables beforehand or brush them with a dressing of seasoning, oil, lemon juice and herbs while grilling. Here are a few guidelines for success:

**COOKED VEGETABLES** Small new potatoes make great kebabs. Boil them in their skins, then thread them with other vegetables or just bay leaves onto skewers. Boiled and sliced corn cobs or whole baby corn cobs also make good kebabs for the barbecue.

**RAW VEGETABLES** Courgettes (zucchini), aubergines (eggplants), green, red and yellow peppers (sweet bell peppers), mushrooms and pickling onions are all suitable for barbecuing. Tomatoes may also be grilled but they can rapidly overcook. Some vegetables, such as aubergines, require a

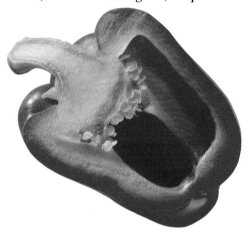

longer cooking time to become tender. If you are including tomatoes for kebabs, select small whole fruit which are ripe but firm.

### Foil-wrapped Vegetables

Another method of barbecuing vegetables is to pack them in foil, season, then place the packages on the barbecue. This is a good way of cooking a selection of vegetables together, such as sliced courgettes (zucchini), chopped spring onions (green onions), small whole mushrooms and cooked new potatoes.

Large whole potatoes can also be foil-wrapped and cooked below the coals; although this is a nice idea if there are just a few of you and there is plenty of time to wait for the potatoes to cook, the more practical approach is to bake the potatoes in the oven first, then finish them off on the barbecue for a few minutes, turning them so they are really crisp and well flavoured.

*Vegetables will cook in no time on the barbecue if they are cut into bite-sized pieces first and threaded onto skewers.*

*Home-made Hamburger with all the trimmings: slices of gherkins (pickles), onion rings, lettuce and a sesame-seed bun.*

## HOME-MADE HAMBURGERS

Good hamburgers can still be the high-light of any barbecue. They are best if you mince (grind) the meat yourself, or buy a piece of braising steak from a butcher and ask for it to be minced. These are the rules for making un-forgettably good burgers:

❖ Season the meat very well with salt and freshly ground black pepper.

❖ Knead the meat together with your hands without any additional ingre-dients, until it binds itself. You can also use the back of a mixing spoon to pound the beef, then lightly knead the meat together with your hands.

❖ Wash your hands and rinse them under cold water to prevent the meat sticking as you shape the burgers. Take a portion of meat and knead it roughly into shape, then press out the burger on your hand, making sure the top and sides are smooth.

❖ Brush the burgers with a little vegetable oil and seal both sides quick-ly near the coals, then move the bur-gers to a cooler part of the barbecue to cook through.

### Burger Garnishes

**BUNS** These should be slit horizontally and toasted. Toast a stack of buns in advance, then warm them through at the last minute on the barbecue, if space allows, or in the oven.

**GHERKINS** Slice gherkins (pickles) or make attractive fan shapes by leaving lengthways slices attached at one end.

**ONIONS** Thinly slice red or white onions which have a delicate flavour and are always popular. Large Spanish onions are particularly tasty.

**LETTUCE** Use shredded crisp lettuce, not a limp lettuce leaf.

## Relishes

**FRESH APPLE RELISH** Mix together 4 cored and diced eating apples, a chopped onion, a seeded and chopped green chilli (chili pepper) and lots of chopped fresh parsley. Add a squeeze of lemon juice, a tablespoon of chopped capers, 2 tablespoons of chopped raisins and a little olive oil. Serves about 4.

**CRANBERRY RELISH** Simmer 450 g/ 1 lb cranberries with 350 g/12 oz (1¾ cups) sugar, 2 large finely chopped onions, 100 ml/4 fl oz (½ cup) white vinegar, a cinnamon stick, a generous pinch of ground cloves and a teaspoon of grated nutmeg. Keep the pan covered during cooking and allow 45 minutes, until the onions and cranberries are tender. Leave covered until cool. Remove the cinnamon stick before serving. Serves about 6.

# BEEF BURRITOS

——— MAKES 12 ———

Burritos are soft wheat tortillas (virtually the same as Indian chapatis) which are filled with meat or beans and topped with sauce, then rolled or folded and eaten. The burritos can be made in large batches and frozen, then heated through on the barbecue or in the oven if grilling space is limited.

*450 g/1 lb lean grilling steak in 1 piece*
*salt and freshly ground black pepper*
*juice of 1 lime*
*2 tablespoons olive oil*

WHEAT TORTILLAS
*225 g/8 oz (2 cups) plain (all-purpose) flour*
*1 teaspoon salt*
*50 g/2 oz (¼ cup) lard (shortening)*
*100 ml/4 fl oz (½ cup) water*

TOMATO SALSA
*450 g/1 lb ripe tomatoes, peeled, seeded and diced*
*grated rind (peel) and juice of 1 lime*
*2 garlic cloves, crushed*
*3 tablespoons chopped fresh coriander leaves (cilantro)*
*2 green chillies (chili peppers), seeded and chopped*
*1 onion, very finely chopped*

TO SERVE
*¼ head iceberg lettuce, shredded*
*250 ml/8 fl oz (1 cup) soured cream (fresh sour cream)*

Beat out the steak thinly with a meat mallet. Lay it in a large dish and season very well. Sprinkle the lime juice and oil over, cover and marinate for 24 hours before cooking. Turn the meat over once during marinating.

Make the tortillas. Mix together the flour and salt, then rub in the lard (shortening). Gradually mix in the water, adding enough to bind the flour in a workable dough which is not sticky. Roll the dough into a sausage shape, then cut it into 12 portions.

Have a folded clean tea-towel (dish-towel) ready to hold the cooked tortillas. Heat a griddle or heavy-bottomed frying pan (skillet). Lightly flour the surface. Roll out a portion of dough into a thin round measuring about 17.5 cm/7 in in diameter. Slap the dough onto the hot griddle and cook until browned in patches underneath – if the griddle is hot enough this should take 50–60 seconds. Turn over the tortilla and cook the second side. Transfer the tortilla to the tea-towel and wrap it loosely while cooking the remainder.

Pack in plastic bags when cool and freeze or keep in the refrigerator for 2–3 days. When you are ready to serve, warm the tortillas on the barbecue or in the oven.

Prepare the salsa no more than a few hours before it is to be served. Simply mix together all the ingredients, adding seasoning to taste. Turn the salsa into a serving dish, cover and chill until ready to serve. Grill the steak on a very hot barbecue: it should sear and brown in 1–2 minutes. Turn and brown the second side. Have a large platter ready and transfer the meat to it. Use a sharp serrated knife to cut the steak into fine strips.

Fill each tortilla with a little lettuce, some steak, tomato salsa and a dollop of soured cream (fresh sour cream). Fold and eat immediately.

**FINISHING OFF WITH FRUIT**
Fruit can be wrapped in foil and cooked on the grill once the main business of barbecuing is over. Try apples, bananas, peaches, apricots, pineapple and plums. Add honey or maple syrup, spices such as cinnamon or grated nutmeg, and a little fruit juice. Make sure the foil packages are tightly closed so that all the precious juices are retained. If the embers are dying away, then leave the packages over the low heat while everyone eats the main course.

Fruit kebabs, however, are more interesting and take only a little more effort. Chunks of banana, apple, pineapple, halved apricots, stoned (pitted) cherries and halved plums can all be skewered. Brush them with a mixture of lemon juice and honey or syrup, adding a little cinnamon or ground mixed spice (apple pie spice), if you like. Turn the kebabs a couple of times while they heat through.

A firm favourite for cooking on the barbecue is bananas grilled in their skins. Pick firm bananas, even verging

on the under-ripe, then place them on the grill when the embers are dying. Turn them often until the skins are completely blackened. The bananas look good with their tops peeled and cream, chopped nuts, honey or maple syrup added. However, they actually taste far better, and are more pleasant to eat, if each diner has a warm plate and the skin is completely discarded. Set out various bowls of toppings so everyone can help themselves. This way, bits of peel do not interfere with the tempting fruit.

## Tissue-lined Lantern

This method makes a lantern about 12.5 cm/5 in deep, but you can adapt the measurements. A group of lanterns of varying sizes and colours looks attractive hanging together. Simple slits or leaf shapes are best for the cut-out 'windows'.

**YOU WILL NEED:** oblong of lightweight craft paper about 45 × 12.5 cm/18 × 5 in, tissue paper, scissors, craft knife and cutting board, sticky (transparent) tape, ribbon for hanging.

**1** Fold 2.5 cm/1 in hems along both long sides of the paper. Then fold the paper in half lengthways. (Using an iron helps to achieve crisp creases.) Next fold it widthways into four.

**2** Draw fluid outlines or leaf shapes for the 'windows'. Cut them out using a craft knife.

**3** Unfold the paper and stick a layer of tissue paper over the cut-outs. Refold the paper and join the two short ends with tape on the inside.

**4** Open the lantern out and press into a diamond shape. Use tape to attach hanging ribbons near the top edge.

## Box lantern

Use fine flecked paper for these lanterns, or decorate plain paper yourself: gilt or silver paint sprayed through a stencil or doily looks especially good.

**YOU WILL NEED:** oblong of paper 75 × 27.5 cm/30 × 11 in, two 80 cm/32 in lengths and four 30 cm/12 in lengths of fine plastic-coated wire, wirecutters, pliers, sticky (transparent) tape, 4 tassels, ribbon for hanging.

**1** Press a narrow hem along both long sides of the paper. Fold a 1 cm/½ in hem along both short sides. Fold the paper widthways into two and press, then fold each half into two again and press to mark the four sides of the lantern. Lay one of the short lengths of wire along each of the three creases and along one of the 1 cm/½ in hems, pushing the ends of the wire through the hems top and bottom. Tape the wires in the creases.

**2** Tape the long pieces of wire under the narrow hems at top and bottom. Bend these wires into three corners to correspond to the creases in the paper. Stick the two short ends of the paper together with tape to make the fourth corner.

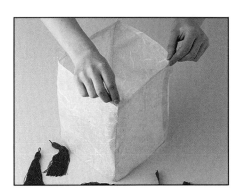

**3** Neaten the ends of the wires on the bottom edge with pliers, making loops at all four corners. Attach tassels to the loops.

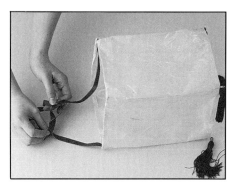

**4** Bend the ends of the wire into loops at two opposite corners on the top edge and attach hanging ribbons. Twist the other wires and trim to neaten.

# PICNIC EXTRAVAGANZA

*A*century ago, a picnic in a wealthy household involved a major feat of planning for the staff: there were tables, chairs, the linen, the silver, crockery (china) and glassware, rugs and cushions, flasks of spirits for mixing aperitifs, wine baskets, bottles of home-made lemonade and burners for making tea or coffee; and that was before beginning on the business of the food!

Sadly, not only has the picnic lost a lot of its glory, but it is often reduced to soggy sandwiches with a can of fizzy drink (soda) or a vacuum flask of stale tea. There are, however, still occasions when the picnic can reign supreme: on the lawn at an open-air concert, perhaps, or at a major horse racing event. But why set the fun aside for such rare occasions? It is still possible to enjoy a stylish meal and share convivial company with a little forethought and less formality.

## PICNIC PLANNERS
The approach depends on the style of picnic, whether it is a fun family occasion or an elegant dining occasion.

### Fun Family Picnic Ideas
❖ No need to resort to sandwiches! Bring cold fried chicken, individual pies, spicy meatballs, a pizza slice that cuts into fingers neatly, a large quiche and a bowl of salad. Take bowls of dip and bought snacks (chips) to dunk.
❖ Pack plastic plates and cups. Try to keep utensil requirements to a minimum, concentrating on finger food and items that can be eaten with a fork.
❖ Take lots of absorbent kitchen paper (paper towels) as well as colourful paper napkins.

### Picnic Checklist

- Finger food
- Wine and/or beer
- Alcohol-free drinks
- Ice
- Plastic plates and cups
- Cutlery (flatware)
- Table linen, if using
- Paper napkins, if using
- Chiller bag (cooler)
- Absorbent kitchen paper (paper towels)
- Plastic ground sheet
- Picnic blanket
- Picnic basket

❖ Use coolers to keep the food fresh and drinks cool. Carry plastic bottles which weigh less than glass and avoid cans which cannot be resealed if the drink is part used.
❖ A plastic ground sheet is a good idea to prevent insects creeping up into a picnic blanket. Lay a blanket on top.

*Straw hats protect picnic-goers from the sun and add a graceful note to the proceedings, especially on special occasions.*

*Bring a colourful assortment of picnicware which is easily packed away and will not break easily. Remember to bring a thick rug too.*

### Simple Cloth Idea

For a large picnic, decorate an old sheet with lots of simple appliqué flower shapes in different colours.

Stitch ribbons on the corners and halfway along the sides, then tie these to meat skewers or tent pegs and hammer them into the ground to prevent the cloth flying away.

❖ A picnic basket looks splendid and it is useful for holding chinaware and utensils, interleaving plates with napkins, wrapping glasses in tea-towels (dish-towels); however, a chiller bag (cooler) is essential for food. A rigid box-type chiller (thick plastic cooler) is best for delicate foods which will be squashed easily.

❖ Prepare a couple of baskets which can also be used to weight down the corners of the picnic cloth. Fill one with fruit and the other with bread, rolls and biscuits (crackers).

❖ When you plan to meet friends for a special picnic, suggest that everyone dresses for the occasion; women in flowing skirts and men in smart but comfortable casual wear. Sun shades and straw hats complete the image.

### Special Occasion Picnic Ideas

❖ Simple foods to transport can make the most elegant picnics: smoked salmon sandwiches, a pot of lumpfish roe, Parma ham (prosciutto) and fragrant melons, smoked fish pâté, a special cold meat pie.

❖ Take a beautiful linen cloth and matching napkins, and lay them on a plain blanket base.

❖ Pack inexpensive flutes for champagne; sparkling wine will do! A dash of bitters with sparkling mineral water (seltzer) makes a good non-alcoholic drink for drivers.

### Fun Drinks for Picnics

Take the opportunity to recapture childhood joys with these fun drinks.

**FLAVOURED MILK** Very sweet fruit syrups make traditional childhood milk shakes. Strong fresh coffee essence or cocoa diluted with boiling water are more sophisticated flavourings. Pour the flavouring into the glass to taste, then whisk in cold milk. Add scoops of ice cream for really special results.

**ICE CREAM SODA** Place scoops of ice cream into tall glasses and top with fizzy lemonade or your favourite fizzy drink.

**NON-ALCOHOLIC FRUIT PUNCH** Base this on grape juice, unsweetened apple juice or exotic fruit juice flavours such as mango, pineapple and passion fruit juice. Add whole strawberries, finely sliced cucumber, orange slices, some seedless green grapes and top up with sparkling mineral water (seltzer) or tonic depending on how sweet a result you require. Angostura Bitters can be added to sparkling mineral water (seltzer). Don't forget sprigs of fresh mint or lemon balm if they are available.

# GRAVADLAX

### SERVES 16–20

A superb dish for an extra special picnic. You really do need a lot of fresh dill to make gravadlax. If you are buying the small 15 g/ ½ oz package of fresh dill, then think in terms of two to go under the fish, four to go between the fillets and another two on top – plus the dill for the sauce.

2.75–3 kg/6–7 lb whole salmon
10 tablespoons sugar
10 tablespoons sea salt
1 tablespoon coarsely crushed black peppercorns
lots of dill

SAUCE
6 tablespoons Dijon mustard
4 tablespoons caster (superfine) sugar
4 tablespoons cider vinegar
250 ml/8 fl oz (1 cup) sunflower oil
25 g/1 oz fresh dill, chopped

Make a point of telling the fishmonger or your fish merchant that you are going to pickle the salmon, as the fish must be really fresh. Have the fish descaled, gutted and filleted. It is important that the fish scales are removed before the salmon is filleted, otherwise it is virtually impossible to keep the scales away from the flesh.

Trim the fins from the fillets and make sure all the fine bones are removed, cutting them away with a very sharp knife. Cut away any small bones running down the length of the fillet. Mix together the sugar, salt and crushed peppercorns. Scatter plenty of dill in the base of a dish which is large enough to hold the salmon fillets. Sprinkle a little of the salt mixture in the base of the dish, then lay 1 fillet skin down on the dill.

Top the fish fillet with a generous covering of dill sprigs, and sprinkle half the salt mixture over. Lay the second fillet on top, skin side up, with the head end to the tail of the fillet in the dish. Sprinkle with the remaining salt mixture and top with a thick layer of dill. Cover with cling film (plastic wrap), then foil. Place a baking dish on top of the fish and weight it down in several places with heavy cans if you do not have any weights. Put the fish in the refrigerator and leave it to slowly pickle for about 3 days.

The sugar and salt create a pickling liquid on

standing. Turn the pair of fillets over twice a day during pickling and baste between them with the liquid. The fish may be removed from the pickle after 2 days and it will keep for 4–5 days in the refrigerator.

When you are ready to serve the gravadlax, scrap all the dill off the fish. Remove it from the pickle and mop the fillets on absorbent kitchen paper (paper towels). The salmon is now ready for slicing very thinly at an acute angle.

To store the fillets, wrap them closely in cling film and chill them at all times.

For the sauce, beat together the mustard, sugar and vinegar in a bowl until the sugar completely dissolves. Gradually trickle in the oil, beating vigorously all the time, as if making mayonnaise. The oil will combine with the mustard mixture to make a thick sauce. Stir in the dill. The sauce will keep in an air-tight container in the refrigerator for several days.

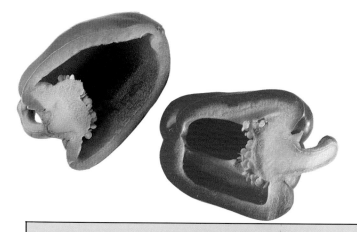

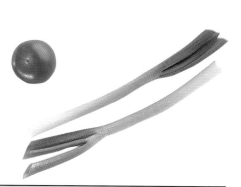

## Decorated Pebbles

Painting and decorating pebbles is a pastime that is ideal for seaside picnics. It also makes the ideal implements for weighting down the corners of a picnic cloth.

**PAINTING** Pick smooth, fairly flat pebbles and begin with small ones. Children like to colour the pebbles with simple mediums like felt-tip pens or acrylic paints. For a more interesting finish, mark out the

design in felt-tip pen, then paint over it with a more exotic medium, such as enamel paint. Metallic gold, silver, bronze, brass, copper and other finishes are available.

A nondescript marbled pattern may be applied or a simple pattern of circles and stripes, even spots, works well. If you want to paint a more complicated image, then try copying a pattern or painting a base and stencilling a design on the stones. Leave the paints to dry completely. The pebbles may be

varnished if desired and allowed to dry for a further 24 hours.

**DECOUPAGE** If you are unsure of your talents with paint and brush, then try an alternative decorative technique. Paint the pebbles with a base colour, then cut out patterns and pictures from glossy magazines or wrapping paper. Use a strong glue to stick the cut-out pieces to the stones, building up your own combination of images. Leave the glue to dry, then varnish.

## RAISED CHICKEN AND HAM PIE

—— SERVES 10 ——

This chicken and ham pie is perfect for any special occasion.

25 g/1 oz (2 tablespoons) butter
1 onion, chopped
50 g/2 oz (1 cup) fresh breadcrumbs
2 tablespoons chopped fresh sage
2 tablespoons chopped fresh parsley
1 tablespoon chopped fresh thyme, or 1½ teaspoons dried thyme
450 g/1 lb (3 cups) lean cooked ham, diced
1 kg/2 lb boneless chicken breasts (chicken breast halves), skinned
salt and freshly ground black pepper
beaten egg
250 ml/8 fl oz (1 cup) chicken aspic, see cook's tip

HOT WATER CRUST PASTRY (DOUGH)
500 g/18 oz (4½ cups) plain (all-purpose) flour
½ teaspoon salt
175 g/6 oz (¾ cup) lard (shortening)
6 tablespoons water
6 tablespoons milk

**1** Melt the butter in a small saucepan. Add the onion and cook for 5 minutes, stirring occasionally. Mix together the onion with the breadcrumbs, sage, parsley, thyme and ham. Cut the chicken breasts into thin slices and season the pieces well. Set the oven at 200°C/400°F/Gas 6. Have a 23 cm/9 in raised pie mould ready, lightly greased and with the base and clips in place.

**2** Now make the pastry (dough): mix together the flour and salt in a bowl. Set a clean, heatproof bowl over a pan of simmering, not boiling, water. Place the lard (shortening) in a saucepan and add the water and milk. Heat gently until the lard melts, then bring the liquid to the boil as quickly as possible. Tip the liquid into the bowl of flour and mix it in immediately.

**3** Gather the dough together and knead it quickly until smooth. Cut off one-third of the dough and place it in the bowl over hot water. Cover tightly with cling film (plastic wrap).

**4** Line the pie mould with the larger portion of dough. Work fairly quickly as the pastry sets, tends to crack and becomes more difficult to manage as it cools. Roll out the pastry into an oval shape which is larger than the top of the mould but thick — do not try to roll out the pastry large enough to line the tin: the technique is to press the pastry into the shape.

**5** Lift the pastry over the mould, keeping the edges around the inside of the top rim, then press it down the sides, stretching the upper part of the dough downwards to avoid breaking it towards the base. As the dough stretches towards the bottom, press it carefully into all the flutes, around the base and press it into the corners.

**6** Layer the chicken in the pie with the ham mixture. Roll out all but a small piece of the reserved dough to cover the pie. Dampen the top edge with hot water. Press on the lid.

**7** Pinch the edges together to seal them well and to flute them in a decorative border. Make a hole in the middle of the pie.

**8** Mould leaves from the remaining pastry and attach with a little beaten egg. Mould a ball of pastry to cover the hole in the middle. Glaze the pastry with beaten egg. Bake for 40 minutes.

**9** Have the egg glaze ready to brush the pie when you remove the sides of the mould: the glaze sets on the hot pastry and helps to strengthen it. Remove the clips and ease the sides of the mould away carefully, using the point of a knife to gently loosen any tiny areas which may be stuck. Working as speedily as you can, brush the sides with egg and return

the pie to the oven. Reduce the oven temperature to 180°F/350°C/Gas 4 and cook for a further 40 minutes. Cover the top of the pie with foil after 20 minutes to prevent it becoming too dark. Glaze the sides of the pie with more egg, if necessary, during this final cooking. Remove the pie from the oven and leave to cool completely. Meanwhile, make up the chicken aspic. Cut around the ball of pastry on top of the pie and insert a funnel into the hole. Pour in the aspic until the pie is full, then replace the pastry ball. Chill for a couple of hours so the aspic sets.

### COOK'S TIP
Either buy a packet of chicken aspic or make good chicken stock, then sprinkle unflavoured powdered gelatine over the hot stock, allowing 1 tablespoon to each 600 ml/1 pint (2½ cups). Sparkling aspic is not essential, if the stock is well strained, you can just clarify it first.

### Lining a Raised Pie Mould

It is important to keep the pastry (dough) hot and to keep your hands warm all the time. Keep the pastry which is not actually being worked covered in a bowl over hot water.

The knack of pressing the pastry into the mould is to try and keep the edges of the dough near the rim of the mould. When the mould is more or less lined, gently ease the edges of the pastry right up to protrude over the top of the mould's rim. Make sure the pastry fits snugly all round.

# CHILDREN'S PARTIES

*Children's parties are arranged for the afternoon, unless there is some reason for having them at a different time of day, for example, combined with an outing at a weekend. They last for about two hours around tea time and consist of food and activities. There may be a sit-down tea (snack) or a buffet or simply cake and ice cream: alternatively, some people opt for one simple, favourite food such as a hot-dog and burger barbecue in summer.*

*You have to be well organized about getting the whole show up and running, but once the children are happy and relaxed they will entertain themselves. Arrange a few games but do try to structure the whole of the party. Remember to have prizes ready and packed and try to make sure that all the age groups get a chance to win something to avoid tears and disappointment. Then there are the essential goodie bags (party favor bags) to be taken home.*

## ENTERTAINMENT

Many parents opt to engage a professional children's entertainer for the afternoon, particularly for the 4–8 age group. The entertainment usually consists of magic tricks, clowning and storytelling – audience participation is welcome! Ideally, the entertainer should be there as the guests arrive so that the entertainment can start as soon as the last guest has been received. The show is usually about an hour long, finishing just in time for refreshments.

Older children, 9–12, enjoy activity birthday parties, and this is an excellent way to get a group of energetic children out of the house. The following pursuits are popular with this age group: skating, swimming, football, baseball, visiting a gymnasium.

## PARTY THEMES

A fancy dress (costume) theme is one way to get the whole party off to a good start. Try to avoid anything too complicated which involves hours of work for parents.

### Pirates

A few simple cardboard swords or daggers and a scarf tied around the head with a patch over the eye does

---

**Children's Party Checklist**

- Invitations
- Organize professional children's entertainer, if using
- Book activity, if using
- Party menu: snack bags or range of children's party foods
- Range of soft drinks
- Ice
- Gift bags (party favor bags)
- Ideas for party games
- Props for party games

---

quite well. Organize a treasure hunt in the house or garden and give each child a little pot of treasure to take home. Dress up plastic tubs as pots of treasure, filling them with sweets, a rubber (eraser) and party toys all wrapped in gold paper. Tie them up in plastic bags with gold ribbon.

---

### Circus Party

Children dress up as the performers and the ringmaster. This goes very well with a trip to the circus!

### Monster Party

All children love pretending to be monsters, but they can be very noisy when they run around roaring! Make a monster-shaped cake from chocolate sponge, then outline the shape with melted chocolate put into a greaseproof paper (waxed paper) piping (pastry) bag. Cut the tip off the bag so that the chocolate flows. When outlined you can fill in the middle. White chocolate can be coloured green, orange and yellow with powder food colouring to pipe details on the monsters.

### Nursery Rhymes

Choose any of the characters from a nursery rhyme: either pick one rhyme as a theme or let each guest pick their favourite rhyme.

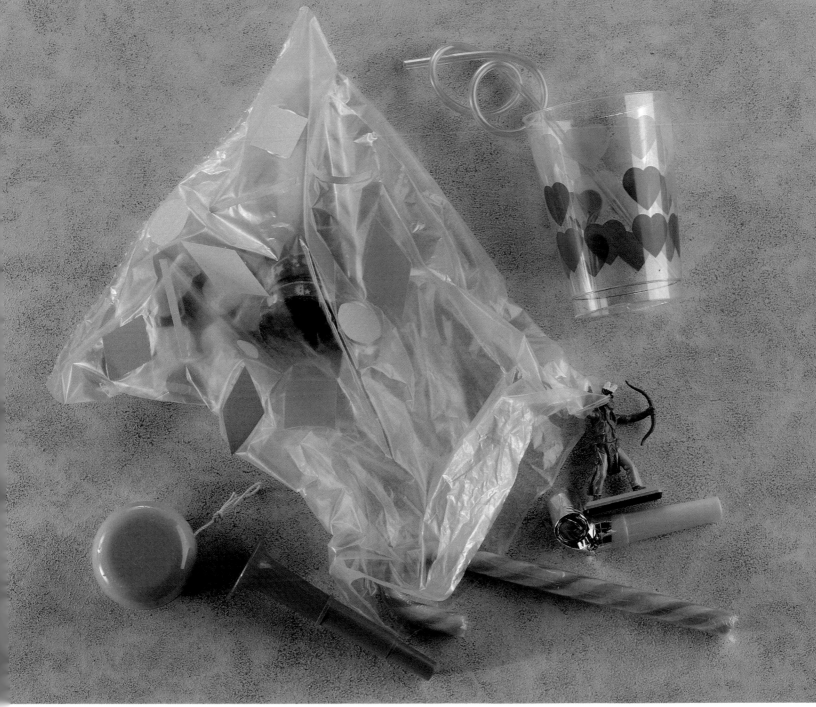

*Fill children's take-away gift bags with an assortment of small toys and candies.*

### Zoo Party

Another theme to combine with a trip! Children dress up as the animals. These do not have to be complicated costumes: a simple T-shirt and tights with lots of pictures of the relevant animal make the point.

### Viking Party

This is a good theme for slightly older children. The helmets are fun to make and robes around the shoulders with swords complete the picture. Long plaits (braids) of string turn little girls into Viking maidens.

### Alice in Wonderland Party

Make playing card outfits by cutting two pieces of card (posterboard) which are then strung from the shoulders of the children. Cover the back of the cards with suitable wrapping paper.

Cut out numbers and the symbols for the suit to stick on the front card. Hold the cards in place on the shoulders and sides with ribbon to keep them in place. Stick the ribbon on the inside of the cards with strong tape or staples. Red or black tights and T-shirts are worn underneath.

Other characters include the Cheshire cat, Alice, the Duchess, the White Rabbit and the Mad Hatter.

### Hat Party

A simple idea for children of all ages: get the youngsters to make their own hats which can be as fantastic as they wish. There must be a hat parade and a prize for the best effort.

### Gift Bags

❖ Buy small colourful carrier (plastic) bags or decorate brown or white paper lunch bags instead.
❖ Buy glued paper shapes and shiny stars or cartoon characters and stick them all over plastic freezer bags before opening them out.
❖ Cut coloured paper labels and write the names of the children on them. Make a hole in each label and thread a plastic-covered wire tie through. Use this to close the bag.
❖ Fill the bags with sweets, small notebooks, pencils, rubbers (erasers) and party poppers (if the children are old enough).

---

**Snack Bags**

An easy way of coping with catering, and a particularly good idea when children are eating outdoors, is to make snack bags.
❖ Decorate plastic bags and fill them with refreshments: an individually wrapped chocolate biscuit (cookie), a peanut butter and jelly sandwich cut into fun shapes, popcorn, a banana, a pot (container) of yogurt and a plastic spoon. The fun is more in the presentation than the food itself.
❖ Pack an individual carton of juice with its own straw and a paper napkin in each bag.

---

## INDOOR ACTIVITIES

Here are some ideas for children's games that can easily take place indoors if the weather is rainy or not warm enough to go outside:

### Musical Hats

A good game for an older children's party. A parent takes charge of the music. The children form a circle. Hats are given to all but one of the children. When the music starts the hats are passed from head to head. When the music stops the child without a hat on his or her head is out of the game (a forfeit prize can be offered). Each time the music stops a hat is discarded. The child to survive with a hat to the end is the winner.

### Pass the Parcel

An old favourite for children's parties. A special prize is wrapped in the middle of the parcel and fun prizes are included in each layer of paper. The parcel moves from person to person until the music stops, then the person who is holding the parcel has to remove a layer.

### Blind Man's Buff

A popular children's game. The child who is picked to start the game has to wear a blindfold. The organizer turns the child around several times and the other children move about. Then the child with the blindfold on moves about until he or she picks out a person. By feeling the hair, face and apparel of the person the child has to guess who it is. If the child guesses correctly, the picked person becomes the next blind man.

### Pinning the Tail on the Donkey

Draw a picture of a donkey without a tail. The tail is made from a length of cord, with a drawing pin (thumb tack) stuck in the end. The donkey should be stuck on a board. Everyone takes it in turns to try to pin the tail onto the picture – with a blindfold on! The person who gets the tail nearest the rear end of the donkey wins a prize.

### Forfeit

The children sit in a circle and one child spins a bottle placed in the centre of the circle. Whoever has the open end of the bottle pointing at him or her when the bottle stops spinning has to perform a dare or forfeit. It's probably best if the organizer has already prepared these in advance. Write a number of forfeits on pieces of paper and place each one in an envelope. The forfeit child then chooses an envelope. The forfeits may include such things as singing a song, miming an animal or dancing a jig. The forfeits should always be achievable ideas which make the child proud to have fulfilled the task.

## OUTDOOR ACTIVITIES

Children welcome outdoor activities. The following also work well for parties with mixed age groups.

### Washing Line Race

A good game that can involve both children and adults. Have two teams and give each team a basket of washing. The basket must contain exactly the same items with some fun things which are difficult to hang. For example, include a couple of towels, 4 socks, and a hat in each basket along with some other items. Each team has a peg (clothespin) bag. When the game starts, the first person hangs up the washing, the second person takes it in, the third hangs it out again and so on, until all the team members have had a go, then the first person takes the washing in again and shouts "dry".

### Cookie Hunt

Cookies are packed and hidden in the garden for an outdoor party. Children and adults alike enjoy the search.

### Egg and Spoon Race

The company is divided into two teams. Everyone has a spoon and an egg (hard-boiled) is given to the first person in each team. At the signal to "go" the egg is passed from spoon to spoon – without any assistance from hands – until it passes along the team and back again. The first to shout "finished" is the winning team.

# ICE CREAM BIRTHDAY CAKE

———— SERVES ABOUT 16 ————

This novel cake is extremely simple to make and it can be partially made a couple of weeks ahead, ready for finishing off at the last minute before serving.

*900 ml/1½ pints (3¾ cups) each of strawberry, vanilla and pistachio ice cream, or any three flavours*
*350 g/12 oz crushed chocolate chip cookies*
*350 g/12 oz (12 squares) chocolate, coarsely grated*
*225 g/8 oz (1 cup) chocolate hazelnut spread*
*100 g/4 oz (½ cup) cream cheese*
*jelly sweets (gum drops)*
*candies and holders*
*indoor sparklers*

Line the base of a 20 cm/8 in square cake tin (pan) with foil. Scoop the strawberry ice cream into the tin and press it down in an even layer. Sprinkle with a third of the cookies, then freeze for about 15 minutes, until firm.

Scoop the vanilla ice cream over the cookies, spread it evenly and cover with half the remaining cookies. Then freeze for at least 15–30 minutes, or until the ice cream is firm. Next add a layer of pistachio ice cream and the remaining cookies. Freeze the cake overnight if it is to be stored, then seal in a plastic bag.

Dip a palette knife (metal spatula) in hot water and slide it between the cake and the tin. Then invert the tin onto a board. Remove the tin and lining paper. Press the grated chocolate on the side of the cake and place in the freezer. Mix the chocolate hazelnut spread with the cream cheese, then spoon some of it into a small greaseproof paper (waxed paper) piping (pastry) bag fitted with a plain piping nozzle (tube). Spoon the remaining cream into a piping bag fitted with a star nozzle.

Use the small piping bag to pipe 'Happy Birthday' and the name of the child on top of the cake. Pipe stars of chocolate all around the top edge of the cake and top them with the jelly sweets (gum drops). Stick the candles in their holders on top of the cake, then add some sparklers. Light the sparklers and candles before carrying the cake to the table.

## THINGS ON STICKS

This may seem old-fashioned, but nibbles (snacks) on sticks are ideal for children's parties, particularly for excited youngsters who are not ready to sit down and eat a meal.

Cut cubes of cheese and ham to skewer on cocktail sticks (toothpicks). Pieces of cucumber, cauliflower and cherry tomatoes are also suitable. Use a grapefruit or orange to hold the cocktail sticks.

### Tasty Sausages

These are popular with most age groups. To make, mix 2 tablespoons of tomato ketchup with a tablespoon of oil, a teaspoon of mild mustard, a finely chopped spring onion (green onion) and a tablespoon of grated onion. Cut 8 skinless link pork sausages into chunks and toss them in the ketchup mixture. Fry in a frying pan (skillet) until browned all over, turning the pieces often with a slotted spoon. Leave to cool before serving on cocktail sticks (toothpicks).

### Ham Rolls

Spread slices of cooked ham thinly with soft cheese, then roll them up neatly, like a Swiss (jelly) roll. Use a serrated knife to slice the roll and stick a cocktail stick (toothpick) in each slice to keep the ham in place.

### Crispy Bread Chunks

Set the oven at 200°C/400°F/Gas 6. Cut a small French loaf into bite-sized chunks. Place in a large plastic bag. Add 6 tablespoons of grated Parmesan cheese, 4 tablespoons of oil, a crushed garlic clove and seasoning to taste. Hold the bag shut and shake it really well. Tip the cubes of bread onto a baking sheet and cook for about 15 minutes, or until lightly browned.

### Sweet Things

Most children have a sweet tooth. Dip cubes of cake, marshmallows, chunks of canned fruit and banana in melted chocolate, then skewer on cocktail sticks (toothpicks).

*Pizza Tray Bake.*

# PIZZA TRAY BAKE

———— MAKES ABOUT 48 PIECES ————

350 g/12 oz (3 cups) strong plain (bread) flour
1 teaspoon salt
25 g/1 oz (2 tablespoons) butter
1 sachet (envelope) easy-blend (quick-rising)
dried yeast
1 teaspoon caster (superfine) sugar
250 ml/8 fl oz (1 cup) lukewarm water
2 large onions, finely chopped
6 tablespoons tomato purée (paste)
4 tablespoons oil
1 teaspoon dried oregano
1 garlic clove, crushed
salt and freshly ground black pepper
225 g/8 oz (2 cups) grated Cheddar cheese

Mix together the flour and salt in a bowl. Rub in (cut in) the butter, then stir in the yeast and sugar. Mix in enough water to form a fairly firm dough. Turn out the dough onto a lightly floured work surface and knead thoroughly for 10 minutes, until it is smooth and elastic. Grease a 33 × 28 cm/13 × 11 in shallow baking pan. Roll out the dough to line the pan. Turn up the edges slightly to form a neat rim.

Mix together the onions, tomato purée (paste), oil, oregano and garlic. Add seasoning to taste, then spread the mixture over the bread dough. Sprinkle the cheese over the top and cover loosely with cling film (plastic wrap). Leave in a warm place for about 45 minutes, or until the base is risen slightly. Meanwhile, set the oven at 200°C/400°F/Gas 6.

Bake the pizza for 40–45 minutes, until it is browned on top and cooked through. Leave to cool, then cut into 4 cm/1½ in squares.

## COOK'S TIP

The basic topping used on the bread base can be varied by adding sliced mushrooms, diced green pepper (sweet bell pepper), flaked canned tuna, diced cooked ham, diced rindless bacon, sweetcorn or spicy sausage, such as pepperoni. The choice of filling is up to you and depends on the age of the children.

Remember, however, that simple flavours are a good option when entertaining a large group of children who may have varied tastes but equally firm ideas about what they will not eat.

## Quick Dessert Ideas

❖ Make a quick banana and orange ice cream by mashing 4 bananas with the juice of an orange. Mix in 6 tablespoons of warmed orange marmalade and 600 ml/1 pint (2½ cups) Greek-style yogurt. Freeze until half frozen, then beat the mixture really well and freeze again until firm.

❖ Make pancakes (crêpes) and spread them with a little orange marmalade, then roll them up. Brush with melted butter and sprinkle with caster (superfine) sugar, then cover with foil. Gently reheat the pancakes in the oven just before serving.

❖ Sweeten plain yogurt to taste with honey. Layer crushed coconut cookies in small dishes with sliced fresh strawberries and the yogurt, ending with cookies. Place a whole strawberry on top of each dessert.

# CHOCOLATE NAME TREATS

MAKES ABOUT 30

*225 g/8 oz (2 cups) plain (all-purpose) flour*
*175 g/6 oz (¾ cup) butter, diced*
*50 g/2 oz (¼ cup) caster (superfine) sugar*
*2 tablespoons cocoa powder*
*1–2 tablespoons water*

DECORATION
*4–6 tablespoons apricot jam, warmed and sieved (strained)*
*100 g/4 oz ready-made sugarpaste (rolled fondant) or roll-out fondant icing (dry fondant)*
*icing (confectioners') sugar, for dusting*
*food colouring pens*

**1** Grease 2 baking sheets. Place the flour in a bowl and rub in (cut in) the butter, then stir in the sugar and cocoa powder. Mix in just enough water to bind the ingredients into a dough. Roll out the dough on a surface lightly dusted with flour and use cutters of various shapes to stamp out biscuits (cookies). Make a hole at the top of each shape with a skewer.

Place the biscuits on the prepared baking sheets, prick them all over, then chill them for 30 minutes before baking. Meanwhile, set the oven at 180°C/350°F/Gas 4. Bake the biscuits for 10–15 minutes, or until firm to the touch. Transfer to a wire rack to cool.

**2** To decorate the biscuits, brush each with a little apricot jam. Roll out the sugarpaste (rolled fondant) or fondant icing (dry fondant) on a surface lightly dusted with icing (confectioners') sugar. Use the same biscuit cutters to stamp out shapes, then press them onto the biscuits, rolling them gently if necessary to cover the surface of each biscuit neatly. Use bright food colouring pens to write the names of the children on the icing.

Take a small piece of the icing trimmings and pound it to a thick paste with a few drops of water in a mug. Use this to stick the sugar decorations on the biscuits. Use food colouring pens to draw in a few details around the decoration. For example, you may apply a pair of sugar flowers to a biscuit and draw in a couple of leaves or stems and leaves.

**3** If you feel artistic, it is also fun to add decorative drawings to the child's name. Strings of balloons float from the tails on some letters or tiny flowers can be drawn to accentuate the dot on an "i". A small cat sits well beside some letters. Use the biscuits as name tags for take-home gifts. Thread each biscuit with ribbon, wrap in cling film (plastic wrap) and tie in place.

## Cool Drinks

As well as the usual fresh fruit juices and fizzy drinks (soda) which most children enjoy, remember these:

❖ Make chocolate milk shakes by mixing 2 tablespoons cocoa powder with 3 tablespoons boiling water and 2 tablespoons sugar. Beat in 600 ml/1 pint (2½ cups) chilled milk.

❖ Fill a glass one-third full with plain yogurt, then top up with a fruit-flavoured fizzy drink (soda).

❖ Drop a scoop or scoops of vanilla ice cream in a tall glass and top up with fizzy lemonade.

❖ Mix 1 sliced orange and 1 quartered, cored and sliced apple with the juice of 2 oranges, then top up with fizzy lemonade to make a light fruit punch. Alternatively, add fresh strawberries and kiwi fruit slices, which also taste good. For teenage parties, add mint sprigs.

## Witch's Hat

The well-dressed witch would never go out without a hat like this one. You can also make wizards' hats from simple cone shapes, decorated with extra stars and moons.

**YOU WILL NEED:** black card (posterboard), pair of compasses, scissors, craft knife and cutting mat, stapler, sticky tape, raffia, silver wrapping paper, paper adhesive.

**1** On a sheet of black card (posterboard), draw a circle large enough for the brim of the hat.

**2** Cut out the circle using scissors.

**3** Draw a second circle inside the first large enough to fit the wearer's head. Cut around this line using a craft knife.

**4** Measure the diameter of the brim and cut another circle of black card measuring about 15 cm/6 in larger for the crown. Cut a slit from the edge into the centre.

**5** Fold this circle into a cone shape to fit inside the brim. Staple the cone in position where the card overlaps.

**6** Tape the cone to the brim on the inside.

**7** Tape raffia inside the cone at the back of the hat to form the witch's hair.

**8** Draw a star shape on silver wrapping paper.

**9** Cut out the paper star.

**10** Using paper adhesive, stick the star on the front of the cone.

## Folded Paper Garlands

These simple two-coloured garlands look like a compact pile of square folds but open out into soft twists of colour.

**YOU WILL NEED:** crêpe paper in two colours, scissors, stapler.

**1** Cut strips of crêpe paper about 7.5 cm/3 in wide in two different colours.

**2** Hold the ends of the two strips at right angles and staple together.

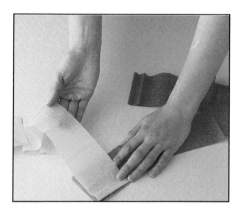

**3** Fold the lower (yellow) strip squarely over the upper (pink) strip. Keep the fold steady with the fingers of your spare hand.

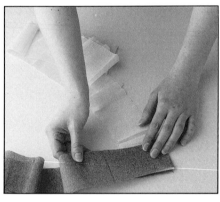

**4** Now fold the lower (pink) strip over the upper (yellow) strip. Continue folding each strip of paper over the other in turn, making a neat square stack of folds.

**5** When all the paper is used, staple the two colours together in the last fold.

**6** When ready to hang the garland, lift one end and the folds will open out.

# Feasts and Festivals

# CELEBRATING EASTER

*E*aster weekend heralds the dawning of spring, new blooms in the garden and a sunny approach to entertaining. Time to perk up under an Easter bonnet, to beat the children at an egg-rolling race or indulge in a chocolate egg hunt.

*Like Christmas, this is very much a family holiday with parties geared towards children and adults alike. Aim for a bright start on Easter Sunday by serving coloured eggs for breakfast, then make the most of seasonal culinary treats by turning out perfect roast lamb. This section includes all the extras you need to plan an old-fashioned Easter, with a cook's checklist too.*

## EASTER ENTERTAINING

Lunch on Easter Sunday is a special occasion for many people, and it is often the focal point of the Easter break. Fortunately, it is usually a re-laxed event, when timings are not critical. This makes the menu a simple decision – a roast of spring lamb, a seasonal delight in some areas, with an assortment of young vegetables such as baby carrots, mangetout (sugar snaps) and new potatoes. End the meal with a light dessert – a fruit salad or lemon mousse perhaps.

Easter is also the time for making sweets (candies) and chocolates, parti-cularly chocolate Easter eggs. If you don't feel inclined to make your own Easter eggs, you can always mould small egg shapes from marzipan (almond paste) and roll them in cocoa powder to make imitation eggs.

### Easter Checklist

- Easter eggs
- Simnel cake, if required
- Easter menu
- Flowers
- Easter games
- Props for Easter games
- House cleaning and tidying

### Home-made Coloured Boiled Eggs

❖ Add home-made colouring to the water when boiling eggs for breakfast but remember that this must be edible. Pick white-shelled eggs for best results. Use a small pan and boil up to four eggs at a time otherwise the colour will not be concentrated enough to tint the eggs. Try turmeric, uncooked beetroot (beets) or the liquid squeezed from cooked spinach.
❖ Paint hard-boiled eggs with edible food colouring and serve them in a basket for a special Easter first course. Serve bowls of mayonnaise and pesto so that everyone can shell their own eggs and coat them with mayonnaise.

## HIDDEN CHOCOLATE EGGS

White-shelled eggs give best results. Blow the eggs and wash them, then dry thoroughly. Use a pin to scrape away the shell around one hole and to enlarge it so that you can fit the point of a small piping tube in.

Seal the hole at the opposite end of the egg by spreading a little butter in it, then stick a small piece of tape across the butter. Stand the egg in an egg cup.

Use a fabric piping (pastry) bag and the tube. Melt plain (semi-sweet), milk or white chocolate in a bowl over hot water. Fill the bag with the chocolate, turning the tip up to prevent it running out. Fill the egg with chocolate through the hole. Leave to harden.

The outside of the egg may be painted. Use edible food colourings to paint the egg. The liquids are fine for brushing large areas but the paste col-ours are more suitable for fine work. Edible colouring pens are useful.

### Easter Egg Hunt

Devise an Easter egg hunt to entertain the children while lunch is cooking on Easter Sunday.
❖ Work out the route of the hunt on paper first, then write out clues on slips of paper and hide them at the chosen stages about the house and/or garden leading to a final hiding place. Small chocolate eggs can also be hidden with each clue.
❖ If more than one age group is involved, it may be best to create a separate, easier hunt for the younger children to avoid tears.
❖ Alternatively, designate one or two rooms as "hunt" rooms and hide small eggs everywhere for the children to find. Give each child a bag or small basket in which to collect their eggs.

*Make the most of spring bulbs to create an Easter basket of flowers. Fill it with a mass of daffodils, tulips and miniature narcissi and use it for the centrepiece of the Easter table.*

## Cook's Checklist

❖ Marinate lamb in rosemary, grated orange rind (peel) and olive oil before roasting. Glaze with a little port heated with redcurrant jelly before serving.

❖ Make a plaited (braided) bread ring using a rich dough made with milk instead of water. Put on a greased baking sheet to rise. Press hard-boiled eggs around the ring and leave, covered, in a warm place. Glaze with beaten egg and bake with the hard-boiled eggs in place. Paint the eggs decoratively when cooled. Fresh boiled eggs may be used to replace the baked eggs if they are to be eaten with the bread.

### MAKING CHOCOLATE EGGS

These chocolate eggs are slightly fussy to make and they take time if you are going to achieve good results. Egg moulds can be found at any good kitchen suppliers (candy-making party supplier or craft store).

Melt the chocolate in a heatproof bowl placed over a saucepan of hot, not boiling, water. The bowl should be smaller than the pan so that it sits on top of the rim. This prevents any steam or drops of water from getting into the chocolate. If water does get in the chocolate it will separate and thicken, then it cannot be used.

Thoroughly polish the inside of the moulds with a pad of absorbent kitchen paper (paper towels), particularly when using metal. Metal moulds are more difficult to use as the eggs are not released as easily.

Use a fine bristle brush to paint the inside of the mould evenly with melted chocolate. Leave until just dry, then paint on another layer. Continue until a thick, even layer is built up, then leave to set thoroughly in a cool place but not in the refrigerator.

Lay out a sheet of greaseproof (waxed) paper on which to invert the eggs. They are released from the moulds by flexing the container gently. Plastic moulds are pressed around the rim; metal moulds have to be carefully flexed and the edge of the egg may be released in parts with the point of a knife, taking great care not to crack the chocolate. Once air breaks the vacuum between the chocolate and the mould the egg will come out.

Handle the eggs as little as possible as fingerprints dull the surface of the chocolate. Keep your hands very cold by running them under cold water and drying them. Fine cotton gloves are worn by confectioners when handling chocolate.

A long wide palette knife (metal spatula) or a large flat metal fish slice (pancake turner) helps with picking up the eggs. Seal the two halves together with a little melted chocolate. Then leave to dry.

Use a plastic egg box to support the egg while decorating it. Melt more chocolate and allow it to cool for piping. Place it in a small greaseproof (waxed) paper piping (pastry) bag fitted with a star nozzle (tube). Fold the end of the bag down to keep the chocolate in, then practise piping a star or

*Brighten up the home at Easter with bowls of spring flowers.*

## Easter Egg Gift

This Easter egg is made of pastillage (gum paste). It is easier to make than a chocolate egg and it may be filled with home-made sweets, chocolates or truffles. It can also be used as a container for a small gift, such as a folded and wrapped tie or a brooch.

Colour pastillage (gum paste) as required, then roll it out and smooth it into a well-polished smooth Easter egg mould: a metal one is best. Work the paste into the mould slowly, easing out the pleats to make sure it is completely smooth. Use a scalpel or sharp knife to trim the edge level. Make two and leave to dry overnight.

Join the two halves with small blobs of royal icing and allow to set.

The join may be trimmed by piping a row of shells over it in royal icing. Alternatively, a long fine plait (braid) of pastillage may be made and used to cover the join. Mould the soft plait around the egg, sticking it in place with an occasional blob of icing. Make a neat join at the bottom of the egg.

The egg may be glazed with confectioners' varnish to give it a hard shiny finish.

two on paper before piping around the join in the egg. The chocolate should be at the point when it is just beginning to set and slightly thickened so that it pipes neat shapes.

Decorate the egg with crystallized violets and a bow of ribbon. You can crystallize rose petals or primroses for the decoration, or alternatively use piped chocolate shapes or flowers.

Present the finished egg in a tissue-lined basket, trimmed with ribbon.

### EASTER ACTIVITIES
Egg and spoon races are a good idea as well as the suggestions below.

### Egg-rolling Race
Mark race lanes with string across the lawn, pegging the string into the ground with meat skewers. Each person is given a hard-boiled egg and a short length of garden cane (bamboo stake). The eggs have to be rolled from start to finishing post using just the canes. Straying into a neighbouring lane means starting again and three such offences cause disqualification!

### Easter Bonnet Competition
A good way of giving a party a theme. Men should take part as well. Encourage the most outrageous creations, laden with flowers, ribbons, eggs and nests. Everyone votes for the winner and the votes are written on pieces of paper which are folded and placed in a ballot box, then the first, second and third prize winners are chosen. Organize a separate Easter bonnet competition for children and have a panel of judges. Every worthy junior contestant should receive a little something for their efforts.

## Easter Nest Table Decorations

❖ Make a simple table decoration from straw, fresh or silk flowers and small chocolate eggs or tiny sugar eggs. Bind the straw to a double-thick length of plastic-covered wire, using raffia to bind it discreetly. Shape the straw into a ring – it should be thin and look sparse initially. Once you have formed the basic shape, attach four pieces of wire diagonally across the bottom, binding them with string or cotton in the middle. Cover the base with a layer of straw, using a large trussing needle and raffia to bind it to the wire struts. Attach more straw to the sides of the nest.

❖ For fresh flowers, trim a small plastic margarine container and cut a piece of wet florists' foam to put in it. Wire the flower stems – miniature daffodils, primroses and freesias are perfect – and arrange them in the foam. Add loops of ribbon and small bows around the flowers, teasing both ribbon and flowers over the edge of the nest.

❖ Alternatively, fill the nest with colourful miniature chocolate eggs, or use a mixture of eggs and silk or dried flowers in the arrangement.

# Painted Eggs

A little basket of blown eggs decorated with paint, ribbon and stuck-on shapes — even sequins — is a charming and permanent Easter gift. It is fun to make and the effect may be as whimsical or sophisticated as you please.

**YOU WILL NEED:** eggs, sharp pin, saucer or basin, soft pencil, paints and paintbrushes, glue, ribbons, adhesive stars, basket.

**1** Wash the eggs in cold water and dry on paper towels. Use a sharp-pointed pin to screw a small hole in each end of an egg.

**2** Shake the egg vigorously to break the yolk and mix it with the white. Then hold the egg over a saucer or basin and blow hard into one hole until all the contents have run out of the other hole. Wash the shell carefully under cold running water, rinsing out several times. Leave to dry. Repeat with the remaining eggs.

**3** Use a soft pencil to mark a design lightly on each shell.

**4** Paint motifs, one colour at a time.

**5** Paint some eggs one colour all over.

**6** Stick a loop of ribbon on the top of an egg for hanging. (This can also help to disguise untidy holes.)

**7** For striped eggs, lightly indicate areas of different colour in pencil.

**8** Paint in the stripes using the pencilled lines as a guide.

**9** Decorate plain painted eggs with bands of ribbon and bows.

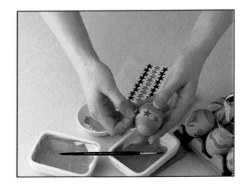

**10** Stick on adhesive shapes such as stars to make a pattern with painted stripes.

# FOURTH OF JULY

*Enjoy a truly American-style celebration for the Fourth of July. Invite friends and family to join in an informal barbecue or prepare the special menu suggested in this section.*

*This is a day for flying the colours – red, white and blue* *reign supreme with an abundance of balloons decorating the garden and streamers and baubles trailing around the house. Fix an early morning outing to a local parade, sporting event or a leisurely swim for all the company to stir up their appetites.*

## CELEBRATION PICNICS

Fourth of July celebrations are casual affairs, with the emphasis on friends and family, and relaxing outdoors. For many, the Fourth of July means a daytime picnic – on the beach or in a park – leading up to a firework display in the evening. No matter what the location, bear in mind that this is an all-day affair and that you will have to plan accordingly, ensuring you provide a varied enough selection of food (and in sufficient quantities) for lunch and afternoon snacks as well.

Whether you plan a barbecue at home or load a picnic basket with cold fried chicken and a selection of salads for eating on the beach, be sure to include enough nibbles and snacks to keep everyone going until the evening

celebrations. Suitable snacks might include raw vegetable sticks and other crudités packed in flasks of iced water to keep them fresh, dips, crisps (chips), crackers and fruit, as well as sweet treats for the afternoon, such as cupcakes, muffins, cookies and easy-to-transport tray bakes such as brownies.

Even if you are not entertaining at home but are hosting a picnic outdoors you can continue the festive theme with a few simple decorations: paper plates and napkins in red, white and blue or with star-spangled patterns and small paper flags on cocktail sticks (toothpicks) for decoration, sandwiches, cup cakes and brownies.

### Fourth of July Barbecue Checklist

- Charcoal, if using
- Firelighters or commercial barbecue lighting fuel if using charcoal
- Gas, if using
- Nibbles (snacks)
- Main course
- Dessert
- Wine and/or beer
- Alcohol-free drinks
- Ice
- Coffee
- Any special dietary needs?
- Skewers
- Table linen
- Cutlery (flatware)
- China and glassware or paper plates and cups
- Decorations

## MENU REMINDERS

Whether you are planning a picnic or a barbecue, keeping the main ingredients simple helps to reduce the amount of advance preparation that has to be done and enables you to be really creative instead with the range of salads you provide.

If you're catering for a picnic, pack the salads in large uncrushable bowls or containers with lids and keep in chiller bags (coolers) until you are ready to eat.

A cold pasta salad is also delicious, especially if made with a selection of vegetables that have either been marinated or, even better, roasted or grilled. Broccoli, red and yellow peppers (sweet bell peppers), courgettes (zucchini) and red onions are all good when treated in this way. Cut the vegetables into small strips or chunks and combine them with the pasta while they are hot to bring out the flavours, and either dress in olive oil with salt and freshly ground pepper, or a mixture of

*Balloons in red, white and blue will contribute to the festive spirit.*

olive oil and a balsamic or flavoured vinegar. Add plenty of stoned (pitted) black olives (ripe olives) and leave to cool so the flavours mingle together well. A handful of chopped coriander (cilantro) leaves or basil gives colour and extra flavour.

A simple bean salad is also a good idea for a picnic as it is easy to make and tastes better if the flavours are allowed to. mingle for a few hours before eating. Mix cooked chick peas (garbanzo beans) with cooked red kidney beans and add crushed garlic, thin slices of red onion, orange, yellow or

red peppers (sweet bell peppers) cut into strips, plenty of stoned (pitted) black olives (ripe olives) and some chopped fresh oregano. Add plenty of salt and freshly ground black pepper and dress with a good-quality olive oil and some freshly squeezed lemon juice.

215

### Salmon Brochettes

These are easy to make and may be prepared the night before ready for threading on skewers and barbecuing. Buy salmon steaks, allowing one per person or the thick end of the fillet, about 175 g (6 oz) to each brochette. Skin the fish, discard bones and cut it into chunks. Marinate with 4 tablespoons of sunflower oil, 2 tablespoons of walnut oil, 6 tablespoons of dry sherry, a tablespoon of honey and 2 finely chopped sun-dried tomatoes, a teaspoon of chopped fresh thyme, seasoning and the juice of an orange.

Thread the fish on metal skewers. Pour the remaining marinade into a saucepan and bring to the boil. Grill the brochettes for 5–7 minutes on each side, until just cooked, brushing with marinade occasionally. Glaze with the remaining marinade before serving.

### Pork Fillet in a Coat of Spinach

A pork fillet weighing about 675 g/1½ lb) will serve four as a barbecue dish. Season the pork the day before and leave it in the refrigerator overnight. Mix together a teaspoon of ground mace, a finely chopped garlic clove, a teaspoon of paprika, a tablespoon of chopped fresh sage and seasoning. Brush the pork with a little olive oil, then sprinkle the seasoning all over it.

Place well rinsed fresh spinach in a saucepan and cover tightly. Cook over high heat for 3–5 minutes, shaking the pan often. Drain well.

Open out the spinach leaves, overlapping them on a board and lay the pork on top, scraping all its seasoning over. Wrap completely with a double thickness of spinach.

Wrap rindless streaky bacon rashers (slices) all around the pork, securing them with string to cover the spinach thoroughly. Grill the pork fairly high over the coals, turning often and brushing the bacon with oil occasionally. The pork should be cooked through in about 30 minutes, depending on the thickness of the fillet. Serve the pork sliced, with a dressing of soured cream (fresh sour cream) and chopped chives.

New potatoes and a three bean salad would be a nice accompaniment.

### Potato Salads

A cold potato salad is a must, and will be best if you use one of the special varieties of waxy-textured salad potatoes that are now so easily available from supermarkets – "Pink Fir Apple" is a good choice and its knobbly shape and red skin increases the visual appeal of the salad. Boil the potatoes in their skins until tender but still intact, drain and then toss them, while still warm, in a vinaigrette made from wine vinegar, olive oil, salt and freshly ground pepper, Dijon or whole-grain mustard and garnish with plenty of chopped fresh dill.

Alternatively, you can dress the hot potatoes with a mixture of mayonnaise, soured cream (fresh sour cream) and a dash of white wine vinegar, salt and freshly ground pepper, chopped fresh chives and lots of chopped celery and green and red peppers (sweet bell peppers) for extra colour and a deliciously crunchy texture.

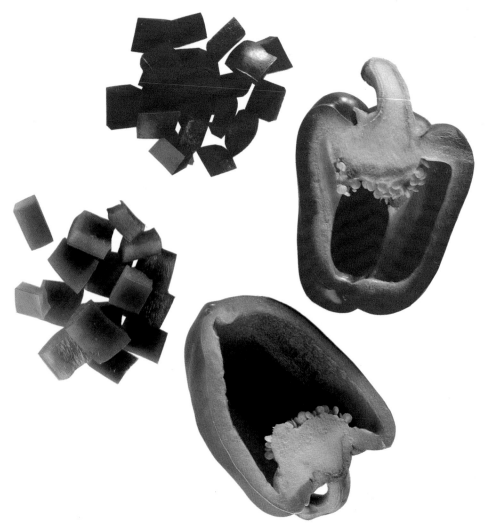

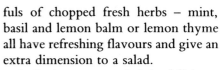

### Other Salad Ideas

A large bowl of a simple green salad is always welcome, and adding different salad leaves takes it out of the ordinary and gives it a festive air as well as a delicious blend of flavours. Adding an interestingly coloured lettuce, such as radicchio or oak leaf, gives extra interest although purists might argue it is no longer a green salad.

You can also add other variations on lettuce, such as baby spinach leaves, crisp watercress, chicory (endive) and rocket (arugula), with generous hand-

fuls of chopped fresh herbs – mint, basil and lemon balm or lemon thyme all have refreshing flavours and give an extra dimension to a salad.

A fresh tomato salad is delicious, especially if you take care to choose tomatoes that are juicy and really ripe, with a good flavour. Slice them thinly and let them marinate for an hour in a simple vinaigrette made from the best olive oil and wine vinegar you have, salt and freshly ground pepper, and garnish with slivers of red onion and chopped fresh mint or basil.

### SAY IT WITH STYLE

Trim white napkins with red and blue ribbon; red with blue and white ribbon; blue with red and white ribbon. Measure the length of one side of each napkin, then buy just over four times that length of 3 mm/⅛ in wide ribbon for each napkin.

Pin one colour ribbon all along one napkin edge, 2.5 cm/1 in from the finished edge on large napkins, slightly less on small squares. Turn the ends of the ribbon under neatly and machine stitch the ribbon down the middle using exactly the same colour thread. Pin

and stitch a line length of ribbon in the second colour alongside the first, about 5 mm/¼ in away. Sew ribbons along all sides of the napkins in the same way, so that they cross at each corner.

Make red, white and blue tissue

flowers and wire them into dry-foam (styro foam) cone shapes. Make ribbon loops in one colour, either red or blue, stitch their ends and wire them, then push them into the cone between the flowers to finish.

The cones may be used as table decorations or they may be speared on lengths of garden cane (bamboo stake) and made into standard arrangements (topiaries) by securing them in pots of gravel. Paint the canes red or blue and spray the top of the gravel with colour. Trim the pot with ribbons. These give the patio a festive air.

# HALLOWEEN HORRORS

*J*ust when everyone is beginning to feel a bit gloomy about the beginning of winter, when the whole world seems to have turned damp and dusky, there's a great opportunity for adding a spark of fun to life by planning a ghoulish party for adults and children alike.

If you are lost for thoughts on the usual theme, then take a look through the next few pages to revive your ideas for creating a truly horror-filled party!

### Pumpkin Serving Bowl

If there are lots of large pumpkins around, pick out one big enough to hold a mixing bowl or container. Slice the top off the pumpkin thinly, then scoop out and discard all the seeds and fibres before cutting out the flesh. Scrape out the flesh from the sides of the shell (this may be used for soups and purées) and make sure it stands level, trimming the base underneath if necessary. Then sit the bowl or container in the shell. Steady the container by packing crumpled foil around it. Scrape out the lid and cut a small hole at one side for the handle of a ladle. Use the pumpkin serving container for soup, stew, or mulled wine.

### DEVILISH TABLE DESIGNS
Take a ghoulish theme for the table decor. Children love this activity:
❖ Cover the table completely with black crêpe paper, running the sheets widthways over the table. Use double-sided tape to tape wide black satin ribbon over the joins in the paper and tie black bows to finish the ends of the ribbon.
❖ Use the pumpkin lanterns to light the table, placing them on small thick cork mats or pot stands.
❖ Cut out witches in black card (poster-board), adding an extra 5 cm/2 in to the bottom and folding this back so that the witches stand up. Weight the flap with a small piece of blue tack (a mouldable adhesive such as Funtac) or plasticine. Stand the witches towards the back of a buffet table set back against a wall.

### Spooky Lights

Scoop out a series of small pumpkins. Cut out holes for eyes, a nose and gappy teeth. Place a small battery-operated bulb in the middle of the shell and replace the lid. Place the pumpkins about the house.

❖ The crêpe paper still looks acceptable on a dimly lit, more sophisticated buffet but plain fabric can be used instead. Inexpensive cotton or lining fabric will do but it should be laid over a cloth for a base. If you do not want to sew the fabric into a permanent cloth, then tack (baste) it together and cover the join with ribbon, tacking it discreetly instead of sticking it. Replace the lanterns with tall iron candlesticks and black candles.

### Halloween Party Checklist

- Invitations
- Pumpkins, if using
- Party menu: First course, main course, dessert
- Wine and/or beer
- Alcohol-free drinks
- Ice
- Coffee
- Apples for Apple Bobbing
- Decorations
- House cleaning and tidying

*Toffee Apples.*

## Toffee Apples

Toffee apples are a traditional offering at Halloween, and home-made ones always taste the best.

Select full-flavoured apples and avoid any that have very tough skins. Buy sturdy wooden sticks and use them to skewer each washed and dried apple. Have a baking tray sheet ready, covered with a sheet of wax paper or oiled foil.

To make the caramel, combine 450 g/1 lb (2 cups) sugar and 150 ml/¼ pint (⅔ cup) water in a saucepan. Heat the sugar and water, stirring, until the sugar has dissolved completely.

Do not allow the syrup to boil until the sugar has dissolved. Dampen the insides of the pan with water to wash all the sugar crystals down into the pan, then bring the syrup to the boil. Continue boiling until the syrup turns to a golden caramel. Do not stir at all while boiling, otherwise the sugar may crystallize. Remove the pan from the heat as soon as the caramel is golden and dip the pan into a bowl of cold water to prevent further cooking, which may make the caramel too dark. Dip the apples in the caramel, turning them on their sticks to coat them all over. Allow excess caramel to drip off, then twirl the apples and place on the lined baking tray to set. This quantity of caramel will coat 4 to 6 apples, depending on their size. Once the caramel has set, wrap each apple in clear cellophane and close the wrapping with a piece of ribbon tied into a pretty bow. Pile the toffee apples into a table basket.

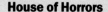

## House of Horrors

Older children love to experience a House of Horrors. Completely darken one room and guide two or three children at a time to the delights of the following:

❖ Bowls of peeled grapes or cooked peas – "fish eyes".
❖ Bowls of cooked, cold spaghetti – "innards" or "brains".

❖ Bowls of yogurt or jelly (jello) – "ghost slime".
❖ Dried pear slices – "ears".
❖ Get an older sibling or parent to dress up as a ghost and pop from behind a chair or out of a cupboard.
❖ Have lots of cobwebs and large spiders hanging everywhere.
❖ Play suitably scary music!

## SPICY PUMPKIN SOUP

— SERVES ABOUT 10 —

A smooth, lightly spiced soup. It can be made a day or two ahead and stored in the refrigerator.

1 tablespoon butter
2 onions, chopped
2 garlic cloves, crushed
1 bay leaf
1.5 kg/3 lb pumpkin, peeled, deseeded and cut into chunks
1 potato, diced (minced)
2 teaspoons good curry powder
1.12 litres/2 pints (5 cups) ham or chicken stock
salt and freshly ground black pepper
300 ml/½ pint (1¼ cups) single (light) cream
croûtons, to serve

Heat the butter in a saucepan. Add the onion, garlic and bay leaf and cook, stirring occasionally, for 5 minutes. Stir in the pumpkin, potato, and curry powder and continue to cook for 10 minutes, stirring occasionally. Pour in the ham or chicken stock and bring to the boil. Cover the pan, reduce the heat and simmer for 30 minutes.

Allow the soup to cool, then, using a food processor or blender, purée until it is smooth. Season to taste, then stir in the cream. Reheat gently without boiling. Sprinkle each portion with croûtons and serve.

## PUMPKIN AND MUSHROOM STRUDEL

— SERVES 8 —

This sounds grand but it is reassuringly simple.

1 tablespoon butter
1 onion, chopped
225 g/8 oz (3 cups) mushrooms, sliced
675 g/1½ lb pumpkin flesh
salt and freshly ground black pepper
fresh nutmeg
1 tablespoon chopped fresh sage
100 g/4 oz (1 cup) grated Cheddar cheese
3–6 sheets ready-made phyllo pastry (dough) depending on size of baking sheet
a little oil or melted butter, for brushing

Heat the butter in a saucepan. Add the onion and cook, stirring occasionally, for 10 minutes. Add the mushrooms and pumpkin and cook for a further 25 minutes, stirring occasionally, until the excess liquid from the mushrooms has evaporated and the pumpkin is almost tender.

Stir in plenty of seasoning, a good grating of fresh nutmeg and the sage. Allow to cool before mixing in the cheese.

Set the oven at 180°C/350°F/Gas 4. Lay 2 small sheets of phyllo pastry (dough) overlapping well on a baking sheet or lay 1 large sheet singly; brush with a little oil or melted butter. Add a second and third layer of phyllo, brushing each layer with a little oil or melted butter. Spread the pumpkin mixture over the phyllo, leaving a gap around the edge. Roll the pastry up to form the strudel, then brush with a little more oil or melted butter. Bake the strudel for about 50 minutes, or until the phyllo is crisp and golden on the outside and cooked through. Serve cut into slices.

*Choose firm, crisp eating apples for Apple Bobbing.*

## Apple Bobbing

There are two ways of organizing this fun family game. The messy version means filling a large bowl or old-fashioned bath (bathtub) almost full of water and floating the apples in it. A large preserving pan or clean babies' bath will do. The contestants have their hands tied behind their backs and they kneel around the bowl. At the signal to begin, each person tries to catch the apples.

Alternatively, and less messily, tie a piece of string in a line across the room. Use a trussing needle to thread a piece of string through each apple and knot it securely, then hang the apples from the line at the appropriate height. The contestants have to eat the apples with their hands tied behind their backs. The game can be made more difficult by making everyone wear a blindfold.

# BEWITCHING TART

Children and adults alike will enjoy this
Halloween theme tart.

175 g/6 oz (1½ cups) plain (all-purpose) flour
100 g/4 oz (½ cup) unsalted butter, diced
50 g/2 oz (¼ cup) caster (superfine) sugar
50 g/2 oz (½ cup) hazelnuts, chopped
and toasted
3 tablespoons cocoa powder
2 eggs, separated
2 tablespoons water
300 ml/½ pint (1¼ cups) milk
25 g/1 oz (3 tablespoons) cornflour
(cornstarch)
1 tablespoon caster (superfine) sugar
225 g/8 oz white chocolate drops
1 teaspoon natural vanilla essence (extract)
150 ml/¼ pint (⅔ cup) double (heavy)
cream
225 g/8 oz (8 squares) plain (semi-sweet)
chocolate

**1** Place the flour in a bowl and rub in (cut in) the butter. Stir in the sugar, hazelnuts and cocoa, then add 1 egg yolk and the water. Use a knife to mix the egg and water into the ingredients to bind them into a chocolate pastry (dough). Use this to line a 25 cm/10 in loose-bottomed flan tin (tart pan). Prick the base all over and chill the pastry for 30 minutes. Set the oven at 200°C/400°F/Gas 6.

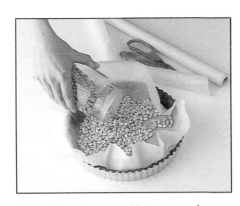

**2** Line the pastry case with greaseproof paper (waxed paper) and baking beans, then bake it for 20 minutes. Remove the paper and beans and cook for a further 10 minutes, until the pastry is cooked. Leave to cool.

**3** Mix a little of the milk with the cornflour (cornstarch) and caster (superfine) sugar until smooth. Bring the remaining milk to the boil, then pour it onto the cornflour mixture, stirring all the time. Return the sauce to the pan and bring to the boil, stirring. Simmer for 3 minutes, stirring all the time until the sauce is very thick. Remove from the heat.

**4** Add the white chocolate drops and the remaining yolk and stir continuously until the chocolate melts. Stir in the vanilla essence (extract), then cover the surface of the sauce with wetted greaseproof paper or cling film (plastic wrap) and leave to just cool but not set.

**5** Beat the sauce to remove any lumps. Whip the cream until it stands in soft peaks, then fold it into the sauce. Beat the egg whites until they stand in stiff but not dry peaks, then fold them into the mixture. Turn the mixture into the pastry case (pie crust), swirl it around evenly and chill for a few hours.

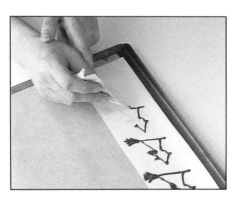

**6** Trace the witch shape several times onto the unwaxed side of waxed paper using a felt-tip pen. Turn the paper over and place it on a board, securing the corners with tape. Melt the plain (semi-sweet) chocolate in a bowl over a small saucepan of hot, not boiling, water. Make a small greaseproof paper piping (pastry) bag and spoon some chocolate into it. Fold the end down neatly, then cut just the tip off the bag. Carefully outline the witch shapes.

**7** Cut a little more off the tip of the bag, then flood in the shapes completely, teasing the chocolate into the corners, if necessary, using a cocktail stick (toothpick). Leave until set, then lift the witches from the paper using a palette knife (metal spatula). Arrange them on the tart and serve.

**NOTE**
If you want to brighten up the tart and make it look as special as it tastes, prepare a piece of ribbon about the same depth as the pastry case and long enough to wrap around it. Make a bow separately and attach a piece of double-sided tape to one end of the ribbon and to the bow. Fix the ribbon around the tart just before serving it and stick the bow over the join.

**COOK'S TIP**
If you want to make the pastry case (pie crust) in advance, it freezes well but should be reheated briefly in a hot oven to refresh the pastry and crisp it. If you are filling the tart the day before it is served, brushing the base of the pastry case inside with melted chocolate prevents moisture from the filling softening it.

## Dancing Witches

Cut out several lengths of these spooky witches and join them together to make chains that are long enough to stretch across the room.

**YOU WILL NEED:** card (posterboard) for template, pencil, black crêpe paper, white or pale-coloured pencil, scissors.

**1** Cut out a rectangle of card (posterboard). Draw a witch on the card, making sure that parts of the shape — hat brim, hair, hands or broomstick — touch the sides of the rectangle. Cut out the witch shape to make a template.

**2** Cut a strip of crêpe paper the same depth as the card. Fold it back and forth, concertina-fashion, in pleats the same width as the card. Place the template on the folded paper, draw around it and cut out the witch, taking care to leave the shapes joined at the sides. Unfold the pleats to reveal the dancing witches.

## Red Devil's Mask

With its evilly glinting eyes and devilish horns, this mask looks dramatic decorating a black tablecloth.

**YOU WILL NEED:** card (posterboard) for template, pencil, scissors, red artists' card, craft knife and cutting board, scraps of silver wrapping paper, sticky (transparent) tape, double-sided tape.

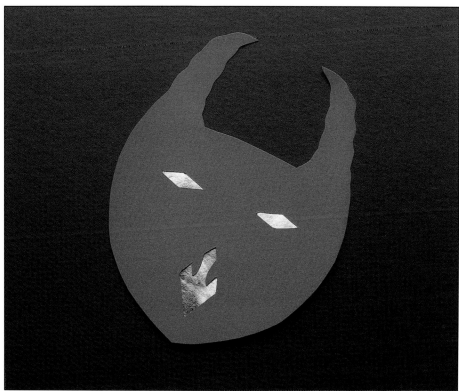

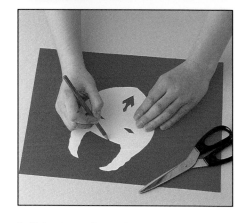

**1** Cut out a mask template in card (posterboard). Draw around the outline on red artists' card.

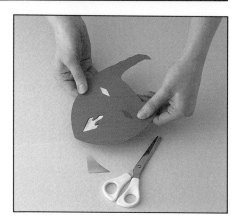

**2** Cut out the red card shape using scissors. Cut out the eyes and mouth using a craft knife. Stick scraps of silver wrapping paper behind the eyes and mouth. Attach the mask to the background using double-sided tape.

# BONFIRE BONANZA

*T*here is nothing like the excitement of bonfires and fireworks to put everyone in the party mood.

Gathering around a fire forms part of a number of celebrations. In many European countries, a bonfire marks the summer solstice, and in Britain, Guy Fawkes' Night in

November commemorates the attempt by Guy Fawkes and his gang to blow up the Houses of Parliament – the Gunpowder Plot. These are occasions for gathering friends together for an informal party with fun entertainment and simple refreshments.

### BONFIRE FUN

Children love bonfires and fireworks, but these are occasions for taking extra care as far as safety is concerned. Keep children well away from the bonfire. Adults should follow the manufacturer's safety instructions when handling fireworks. Never allow children to handle fireworks. If you are in any doubt about safety especially as far as the siting and management of a bonfire is concerned, contact your local fire department for advice.

Organize lots of added attractions for children. Party games that can be played either outside or indoors are a good idea on such occasions.

### AFTER-BONFIRE SUPPER

Appetites will have been sharpened after an hour or so outside in crisp winter weather. Devise a menu that is warming and filling. Here are a few suggestions for quick and easy snack food:

### Vegetarian Herb Sausages

These are a good meat-free alternative to burgers. Although there are specific recipes, it is not difficult to create your own speciality version. They consist of lots of grated cheese and fresh breadcrumbs, with some chopped fresh sage and seasoning, bound to a stiff mixture with milk. Grated onion, chopped fresh parsley and chopped fresh thyme or tarragon are flavoursome additions. Shape the mixture into link sausages, coat them with egg and dry white breadcrumbs, then deep-fry them until they are golden. Drain well on absorbent kitchen paper (paper towels).

### Sausage Patties

Make these instead of burgers. Mix sausage meat with chopped onion, some fresh breadcrumbs, a little chopped fresh sage and 1 beaten egg. Shape into patties and grill (broil) until golden and cooked through. Good in toasted buns with salad.

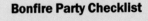

### Hot Cinnamon Chocolate

A delicious bonfire drink: flavour the milk with cinnamon well in advance of making drinking chocolate. Pour 600 ml/1 pint (2½ cups) milk for each 2 or 3 mugs (depending on their size) into a saucepan. Add a cinnamon stick or two if you are heating more than 1 litre/35 fl oz (4½ cups) milk. Stir in a teaspoon of natural vanilla essence (extract) for each 600 ml/1 pint (2½ cups) or add a vanilla pod (bean) to the pan. Heat gently until just boiling, then remove from the heat and cover the pan. Leave until completely cold. Strain the milk and use to make hot chocolate or cocoa using powdered chocolate or cocoa and sugar added to taste. Top with whipped cream and a little ground cinnamon and grated chocolate.

### Bonfire Party Checklist

- Material for bonfire
- Fireworks
- Check safety
- Party menu: First course, main course, dessert
- Wine and/or beer
- Alcohol-free drinks
- Ice
- Coffee
- Party games for children
- Props for party games
- House cleaning and tidying

*Warming Punch.*

## Warming Punch

Offer this hot punch to guests. Mix all these ingredients in a large flameproof casserole, warm the punch through, then ladle it into heatproof glasses: 1 litre/35 fl oz (4½ cups) dry (hard) cider, 2 tablespoons of honey (or to taste), a cinnamon stick, 100 g/4 oz (¾ cup) shelled almonds, pared rind (peel) of an orange, 4 cloves, 150 ml/¼ pint (⅔ cup) brandy and a little grated nutmeg. Serves 10.

*Autumnal colours and streamers decorate a table for Bonfire night.*

### Tips for a Spicy Meat Stew

We all have our favourite recipes – here are some tips for a really good chilli (chili) con carne.

❖ Always boil red kidney beans rapidly for 10 minutes before the main cooking. Never add salt until the red kidney beans are thoroughly tender, otherwise they become tough.

❖ Cook a little diced bacon with the onions: note the "onions" – allow 2 good ones to every 450 g/1 lb meat.

❖ As well as chilli (chili) powder, use ground cumin and coriander to flavour the mixture. Add about 2 tablespoons of coriander and a tablespoon of cumin to 450 g/1 lb minced (ground) beef.

❖ Add some robust red wine and tomato purée (paste), as well.

❖ Taste the mixture for seasoning and add salt and freshly ground black pepper to taste, then simmer, covered, for 10 minutes before serving.

❖ Soured cream (fresh sour cream) goes well with this.

### Toffee Bananas

These are an irresistible Chinese-style dessert. Make a caramel: place 450 g/1 lb (2¼ cups) sugar in a saucepan. Add 150 ml/¼ pint (⅔ cup) water and heat, stirring, until the sugar completely dissolves. Do not allow the syrup to boil until the sugar has dissolved. Dampen the sides of the pan with water to wash all the sugar crystals down into the pan, then bring the syrup to the boil. Continue boiling until the syrup turns to a golden caramel. Do not stir while the syrup is boiling or the sugar may crystallize. Remove the pan from the heat as soon as the caramel is golden and dip into a bowl of cold water to prevent further cooking. Do not leave the pan of caramel in cold water, or it will cool too much and begin to set. Once you have dipped the base of the pan in water, set it aside ready for coating the bananas.

Cut each banana into 2 or 3 chunks, then coat in a batter made from 100 g/4 oz/1 cup flour, 100 ml/4 fl oz/½ cup cold water and a beaten egg. Deep-fry until crisp. Drain on absorbent kitchen paper (paper towels) and coat each fritter with caramel. Transfer them to a plate and sprinkle with sesame seeds.

## BONFIRE GAMES

Here are some energetic games to warm everyone up after the fireworks are over.

### Farmyard Noises

Younger children especially enjoy this boisterous and noisy game. One player is designated the farmer and blindfolded. The rest of the players move around him in a circle. When the farmer claps his hands, they stop. The farmer points at a player (he cannot see who it is of course), who must then make the noise of a farmyard animal, such as a sheep, a chicken or a pig. The farmer has to guess who is pretending to be the animal. If he guesses correctly, the two players change places. If not, the players continue to move around the farmer until he stops another player for an impersonation.

### Musical Chairs

Chairs are placed back to back to form a row – there should be one chair less than there are players. The players form a circle around the chairs and when the music begins start to move from chair to chair. When the music stops each player races to sit on a chair. The player who fails to reach a chair leaves the group and one chair is removed. The player who manages to gain the final chair is the winner.

### Rope Race

The players divide into two teams. Each team is given a length of rope knotted into a large circle (make sure that the knot is secure and cannot be "slipped"). On the word "go" the first player in each team passes the rope circle over his or her head, over his or her shoulders and down to the ground. It is picked up by the next player who does the same, and so on down the line and back again, to the first player in each team. The side which finishes first are the winners.

### Spin the Tray

Everyone sits in a large circle on the floor. There should be a piece of wood, such as a wooden bread board, positioned in the centre of the circle. The first player spins a small circular tray on the board at the same time calling out the name of another player. The second player must catch the tray before it falls to the ground, otherwise he or she is out of the game. If the player succeeds in catching it, he or she spins the tray in turn.

### Spoon a Balloon

This is a game of gamesmanship. The players each have a spoon, and stand in a circle with about a metre (a yard) between each of them. A balloon is placed on one spoon and is then tossed from spoon to spoon around the circle. The other players, without moving from their posts, do all they can, in the way of verbal discouragements, to make the receiving player lose concentration. Any player who fails to catch the balloon on his or her spoon is out, and the others close ranks.

### Pass the Orange

This is a game that is almost as much fun to watch as it is to play! You will need two teams and two oranges. The first player at the front of each team tucks a large orange under his or her chin. He or she then attempts to pass the orange to the next player along the line without using any hands. The aim is to pass the orange from chin to chin to the end of the line and back again as fast as possible. The first team to do so is the winner.

## Lucky Dip

The element of surprise makes this an amusing side attraction at parties for children or adults. Instead of dipping into this box of goodies, each guest selects one of the dangling labels, then fishes out the small gift or bag of sweets (candies) attached to the other end of the string. The design of the tags can be varied according to the party theme and the interests of the guests.

**YOU WILL NEED:** large cardboard box, brown wrapping paper, coloured paper, sticky (transparent) tape, scissors, coloured card (posterboard), coloured pens or crayons, craft knife or skewer, tissue paper, gifts or sweets (candies), narrow ribbon, string.

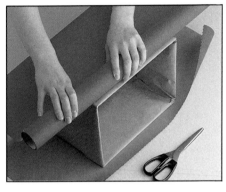

**1** Cover the cardboard box first with brown paper and then with coloured paper, securing it neatly with sticky tape.

**2** Make card (posterboard) templates for the tags. You will need each shape in two sizes, a larger one to attach to the gift and a smaller one to tie to the other end of the string. Draw around the templates onto coloured card.

**3** Cut out the tags.

**4** Use coloured pens or crayons to decorate the tags.

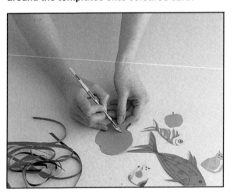

**5** Make a small hole in each tag using a craft knife or skewer.

**6** Pack up the gifts in colourful tissue paper.

**7** Tie the packages with colourful ribbons, knotting them with bows.

**8** Thread a piece of string through the hole in a large tag, then knot the end. Thread the opposite end through a matching small tag, then knot that end.

**9** Tie the string near the large tag securely around the gift. Put the gifts in the box with their small tags dangling around the sides. Pack the box with crumpled tissue paper to hide the packages.

# GOLDEN THANKSGIVING

*This annual American celebration is a feast for giving thanks for the bounty of the harvest and all other blessings throughout the year. It dates back to several years after the arrival of the first Pilgrim Fathers at Plymouth, Massachusetts, in the seventeenth century.*

*It is a family occasion with roast turkey and pumpkin pie as the accepted fare, while oysters and succotash (in its true form as a dried bean dish) were among the original specialities for the feast. In American homes this is an opportunity to listen to tales from the older generation and spend time together relaxing.*

## THANKSGIVING DINNER

In the United States, the Thanksgiving dinner is the most tradition-bound of holiday meals. Whereas the components of the Christmas dinner are influenced by the rich cultural diversity of the country, at Thanksgiving the menu is unlikely to vary much from coast to coast. Dishes which are served to accompany the turkey are a medley of harvest fare: bowls heaped high with squash, sweet potatoes, turnips, wild rice, carrots, sweet corn and beans of all kinds. Often these are simply prepared and only require a pat of butter, and a pinch of salt and black pepper. The challenge for the cook is to organize the preparation so that everything is ready to serve at the same time.

### Thanksgiving Checklist

- Order turkey, if necessary
- First course
- Main course
- Dessert
- Wine
- Alcohol-free drinks
- Ice
- Coffee
- Brandy and liqueurs, if required
- Table linen
- Cutlery (flatware), china and glassware
- House cleaning and tidying

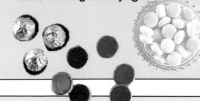

### Menu Reminders

With the main dish of the day being the traditional turkey, think ahead to plan alternative appetizers and side dishes.
❖ The following are light first course suggestions: a tomato salad (variations include a sprinkling of shredded cooked ham, cheese or olives), a consommé, prawn (shrimp) and avocado salad.
❖ Try roasting sweet potatoes with the turkey, or roast small salad potatoes in their skins.
❖ Vegetables such as carrots and Brussels sprouts can be glazed with a little butter and orange juice.
❖ Alternative desserts to the classic pumpkin pie include a mincemeat pie, a cherry pie or an apple pie.

## THANKSGIVING TABLE

Thanksgiving decorations make use of the bounty of the autumn harvest, employing a spectrum of warm, seasonal colours. Table decorations may entail nothing more than a casual grouping of gourds and small pumpkins, with sheaths of wheat and colourful Indian corn gathered into bunches and hung on a door or wall. A cornucopia could grace a buffet table with gleaming apples, nuts and vegetables spilling out in glorious profusion.

Alternatively, make an everlasting bunch of golden grapes. Buy modelling clay to bake or make salt dough using an equal weight of plain (all-purpose) flour and salt bound to a stiff dough with cold water. Roll small

*Among the many seasonal fruit pies, apple pie with ice cream is a favourite.*

*A golden table centrepiece made of gleaming apples and pears and gilded grapes. This is for decoration only: the fruit must not be eaten.*

balls, the same size as grapes. Stick a piece of heavy floral wire into each 'grape' and place on a baking sheet. Set the oven at the lowest heat setting and leave the grapes to dry out for 3–4 hours or until they are completely dry. Prepare a triple-thick length of plastic-covered tying wire for the middle of

the bunch and cover this with floral tape. Tape the ends of the wire which comes out of the grapes but do not work too far down. Twist the grapes onto the central wire, trimming off the ends when the grapes are secure. Leave a short piece of wire for the stem. Build up the shape of the bunch, work-

ing mainly on the top and curving it around underneath but leaving a fairly flat base. Trim off excess central wire, then tape the stalk end. Spray the bunch of grapes completely with gold spray paint, applying it in several layers and allowing each to dry before applying the next.

*Roast Turkey with Harvest Parsnips and Two-potato Gratin.*

## THANKSGIVING MENU

Make the main meal of the day a traditional one, but invite friends or the wider family circle for an early brunch or late supper with cold roast turkey and salad trimmings.

## Roasting Turkey

Trim the wing and leg ends from the bird and place them in a saucepan with the giblets, an onion and a carrot. Add water to cover, bring to the boil, then simmer for half an hour. Strain and reserve the stock for making gravy.

Cut away any lumps of fat from the vent flap of the bird, check that it is well cleaned and thoroughly rinse it under cold running water. Dry well inside and out.

Loosen the skin over the breast of the bird and use a small metal spoon to push stuffing between the breast meat and the skin. Fill the body cavity with stuffing (chestnuts and sausage stuffing is popular), if liked, or place an onion studded with 5 cloves in the body instead. Truss the bird neatly.

Season the turkey all over and dot with pieces of butter or margarine. Place the bird in an oiled roasting pan. Tuck bay leaves between the joints and the body of the bird and around it in the pan.

Calculate the cooking time according to the weight of the stuffed turkey. Allow 20 minutes per 450 g/1 lb plus an extra 20 minutes at 180°C/350°F/ Gas 4 for birds weighing up to 4.5 kg/10 lb; for birds weighing up to 6.8 kg/15 lb, reduce the time to 15–18 minutes per 450 g/1 lb and still allow the extra 20 minutes.

Keep the bird covered with foil for the majority of the cooking time. Baste the turkey often during cooking and remove the foil and bacon for the final 30 minutes, so the skin browns well.

To make gravy or a sauce, discard the bay leaves from the pan and drain off the majority of the fat, leaving the sediment. Add enough flour to just absorb the fat and juices in a thin paste. Cook, stirring, for a few minutes, then pour in the giblet stock, stirring or beating all the time. You should add enough liquid to make a thin sauce at this stage: cooking water from potatoes may be added or water usually makes up the giblet stock as the sauce will be flavoured by the sediment in the pan. Scrape all the sediment off the pan to flavour the sauce, then bring it to the boil and allow it to boil, uncovered, for 15–20 minutes, or until it is reduced and thickened slightly. Taste for seasoning.

Instead of the usual gravy, make a delicious wine sauce by using half red wine with the stock. Alternatively, enrich a plain gravy by adding a generous dash of dry sherry and boiling for 2 minutes before serving.

Accompany with Two-potato Gratin, sautéed green beans with pecans, and Harvest Parsnips.

## Two-potato Gratin

An easy-to-prepare alternative to roast or mashed potatoes, prepare this gratin the night before and chill it ready to go into the oven with the turkey.

Boil an equal weight of sweet potatoes and ordinary white potatoes in their skins until tender, about 20 minutes. Leave them to cool until you can just handle the vegetables, then peel them. They are easier to peel thinly when hot. Slice the potatoes and layer the sweet and plain types alternately in a large ovenproof serving dish. Sprinkle each layer with a little seasoning and some snipped fresh chives, and dot with butter.

Before baking, trickle a little single (light) cream or milk over the top of the gratin to keep it moist during cooking. Cover with foil and bake for 45 minutes. Mix together some fresh breadcrumbs with a little freshly grated Parmesan cheese and 2 tablespoons melted butter. Sprinkle this over the top of the potatoes, return to the oven and bake for a further 20 minutes, until crisp and golden.

## Harvest Parsnips

This bright vegetable dish can replace the more traditional succotash of lima beans and sweetcorn. Cook chopped onion, red and green peppers (sweet bell peppers) and sweetcorn in butter, then add cooked and cubed parsnips. Toss well with salt and freshly ground black pepper to taste.

# PUMPKIN PIE WITH BRANDY CREAM

---

### SERVES 8–10

---

Pumpkin pie is probably one of the best known of American recipes and it can be superb. Rich with cream and spices, the filling should set to a light, custard-like consistency.

*225 g/8 oz (2 cups) plain (all-purpose) flour*
*175 g/6 oz (¾ cup) butter, diced*
*50 g/2 oz (¼ cup) caster (superfine) sugar*
*2–3 tablespoons water*

FILLING
*350 g/12 oz (1½ cups) cooked and puréed pumpkin*
*3 large eggs, well beaten*
*1 teaspoon natural vanilla essence (extract)*
*100 g/4 oz (¾ cup) light soft brown sugar*
*1 teaspoon each ground cinnamon and ginger*
*½ teaspoon each grated nutmeg and ground mace*
*pinch of ground cloves*
*grated rind (peel) of ½ orange*
*300 ml/½ pint (1¼ cups) single (light) cream*
*3 tablespoons brandy*

BRANDY CREAM
*300 ml/½ pint (1¼ cups) double (heavy) cream*
*2 tablespoons icing (confectioners') sugar*
*3 tablespoons brandy*

Set the oven at 200°C/400°F/Gas 6. Place the flour in a bowl and rub in (cut in) the butter, then mix in the caster (superfine) sugar and water to make a shortcrust pastry (piecrust dough). Use this to line a 25 cm/10 in loose-bottomed tart pan. Prick the pastry all over and chill it for 10 minutes. Line with greaseproof paper (waxed paper) and fill with baking beans. Bake for 20 minutes. Remove the paper and beans, reduce the oven temperature to 180°C/350°F/Gas 4 and cook the empty pastry case for a further 5 minutes.

Meanwhile, mix together the pumpkin purée, eggs, vanilla, sugar, spices, orange rind (peel), cream and brandy. Pour this mixture into the pastry case and bake for about 45 minutes, until the filling is set. Leave to cool.

For the brandy cream, whip the cream, icing (confectioners') sugar and brandy together until the mixture stands in soft peaks. Serve spooned over individual portions of pie.

# Wheat Napkin Ring

This simple napkin ring adds a rustic charm to Thanksgiving, harvest suppers or any mealtime occasion when the nights are drawing in.

**YOU WILL NEED:** (for each ring) three small dried leaves, fine florists' wire, paper varnish and brush, three ears of wheat with 25 cm/10 in stems attached, three 25 cm/10 in lengths of stalk without heads, hot water, ribbon.

**1** Wire the stems of the dried leaves.

**2** Paint the leaves with paper varnish and allow to dry.

**3** Soak the wheat stalks for about 30 minutes in very hot water to soften them. Drain and then blot dry.

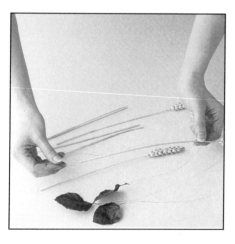

**4** Very gently insert a length of florists' wire into each stalk, leaving a little wire protruding at the ends.

**5** Attach a leaf to the base of each wheat ear, then wire in one of the headless stalks.

**6** Plait (braid) the wheat stalks together as evenly as possible.

**7** Twist the plait into a ring and wire in place. Neaten the end.

**8** Tie a ribbon bow below the leaves and wheat ears to conceal the join.

# CHRISTMAS AROUND THE WORLD

*C*hristmas is the annual party season, when every small assembly takes a festive turn. Each household has its own set of family traditions and favourite activities, times when friends are invited and days are for sharing with the family. Dark wintry evenings provide the perfect excuse for playing card games and board games, and after a glass of warming Glog even the least energetic of participants will join in a happy hour or two of charades!

**CHRISTMAS CAROL EVENING**

Start the festive season with a carol evening for friends and family who enjoy a sing-song. This is ideal if you have a piano and someone who can play, or buy a Christmas carol sing-along tape or CD from any leading music store. Select the carols in advance so that the pianist has time to practise, but do not worry too much about the standard as even a simple accompaniment will bring the guests together. Invite other musicians to join in, giving them plenty of warning.

This is a great party for the week before Christmas. Keep numbers fairly small so that everyone present has to join in. Having too large a crowd can result in some of the less enthusiastic singers forming a separate party in another room.

Make attractive invitation cards, hand written on plain cards and trimmed with red and green ribbon. Type out or write the carols and photocopy them in advance so that every guest has a song sheet – try to include a selection of old favourites along with some contemporary tunes. The house should be decorated and a holly wreath hung on the front door. Make sure there is a table lamp near the piano. Have chairs for the elderly but encourage others to stand for the singing.

Plan simple refreshments, with

### Christmas Bell Invitations

Cut out a pair of bells from card (posterboard). Paint a decorative pattern on one side of each and apply glue, then sprinkle with glitter. Leave to dry. Write the invitation to the carol evening on the undecorated side of one bell. Tie the bells together with red and green ribbon, decorated sides out. These are also fun for a children's carol evening or party.

### Menu Reminders

Roast turkey is the traditional main course for the Christmas Day lunch, accompanied by stuffing, a range of vegetables, gravy, and cranberry sauce. Extras may also include small sausages, bacon rolls and apple sauce.
• For a starter (appetizer), choose something simple, such as a dressed salad: Parma (prosciutto) ham with chichory (endive) and grapes; sliced oranges and tomatoes; smoked ham with blanched baby leeks and coarsely grated carrot; or grapefruit with seedless tangerines, watercress and walnuts are just a few good choices.
• In some countries it is traditional to serve a Christmas plum pudding with brandied butter or a white brandy sauce for dessert. If this doesn't appeal,

warming Glog to greet everyone, a selection of nuts and crisps (chips), sandwiches and perhaps some Stilton cheese spread on crackers. Offer mince pies or a mincemeat tart or wonderful Italian panforte and have a break for sweet food halfway through the singing to revive flagging guests, or towards the end of the evening.

The most difficult part of a musical evening is getting everyone warmed up, for this reason it is a good idea to have one or two people who are confident and keen enough to lead the singing.

consider a classic English trifle, a mincemeat pie served with freshly whipped cream, or serve a family favourite for dessert.
• Some form of special Christmas cake is also traditional to serve with coffee or tea. In England, this is a rich fruit cake covered in marzipan (almond paste) and icing; in Italy they have panforte, a deliciously spicy fruit and nut sweetmeat; and in France they serve Buche de Noel, which is a chocolate sponge log filled with a puree of chestnuts and coated with a chocolate ganache.

## TREE-DECORATING PARTY

A tree-decorating evening is a fun way of entertaining a small group of close friends a week or so before Christmas. Make it an opportunity for exchanging gifts and relaxing together. When you send out invitations, add a note to let guests know that they are expected to participate in decorating the home.

The tree should be ready with electric lights fitted but not switched on, and the decorations should be neatly laid out on a table nearby or place a range of decorations in a series of small boxes. It is a good idea to have other decorations ready to be fixed around the downstairs rooms. Avoid complicated decorations or any that are very time-consuming to fix.

Greet guests with a warming drink such as mulled wine or Glog, then get straight down to the business of the evening. One of the best ways of involving all the company is to hand each person a small box of decorations which have to be hung up.

### Glog

A hot glog is the perfect way to welcome your guests on a cold winter's evening. This traditional Swedish punch is usually served with a silver spoon in the glass to prevent it from cracking when the hot drink is poured in and for eating the almonds and raisins. Combine the following in a large pan: one bottle of red wine, 150 ml/¼ pint/⅔ cup brandy, the juice of 4 oranges, 4 tablespoons of raisins, 6 tablespoons of blanched almonds, 1 cinnamon stick, 4 cloves, pared rind (peel) of 1 orange and 25–50 g/1–2 oz/⅛–¼ cup of granulated sugar, to taste. Stir over a low heat until the sugar has dissolved. Makes enough for 10 glasses.

### Trinkets on the Tree

Each household has its own ideas about the Christmas tree. Building up a collection of beautiful trinkets over many years adds its own significance to the decorations. Even with the best attention, they will eventually begin to look rather tired, so take the opportunity to introduce a new style.

Here are a few ideas! Opt for decorations of one colour only – deep blue, red, gold or silver can look stunning; or try a combination of red and silver, blue and gold or more unusual, purple and gold.

Make gilded cones a special feature of the tree. Collect and dry them well in advance – do not reject closed cones found on the ground as they open on drying. Wire them carefully with hanging loops on the top, then spray them with gold paint. Make lots of small sprays of red berries and tie them to the tree with red ribbon in between the cones. Add red and gold bows.

Cover the tree in golden spices, nuts and blue bows. String gilded star anise and cinnamon sticks. Spray walnuts gold and stick red ribbon loops on top for hanging. Make miniature pomanders by studding miniature clementines with cloves and pinning red ribbon loops into them with large notice-board pins. Add blue bows to the edges of the branches.

### COUNTDOWN TO CHRISTMAS

The trick to enjoying Christmas when you are entertaining a crowd is to have everything planned and prepared as far as possible. Here are some tips to organizing your time running up to Christmas Day.

**THREE MONTHS AHEAD** Make items that need time to really mature, such as a Christmas plum pudding, a traditional fruit cake and mincemeat. Collect autumnal leaves, horse chestnuts, attractive twigs and other natural materials for decoration.

**ONE MONTH AHEAD** Begin to freeze useful dishes for the holiday period. If you have made a traditional fruit cake, now is the time to cover it with marzipan (almond paste) and icing. Order the turkey. Buy Christmas decorations, if necessary. Order the Christmas tree, if necessary. Buy wrapping paper, ribbons and gift tags.

**TWO WEEKS AHEAD** Buy in wines and other drinks. Complete Christmas present shopping, if not already done.

**CHRISTMAS WEEK** Check the store cupboards and do any last-minute food shopping. Collect the turkey. Check defrosting times for the turkey if it is frozen. Collect the Christmas tree and decorate it – tradition may dictate which day the tree is decorated.

### Christmas Eve

❖ Make and chill a stuffing for the turkey (but do *not* stuff the turkey until Christmas Day).

❖ Clean and trim the turkey, ready for adding the stuffing.

❖ Prepare bacon rolls, if serving, by threading them onto wooden cocktail sticks (toothpicks).

❖ Make stock from the turkey giblets, then strain and chill.

❖ Prepare the vegetables. Vegetables like Brussels sprouts and carrots can be placed in plastic bags and stored in the refrigerator. Cover peeled potatoes with iced water to which lemon juice has been added and also store in the refrigerator.

❖ Make a cranberry sauce, if using, and cover and chill.

❖ Make a dessert if not serving a Christmas plum pudding.

❖ Lay the table and set a tray with coffee cups.

### Christmas Day

❖ Stuff the turkey and roast.

❖ If serving a Christmas plum pudding, make a sauce to accompany it and cover with dampened greaseproof paper (waxed paper) and set aside.

❖ Assemble the starter (appetizer) on plates, if serving. A salad starter should be stored in the refrigerator on plates without added dressing.

❖ If serving roast potatoes, par-boil the potatoes, then place in an oven-proof dish. Brush with butter. Add to the oven 1 hour before the turkey is due to come out.

❖ If serving mashed potatoes, put the potatoes on the boil about half an hour before the turkey is ready to come out of the oven.

❖ Prepare all the vegetables ready to cook.

❖ If serving a Christmas plum pudding, allow 1–2 hours for steaming.

❖ When the turkey is cooked transfer it to a serving platter, cover with foil and keep hot.

❖ While the turkey is resting, cook the rest of the vegetables and make the gravy. Have all the vegetables ready for serving before sitting down to the first course.

❖ Turn off the Christmas plum pudding, if serving, before serving the main course.

❖ Gently reheat the dessert sauce for the Christmas plum pudding, if serving, while clearing the main course and turning out the pudding.

*Tiny flower pots are turned into candle holders, and finished with decorative wreaths. Remember: never leave lit candles unattended.*

**To Cook a 4.5 kg/10 lb Turkey**

Set the oven at 180°C/350°F/Gas 6. Trim off the leg and wing ends, rinse the bird inside and out with cold water and mop it all over with absorbent kitchen paper (paper towels) to dry. Cut away any visible fat from the bird.

Spoon the stuffing into the neck end of the bird or under the skin covering the breast, as you prefer. Truss the bird neatly and sprinkle it with seasoning, then cover the breast completely with bacon rashers (slices). Trickle a little oil over the top.

Cover the bird with fresh bay leaves and foil, then place it in the oven. The roasting time is calculated at 20 minutes per 450 g/ 1 lb, plus an extra 20 minutes. However, it is important to allow for the weight of the stuffing, so the

total cooking time for a 4.5 kg/10 lb stuffed bird should be about 4–4¼ hours.

Roast the bird, basting it every 30 minutes, for 3½ hours. Drain off any excess fat occasionally during cooking, if necessary, leaving only a shallow covering in the bottom of the roasting tin (pan). Add the bacon rolls, if serving, to the roasting tin at this stage and continue to cook for the remaining time. Small balls of sausagemeat stuffing may also be added to the roasting tin or a dish of extra stuffing added to the oven.

Remove the foil and bacon covering the breast for the final 30 minutes' cooking time to allow the skin to brown and crisp.

Transfer the turkey to a warmed meat dish and cover it closely with foil, placing the shiny side inwards, then keep hot. Drain

the bacon rolls well on absorbent kitchen paper (paper towels).

Drain excess fat from the roasting tin (pan). Stir in just enough flour to absorb the cooking juices in a thin paste. Cook, stirring, for 2 minutes, then pour in stock, stirring or whisking all the time, until the mixture forms a thin gravy. Bring this to the boil, adding a little extra stock, if necessary, so that the gravy is just too thin for your liking. Boil the gravy for about 10 minutes, stirring often, until reduced and well flavoured. Taste for seasoning before straining into a warmed jug.

**To Check if a Turkey is Cooked**
Pierce the flesh on the thickest area of meat, found behind the leg joints of the bird. If there is any sign of blood in the juices, or any pink flesh, then the turkey should be returned to the oven.

**Thawing a Frozen Turkey**

Frozen turkey must be thoroughly thawed before cooking and it must be thawed in the refrigerator. Small turkeys may be left in a cool room to complete the thawing overnight, but they must be covered. Never leave a bird at normal (warm) room temperature for any length of time.

Remove the turkey from its wrapping and place it in a large bowl or deep dish. Cover completely with aluminium foil or cling film (plastic wrap) and place in the refrigerator. Allow 2–3 days, thawing for a 2.5–3.5 kg/5–8 lb turkey; up to 4 days for a bird weighing 7 kg/15 lb. A turkey weighing between 7–9.5 kg/15–20 lb needs a full 4 days to thaw.

Drain the drips from the turkey, then wash and dry the container before replacing the bird in it.

## CHESTNUT STUFFING

——— MAKES ABOUT 400 G/14 OZ ———

This is a delicious stuffing to accompany a traditional sausagemeat stuffing for the turkey. Bring the stuffing to room temperature before using it to pack the bird and only pack the bird just before cooking.

40 g/1 lb butter
1 large onion, chopped
2 celery sticks, finely chopped
450 g/1 lb chestnut puree
100 g/4 oz/2 cups fresh white breadcrumbs
2 tablespoons fresh sage, chopped
1 tablespoon fresh thyme, chopped
1 cooking apple, peeled and diced (minced)
3 tablespoons orange juice
salt and freshly ground black pepper

Heat the butter in a pan and cook the onion and celery gently for about 10 minutes until translucent.

Remove from the heat and mix with the chestnut puree, breadcrumbs, herbs, diced apple, orange juice, port or sherry and a little freshly grated nutmeg. Season to taste. Use to pack the neck end of the turkey.

## WONDERFUL MINCEMEAT

———— MAKES ABOUT 5 KG/10 LB ————

This is deliciously different from many traditional mincemeat recipes – the tangy apricots, peaches and dried pears combine with zesty ginger to give the occasional unexpected, lively zing to a mincemeat tart or small pies. Make this at least 3 weeks before it is needed, but it is best left for a couple of months, if not more.

450 g/1 lb (1⅓ cups) raisins
450 g/1 lb (1⅓ cups) currants
225 g/8 oz (1⅓ cups) ready-to-eat dried apricots, chopped
450 g/1 lb (2⅔ cups) ready-to-eat peaches, chopped
225 g/8 oz (1⅓ cups) ready-to-eat dried pears, chopped
225 g/8 oz (1⅓ cups) dried prunes, chopped
225 g/8 oz (1⅓ cups) stoned (pitted) dried dates, chopped
225 g/8 oz (1⅓ cups) glacé (candied) cherries, chopped
225 g/8 oz (1⅓ cups) candied orange peel, chopped
100 g/4 oz (⅔ cup) candied stem ginger, chopped
grated rind (peel) and juice of 1 lemon
1 kg/2 lb cooking apples, peeled, cored and chopped
225 g/8 oz (1⅓ cups) shredded suet
225 g/8 oz (⅔ cup) honey, warmed
500 ml/16 fl oz (2 cups) brandy
1 teaspoon grated nutmeg
2 teaspoons ground allspice
225 g/8 oz (heaped 1 cup) demerara sugar

Mix together all the ingredients in a large bowl. Cover tightly and leave for 2 days, stirring occasionally. Pot into thoroughly clean, sterilized jars and put on airtight lids which are coated in plastic so they do not react with the fruit acid. Store in a cool dry place.

The mincemeat will keep well for several months or up to a year if the edges of the lids are sealed with freezer tape. Stretch the freezer tape hard as you apply it so it shrinks back to prevent evaporation around the edge of the lids.

## MINCEMEAT TART

———————— SERVES 8 ————————

A mincemeat tart is a perennial favourite at Christmas. Serve it hot or cold with lashings of whipped cream.

350 g/12 oz (3 cups) plain (all-purpose) flour
175 g/6 oz (¾ cup) butter, cut into small pieces
50 g/2 oz (¼ cup) caster (superfine) sugar
grated rind (peel) of 1 orange
1 egg yolk
1 tbsp natural vanilla essence (extract)
a little orange juice
450 g/1 lb Wonderful Mincemeat
milk to glaze
icing (confectioner's) sugar to dust (optional)

Place the flour in a bowl. Rub in the butter finely, then stir in the caster (superfine) sugar and orange rind (peel). Mix the egg yolk with the vanilla essence (extract) and 1 tablespoon of the orange juice. Add this mixture to the dry ingredients and mix well, adding a little extra juice if necessary to just bind the ingredients into a dough.

Use half the dough to line a 23 cm/9 in flan tin. Prick the base all over and chill for 30 minutes. Wrap the remaining dough in cling film (plastic wrap) and chill it. Set the oven at 200°C/400°F/Gas 6. Line the pastry shell with greaseproof paper (waxed paper) and baking beans. Bake the pastry shell blind for 15 minutes, then remove the paper and beans. Reduce the oven temperature to 180°C/350°F/Gas 4.

Turn the mincemeat into the flan, spreading it out evenly. Roll out the remaining pastry thinly into an oblong shape, then cut this into 1 cm/½ in wide strips. Dampen the edge of the part-baked pastry shell, then lay the strips of pastry over the top, weaving them into a lattice as you lay them on the flan. Press the ends of the pastry onto the edge of the flan case, then trim them. Brush the lattice with a little milk and bake the flan for about 40 minutes, or until golden brown and cooked through. Serve hot or cold, dusted with a little icing (confectioner's) sugar if liked.

*Mincemeat Tart.*

## PARTY GAMES

There's nothing quite like a good game to liven up a party. Here is a brief selection of guessing, memory and team games that are bound to please children and adults alike.

### Drawing Game

For this popular guessing game you will need two teams of at least three people each, plus an organizer who is out of the game. You will also need a list of subjects to be guessed, and plenty of pencils and paper placed in two separate rooms. Allocate a room to each team. The organizer stands in a central position between the two rooms (say, in the hallway) and a player from each team is sent out to get the first subject. The players return to their respective teams and then communicate the subject by drawing alone – no talking by the drawer is allowed, although nodding or shaking of the head is allowed for yes and no. The rest of the team shout out their guesses, and the person to guess correctly has the next go. The team to guess all the subjects first wins. Some suggested subjects: the Eiffel Tower, King Kong, Laurel and Hardy, any popular children's characters, the Queen of England, Concorde, any topical subjects.

### Ten Things Under The Table

A good after-dinner game. The best way to involve everyone is for the host or hostess to fill two containers with five items each some time ahead of the party. At the table each guest is given a piece of paper and a pencil. The items are passed around under the table, one container's worth in one direction and the other in the opposite direction, and each person is given a few seconds to feel but not look at the item. When the items have been around all the guests they are returned to the containers. The winner is the person who has guessed the most items correctly. Suggestions: a rubber glove packed with cotton wool (batting), unravelled wool, pipe cleaners, peeled grapes in a bowl, a wig, a natural sponge slightly dampened, a woolly hat, a nail brush, a child's toy, buttons, bag of rice or couscous, lump of child's play dough or clay, globe artichoke, piece of root ginger, clothes pegs – the possibilities are endless!

### My Aunt Went Shopping

One player starts by saying 'My aunt went shopping and she bought . . .' It may be that her purchase was a pair of fun-fur gloves. The next player repeats the line about his aunt's expedition, and her first purchase, then adds his own. Her next good buy might be a second-hand pink and blue feather boa. And so it goes on. As each player's memory fails or even an adjective is forgotten, he or she drops out of the game until eventually the only niece or nephew who accurately repeats the shopping list wins.

### Charades

This is an after-dinner game which a small gathering may well happily fall into. Everyone writes a subject on a piece of paper. The papers are folded and placed in a hat. One player picks a paper from the hat, then he or she has to mime the subject which is written on the paper.

The player is not allowed to speak beyond saying whether the subject is a book, film or a play, if this is relevant. The following system of symbols is used: To indicate the number of words in the subject, one, two, three or more fingers are held up. Once the miming is in progress, the player taps the shoulder with the number of fingers which refer to the relevant word – one finger for the first word, two for the second and so on. To indicate the number of syllables in a given word, and to indicate which syllable is being mimed, the relevant number of fingers are tapped on the forearm.

If the word is very short, this is indicated by holding up the thumb and index finger very slightly apart. If a word sounds similar to another, the player may hold his or her ear and mime a word that sounds like the one to be guessed. The word 'the' is indicated by making the letter T with both forefingers, and 'a' and 'an' by holding up an index finger and thumb together.

Throughout the game the gathered company respond to each piece of mime by shouting out what they think the word is or by indicating that they understand what they should be guessing.

The winner is the person who guesses the subject, and that person mimes the next round.

### Balloon Race

This is a lively game for all the family. Divide into two teams (it may be more practical to divide into even more teams if there are more than three or four players per team). Each player is given an inflated balloon and a short, thin stick with which to pat it across the room and into a bowl on the other side. If a player touches the balloon or allows it to fall to the ground, then he or she is disqualified. If liked, play the game in heats, the winners of each event meeting in the semi-finals and the finals.

## GINGERBREAD TREATS

### MAKES ABOUT 30 BISCUITS (COOKIES)

Gingerbread cookies are traditional at Christmas, and cut into attractive shapes and piped with icing (frosting) they make excellent Christmas tree decorations. This is a Christmas activity that older children can enjoy, although an adult will have to help with the baking part.

225 g/8 oz (2 cups) plain (all-purpose) flour,
plus extra for dusting
pinch of salt
1 tsp baking powder
2 tsp ground ginger
½ tsp ground cinnamon
125 g/5 oz (½ cup) unsalted butter at room
temperature, cut into small pieces, plus extra
for greasing
100 g/4 oz (½ cup) caster (superfine) sugar
2 tbsp golden (dark corn) syrup
1 small egg, beaten, to mix

DECORATION
50 g/2 oz (½ cup) icing (confectioners') sugar
about 2 tsp water or lemon juice
2–3 drops edible food colouring (optional)
chocolate drops and candies (optional)

Sift together the flour, salt, baking powder, ground ginger and ground cinnamon into a mixing bowl. You will have to do this in several batches. Using your fingertips, rub in (cut in) the butter until the mixture looks like breadcrumbs. Add the sugar and golden (dark corn) syrup and mix it well. Add just enough of the egg to make a stiff dough.

Sprinkle a little flour onto a pastry board, turn out the gingerbread dough and knead it with your hands until there are no more cracks. Put the ball of dough in a plastic bag and leave it in the refrigerator for about 30 minutes.

Take the dough out of the refrigerator. Sprinkle a little more flour onto the pastry board and roll out the dough until it is about 3 mm/½ in thick. Set the oven to 180°C/350°F/Gas 4.

Using cookie cutters, cut out star, heart and other shapes from the dough. Gather up the pieces left over, roll them into a ball, sprinkle a little more flour onto the pastry board and roll them out to the same thickness as before. If you want to use the cookies as tree decorations, make a hole near the top of each

one with a skewer. Lift the shapes onto the baking sheet.

Bake the gingerbread in the oven for 12–15 minutes, until it is pale golden brown and just beginning to darken at the edges. Take the baking sheet from the oven and leave the gingerbread to cool thoroughly on the sheet. Use a spatula to transfer the shapes to a cleaned pastry board.

Sift the icing (confectioners') sugar into a small bowl, and add just enough water or lemon juice so that it makes a stiff paste when you mix it. If you want to add food colouring (an adult should help children with this) divide the mixture into two or three and add 1 drop of each colour to each. Mix well, to achieve an even colour.

Put a star nozzle (tube) on an icing (pastry) bag, spoon some of the icing (frosting) mixture into it and pipe blobs of icing onto the shapes.

Use a little of the icing to stick chocolate drops or other candies to the shapes, if using. For tree decorations: when the icing is dry, thread a narrow ribbon through the holes in the cookies to hang them on the tree.

## PANFORTE

### MAKES 144 SMALL PIECES

This is an Italian dessert speciality which is so rich that small squares are quite adequate portions. It is made from lots of fruit and nuts with honey and spices, so it can be prepared well in advance and it will keep well in an air-tight container in a cool place for several weeks. I have also prepared batches as Christmas gifts, baking the mixture in shallow round foil containers which I first line with non-stick baking parchment. Neatly wrapped in cling film (plastic wrap) sealed underneath with freezer tape, and tied with ribbon, the panforte looks most festive.

1 kg/2 lb (5⅓ cups) shelled walnuts, brazils
and hazelnuts, chopped
450 g/1 lb (2⅔ cups) good-quality candied
peel, chopped
225 g/8 oz (1⅓ cups) dried figs, chopped
225 g/8 oz (1⅓ cups) sultanas (golden raisins)
225 g/8 oz (2 cups) ground blanched almonds
75 g/3 oz (⅓ cup) soft brown sugar
1 tablespoon ground coriander
1 tablespoon ground allspice
2 tablespoons ground cinnamon
grated rind (peel) and juice of 3 oranges
225 g/8 oz (⅔ cup) honey
4 tablespoons brandy
icing (confectioners') sugar to dredge

*Panforte.*

Set the oven at 180°C/350°F/Gas 4. Line the base of a 30 cm (12 in) square tin (pan) with rice paper. Roast the mixed nuts in a heavy-based saucepan over low to medium heat, stirring often to prevent them overcooking, until lightly browned.

Turn the nuts into a bowl and add all the remaining ingredients, except the orange juice, honey and brandy. Stir well to distribute the spices evenly, then add the liquids and mix

until thoroughly combined. Turn the mixture into the tin and press it down well with the back of a metal spoon. Bake for 30 minutes, or until the panforte feels firm and lightly crusted. Leave to cool.

Wrap the panforte tightly in cling film (plastic wrap), then seal it in a plastic bag and leave to mature for at least 2 days before cutting. Dredge the top with icing (confectioners') sugar and cut into 2.5 cm (1 in) squares.

## Decorative Candle Wreath

Highlighted with touches of gold, natural colours and forms glow appealingly in this table centrepiece. Remember that the lit candles should never be left unattended, and make sure they do not burn down to within reach of the wreath.

**YOU WILL NEED:** dry foam (styro foam) ring, four candles, florists' wire, nuts, strong glue, small fir cones, dried hydrangea head, tiny gold baubles, berries or rose hips.

**1** Twist two lengths of wire around the base of each candle, leaving double ends of wire projecting downwards. Spear these wires firmly into the foam ring, spacing the candles evenly.

**2** Stick nuts to the foam in attractive groups.

**3** Add clusters of fir cones between the nuts. Twist wire around the base of cones that have no stalks, or use strong glue to stick them in place.

**4** Fill spaces in the ring with hydrangea florets (flowerets), sticking them in place with glue. Add baubles and berries as finishing touches.

**NOTE:** Never leave lit candles unattended, and never allow candles to burn down too close to the decorations.

## Holly Table Arrangement

Use an attractive bowl or pot as the base for the arrangement. Poinsettia flowers, real or silk, make an attractive decoration at the base to cover the gravel.

**YOU WILL NEED:** a length of garden cane (bamboo stake), a dry florists' foam (styro foam) sphere, sticky (transparent) tape, florists' ribbon, scissors, small block of dry florists' foam, container, gravel, florists' wire, holly sprigs, artificial florists' pine sprigs, ivy leaves, real or silk poinsettias, narrow satin ribbon (optional), wide decorative ribbon for container.

**1** Insert one end of a length of garden cane (bamboo stake) into the foam sphere.

**2** Tape the end of a piece of florists' ribbon to the top of the cane, then wrap ribbon around the entire length. Secure with tape at the base.

**3** Insert the end of the garden cane into a piece of dry foam (styro foam) placed in a decorative container. Fill with gravel.

**4** Make a loop at one end of a length of florists' wire and wire individual holly sprigs. Also wire artificial florists' pine sprigs.

**5** Push the wired stems into the foam to cover it evenly. Add wired individual ivy leaves to fill any gaps.

**6** Insert the poinsettias into the gravel to disguise the pebbles. Tie a wide ribbon around the container. If liked, a few red ribbon bows can be added to the holly arrangement.

# NEW YEAR'S CELEBRATIONS

*O*ut with the old, in with the new; a time for reflection and resolution, for sharing with close friends or family. In many communities this is when everyone sheds inhibition and dances into the new year. Busy people often make this their annual commitment to entertaining, planning parties which flow through the night to end with an extremely early breakfast.

Alternatively, plan brunch or lunch on New Year's Day. This brief section offers a few reminders, hints and tips on leaping from year to year.

### NEW YEAR GATHERINGS

New Year's Eve celebrations are either a night of revelry or quieter get-togethers with family and friends.

❖ If you are serving a supper on the eve of the new year, it should be set out in readiness for serving immediately after midnight, when everyone has wished each other well. A buffet-style meal would be suitable, and could include platters of cold meats, a cheese-board, meat and fish pâtés, quiches, and a range of mixed salads.

❖ Have chilled champagne or sparkling wine ready and pour into glasses and hand them round as midnight begins to strike.

❖ New Year's Day is often a time for brunch or early afternoon open house parties. For brunch, offer crusty rolls, bagels, speciality breads, a range of cheeses, salami and other cured meats, followed by fresh fruit, nuts and dates. Drinks could include hot chocolate with whipped cream and cinnamon, freshly brewed coffee, a variety of teas, and fruit juices or a low-alcohol punch.

### New Year's Eve Party Checklist

- Invitations
- Nibbles (snacks)
- Party menu, if serving: first course, main course, dessert
- Wine and/or beer
- Alcohol-free drinks
- Ice
- Decorations
- House cleaning and tidying

### NEW YEAR'S TRADITIONS

❖ "Auld Lang Syne" is sung the world over. Everyone crosses their arms in front and joins hands with the next person, then they form a circle to sing the words.

❖ To let out the old and bring in the new, open doors or windows at the front and back of the house to let the air blow through.

❖ This is an old Scottish custom. To ensure warmth and food for the coming year, invite a man with dark hair to enter the house through the front door and out through the back carrying a lump of coal and some bread. He must be the first person to enter the house at the beginning of the year, so send out the chosen guest to walk through to the cheers of the gathered party.

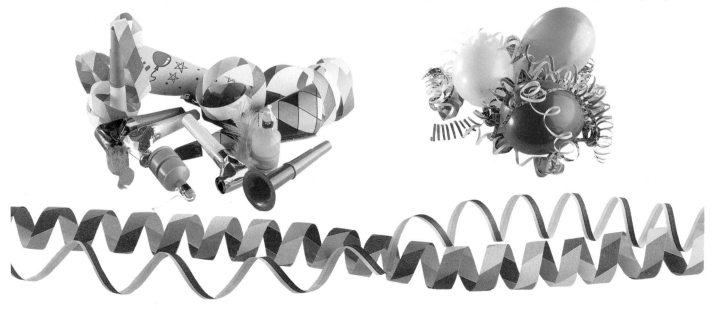

*Bring in the coming year with plenty of colourful streamers and party poppers. Masks and paper hats add to the party mood.*

### Het Pint (Mulled Wine)

The het pint was a container of mulled ale which was taken through the streets of Scottish towns to warm everyone in readiness for seeing in the new year. The original included eggs but the following recipe is an updated version, and very successful it is too!

Pour 1.2 litres/2 pints (5 cups) beer (pale ale or bitter, not a light beer like lager) into a saucepan. Add 50 g/2 oz (¼ cup) sugar, some freshly grated nutmeg and a cinnamon stick. Heat this gently over low heat without allowing the beer to boil. Then add about 8 tablespoons of whisky . . . or more if you wish . . . and heat gently for a few minutes, but do not prolong this or the alcohol will evaporate. Pour the het pint into heatproof glasses and serve at once.

## Cocktail-glass Paper Chain

This simple cut-paper decoration has a slightly tipsy air that sets the party mood at the outset.

**YOU WILL NEED:** crêpe paper in contrasting colours, pencil, scissors, sticky (transparent) tape or stapler.

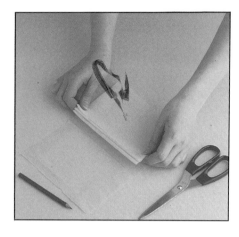

**1** Cut strips of crêpe paper about 17.5 cm/7 in deep. Fold back and forth in even pleats about 12.5 cm/5 in wide.

**2** Draw the outline of a cocktail glass on the outside pleat, making sure that the sides of the bowl meet the folds of the paper about 1 cm/ ½ in from the top edge.

**3** Cut out the glass shape through all layers.

**4** Carefully unfold the chain of glasses. Join separate lengths with sticky (transparent) tape or staples to make streamers long enough to decorate the room.

## HOPPIN' JOHN

—————— SERVES 6 ——————

Early rising seems to be the universal key to New Year's Day celebrations, as they all seem to be executed before noon. For example, this traditional American dish of black-eye beans (peas) and rice, from the Deep South, has to be served up before mid-day to bring good luck for the year ahead. It will certainly cure any midnight revellers' hangovers from New Year's Eve.

225 g/8 oz (1⅓ cups) black-eye beans (peas),
soaked overnight
1 bacon hock
1 bay leaf
1 large carrot, diced
2 celery sticks, diced
2 large onions, chopped
225 g/8 oz (1⅔ cups) long-grain rice
salt and freshly ground black pepper
4 tablespoons chopped parsley

Drain the black-eye beans (peas) and place in a large saucepan with plenty of cold water. Bring to the boil, and boil rapidly for 5 minutes, then reduce the heat and cover the pan, then simmer the beans for 30 minutes, until just tender.

Meanwhile, place the hock in a large saucepan with the bay leaf, carrot, celery and onions. Add cold water to cover and bring to the boil. Skim any scum off the surface of the water, then reduce the heat and cover the pan. Boil the hock for 1 hour. Add the drained black-eye beans to the pan and bring the water back to the boil. Reduce the heat so that the water simmers, cover the pan and cook for 30 minutes, or until the hock is very tender and the meat comes away from the bone easily. Remove the hock from the pan, cut off all the meat, discard the skin, fat and bone, then dice the meat and return it to the pan.

Add the rice and bring the mixture back to the boil. Cover the pan, reduce the heat to the lowest setting and cook for 25 minutes, until the rice is tender. Depending on the size of pan, you may have to add a little extra water to ensure that the rice does not dry up. At the end of cooking the mixture should be moist but not too wet.

Taste for seasoning — most hocks are salty enough to flavour the dish and pepper is the only requirement. Fork the parsley into the mixture and serve at once.

*New Year Kissing Ring.*

### New Year Kissing Ring

To make this golden ring, use a stem wreath form as a base. Secure uneven lengths of evergreens such as cypress, ivy, mistletoe and eucalyptus to the wreath form using bent stub (floral) wire staples.

Position in such a way that the head of each bunch overlaps the tail of the previous bunch, and work your way around the ring until it is covered. Finally, fix bunches of gilded wheat and artificial Christmas roses with stub wires, and finish with ribbon bows.

# SUPPLIERS AND USEFUL ADDRESSES

## Catering Equipment

Brandon Hire
Tudor House
24 Clothier Road
Brislington
Bristol BS4 5PS
UK
0272-716274
(Hire of catering, furniture and marquees)

Taylor Rental companies
USA
Call 800-833-3004 for details of your nearest supplier. (Rental of tents, tables, chairs, canopies, silverware, dishes, dancefloors, champagne fountains, wedding specialities, glassware, etc.)

Gervais Rentals Inc
6570 Esplanade
Montreal
Canada
514-273 3677

Local Party Hire
38 Arden Street
Waverley NSW 2024
Australia
02-664 1399
Fax 02-664 1912

Catering Suppliers and Equipment
84 Newton Road
Ponsonby
Auckland
New Zealand
09-309 0169

Zissis Catering Equipment cc
Box 260 888
Johannesburg
South Africa
011-331 3043

## Tents, Canopies and Marquees

Brandon Hire
Tudor House
24 Clothier Road
Brislington
Bristol BS4 5PS
UK
0272-716274
(Hire of marquees; also offer catering and hire of furniture)

Taylor Rental Companies
USA
For details, *see* Catering Equipment.

Industrial Fabrics Association International
345 Cedar Street
Suite 800
St. Paul
Minnesota
USA 55101-1088
Call 800-225-4324 for details of your nearest supplier.

Acme Tent
6999 Victoria Avenue
Montreal
Canada
514-342 5272

Walders Hire
352 Liverpool Road
Ashfield
Sydney
Australia
02-797 9200
Fax 02-797 9588

Hire Master
246 Taranaki Street
Wellington
New Zealand
04-385 8632

Marquees, Tent and Tarpaulin
34 Downie Crescent
Queensmead
Queensburgh
South Africa
031-446 415

## Catering Services

Feathers
UK
Call head office on 051-709 9655 for details of your nearest supplier.

Leith's
86 Bondway
Vauxhall
London SW8 1SF
UK
071-735 6303

Riverview Caterers
1 Warburton Ave
Hastings-on-Hudson 10706
New York
USA
914-965 7220

Daniel Durand Caterer
2935 de Miniac
Montreal
Canada
514-332 4911

ACS Australian Catering Services
11 Edward Street
Sandringham
Melbourne
Australia
03-587 2511

Anders Fine Catering
46 Mitchell Road
Alexandria
Sydney
02-698 3198
Fax 02-319 3048

Food Management Services
22 Hanbury Avenue
Landsdowne
Cape Town
South Africa
021-696 2984

McLeods Hiring and Banqueting
625 Smith Street
Durban
South Africa
031-301 1991

## Wedding Services

National Wedding Information Services
FREEPOST
121/123 High Street
Epping
Essex CM16 4BD
UK
Contact 0992 576461 for details of local firms.

Modern Bride Magazine
249 West 17th Street
New York
NY 10011
USA
212-337 7000
(Contains all the current information and names and addresses of wedding services nationwide.)

Canadian Wedding Services
14240-111 Avenue
Edmonton
Canada
403-451 1244

Apricot Corporation Pty Ltd
135 Leicester Street
Carlton
Melbourne
Australia
03-349 2277
(Complete wedding planning services)

Alegro Wedding and Function Organizers
47 Reserve Street
Smithfield
Sydney NSW
Australia
02-604 6067

The Wedding Connection
PO Box 38-857
Wellington
New Zealand
04-565 1081
(Wedding advisory service)

Weddings and Functions Pty
Ltd
Durban
South Africa
031-305 1963

## Party Hire

Non Stop Party Shop
214-216 Kensington High
Street
London N8
UK
071-937 7200

Cedarhurst Paper
USA
Call 516-368 5200 for details of
your nearest retailer. (Offers
papers and plastics ware, party
favors, hats, etc.)

Hallmark Cards and Gifts
USA
Call 800-HALL MARK for
details of your nearest retailer.

A Party Decor Inc
1434 Sauvé W
Montreal
Canada
514-335 0841

TVN Party Goods
487 Toorak Road
Toorak
Melbourne
Australia
03-827 7161

One Stop Party Shop
Lychgate Centre
100 Riddiford Street
Newtown
Wellington
New Zealand
04-389 8802

## Ladies' Wear

One Night Stand
44 Pimlico Road
London SW1
UK
071-730 8708
(Formal wear for hire)

Jandi Classics
P.O. Box 11463
Knoxville
Tennesee 37939-1463
USA
Call 800-342-1544 for details of
your nearest retailer.
(Formal wear for rental)

One Night Stand
905 Madison Avenue
New York
NY 10021
USA
212-772 7720
(Formal wear for rental)

Grace Bros Formal Hire
213 Pitt Street
Sydney
Australia
02-238 9111

Jills Evening Wear Hire
Wellington
New Zealand
04-475 9868

## Men's Wear

Moss Bros
27/28 King Street
London WC2
UK
071-240 4567
or contact Head Office on 071-
924 1717
(Formal wear for sale or hire)

Full Dress Formals
USA
Call 800-522 4338 for details of
your nearest retailer.
(Formal attire for rental)

Fran Myers
USA
Call 800-626 6305 for details of
your nearest retailer.
(Formal attire for rental)

Grace Bros Formal Hire
213 Pitt Street
Sydney
Australia
02-238 9111

Rent a Tux cc
256 Bree Street
Johannesburg
South Africa
011-293 794

## Arts Supplies

Paperchase
213 Tottenham Court Road
London W1A 4US
UK
071-580 8496

Pearl Paints
308 Canal Street
New York
NY 10013-2572
USA
212-431 7932

Oxford Art Supplies Pty Ltd
221-223 Oxford Street
Darlinghurst
NSW
Australia
02-360 4066
*Fax* 02-360 3461

Karori Art, Craft and
Wallpaper Centre
264 Karon Road
Karori
New Zealand
04-476 8426

Academy of Crafts
28 Goldman Street
Florida
South Africa
011-472 4884

Arts and Crafts Depot
40 Harrison Street
Johannesburg
South Africa
011-832 2286

## Cake Decorating
## Suppliers

Squires Kitchen
Squires House
3 Waverley Lane
Farnham
Surrey GU9 8BB
UK
0252-711749/734309
(Mail order service available)

Woodnutt's
97 Church Road
Hove
Sussex BN3 2BA
UK
0273-205353
(Mail order service available)

Country Kitchens
Fort Wayne
Indiana 46825
USA
219-482 4863
(Manufacturers of fine cake
decorating supplies and
accessories)

Wilton Enterprises Inc
2240 West 75th Street
Woodridge
Illinois 60517
USA
708-963 7100

McCall's School of Cake
Decorating Inc
3810 Bloor Street
Islington
Ontario
Canada M9B 6C2

Australian National Cake
Decorators' Association
PO Box 321
Plympton
South Australia 5038

Decor Cakes
RSA Arcade
435 Great South Road
Otahuhu
New Zealand
09-276 3443

South African Sugarcraft Guild
National Office
1 Tuzla Mews
187 Smit Street
Fairlan 2195
South Africa
011-825 8080

Jem Cutters
PO Box 115
Kloof
3 Nisbett Road
Pinetown 3600
South Africa
031-701 1431

# INDEX

# ACKNOWLEDGEMENTS

The publishers would like to thank the following suppliers for loan of materials photographed in the book:

Nice Irma's
46 Goodge Street
London W1
UK
071-580 6921
(Ceramics, glassware, Asian gifts and fabric furnishings)

General Trading Co (Mayfair) Ltd
144 Sloane Street
London SW1
UK
071-730 0411
(Antique china, glass gifts, fabrics)

Les Olivedes
7 Walton Street
London SW3
UK
071-589 8990
(Furnishing fabrics and accessories)

Papyrus Stationers
48 Fulham Road
London SW3
UK
071-584 8022

Waterford Wedgewood
158 Regent Street
London W1
UK
071-734 7262
(Fine china)